Admiral Byng

To my brother Hugh

Admiral Byng

His Rise and Execution

Chris Ware

Pen & Sword
MARITIME

First published in Great Britain in 2009 by
Pen & Sword Aviation
an imprint of
Pen & Sword Books Ltd
47 Church Street
Barnsley
South Yorkshire
S70 2AS

Copyright © Chris Ware 2009

ISBN 978-1-84415-781-5

A CIP catalogue record for this book is available from the British Library.

Typeset in 11.5pt Ehrhardt by
Mac Style, Beverley, E. Yorkshire

Printed and bound in the UK by the CPI Antony Rowe, Chippenham, Wiltshire

Pen & Sword Books Ltd incorporates the imprints of Pen & Sword
Aviation, Pen & Sword Maritime, Pen & Sword Military, Wharncliffe
Local History, Pen and Sword Select, Pen and Sword Military Classics and
Leo Cooper.

For a complete list of Pen & Sword titles please contact
PEN & SWORD BOOKS LIMITED
47 Church Street, Barnsley, South Yorkshire, S70 2AS, England
E-mail: enquiries@pen-and-sword.co.uk
Website: www.pen-and-sword.co.uk

Contents

Acknowledgements

First I would like to thank the man who commissioned this book, Philip Sidnell, who has been a model editor and kept a wayward academic on task. In a similar vein my partner Carol has tried to keep me on the straight and narrow and in the process created a new verb 'to Byng', thanks for everything. A very special thanks goes to my friend Vicki Carolan, who valiantly read almost every single word, and in the process improved the text greatly. Thanks also to Ian Hughes, my copy editor, for doing such a sterling job with the text.

My academic peers have been no less generous: to Professor Roger Knight who has been my colleague and friend for more than thirty years and Professor Sarah Palmer for many kindnesses thank you both. To Glyn Williams, an exemplary scholar, who suggested I write a book on Byng and helped with references, I am grateful. A special mention has to be made for my late colleague Alan Pearsall, the last conversation we had two days before his death was about John Byng. None of the above is responsible for any errors of fact or interpretation: they lie with me alone.

List of Plates

Prelude

The wind blew hard, clouds scudded across the night sky, it was barely after 9pm and 30 Royal marines had just disembarked before being rowed across Portsmouth harbour from the ship to the shore.[1] There was little unusual about this: it was after all wartime and Portsmouth, as with all the Royal Dockyards, was busy fitting, victualling and manning ships of war.[2] Many such men would cross and re-cross the ruffled water of the harbour, both now and in the future. As the wind took their footsteps and carried them away they would have been unaware that the events which had unfolded some nine hours earlier would, amongst so many other things which had already happened during the brief course of the war, still be the subject of debate some 250 years later, and in some circles at least would leave the feeling of injustice.[3] These anonymous Marines had taken part in a major event, and, although what they thought of it is lost to history, there were plenty of observers who did record all, or nearly all, that transpired both on this March day in 1757 and during all of the events which led up to it. Yet none would quite literally have had their fingers on the trigger as nine of those Marines had at 12 O'clock on 14 March 1757.[4]

At 6 pm the body of a flag officer was rowed ashore from one of the ships moored in the harbour. Along with his mortal remains was his baggage.[5] At 52 he had had a good life; he had outlived his elder brother by some years and another of his brothers had predeceased a year earlier. His mother was to die in 1756 in her mid eighties, just one year before her son's death.

The flag officer was the Hon. John Byng, Admiral of the Blue, and unlike his brothers his death was not from natural causes but from execution. The marines who formed the firing squad may have slipped into historical obscurity, but not so John Byng. He was put to death aboard the *Monarch*, a ship of the line which in March 1757 was fitting ready for service in the Mediterranean.[6] The vessel chosen by the Port Admiral for the place of execution was, with exquisite irony, a ship captured from the French at the battle of Cape Finisterre in 1747. Perhaps Boscawen, the Admiral in question, was being more than ironic in his choice of place of execution but, if that were the case, why so?

What was Byng's crime? Had he, as many a noble and commoner before, followed the cause of the exiled Stewarts and paid the price many of them had with his life? No. He, like his father, had supported the Hanoverians and in the last rising in 1745–6 had served off the coast of Scotland to help defeat the Jacobite threat.

It was not treason which brought Byng to his execution on that stormy March day: it was both devastatingly simple and, at the same time, far more complex than that. What brought him down was the one thing which could destroy any British admiral: failure to defeat the enemy in battle. How and why that lack of success came about was much more complex, involving both high politics and the minutiae of Admiralty regulations on the one hand, and low cunning and 'King Mob' on the other.

Chapter One

Destined for the Navy

The Honourable John Byng was christened on 29 October 1704. He was the ninth child and fifth surviving son of George Byng Viscount Torrington and Margaret Masters. John's father was, by the time that his son John was born, becoming very successful in his career in the Navy. Sir George was the son of a draper, also called John Byng, who does not appear to have been successful in trade. The elder John Byng is supposed to have lost money on his venture and had to part with some of his estate at Wrotham in Kent, and then to have taken up residence in Ireland where he appears to have had a similar lack of success in his business dealings.[1]

On the elder Byng's return to England in 1672, he and his wife Philadelphia Johnson took up residence not far from the Countess of Middleton, the wife of a Scottish general, with whom the Byng's seem to have been on intimate terms to such an extent that the young George Byng was part of her household for some time. George Byng, father of the future Admiral, had been born in 1663 and he was to enter the Navy in 1678 at the age of fifteen. This was done via patronage, when Byng's father applied to Lord Peterborough who in turn brought George Byng's case to the attention of James Duke of York, who was the Lord High Admiral and as such someone who could grant the Byng family's request that he be given an appointment in the service.[2] George Byng was made a King's Letter Boy, which meant that he was a volunteer, and went aboard the *Swallow*. What happened subsequently showed that the boundary between the Army and the Navy was not as impermeable as it was to become later on. In 1680 whilst on service in the Mediterranean Byng was not happy with his commanding officer and he was discharged at Tangier, which at that time was an English possession, having been part of the dowry of Catherine of Breganza.

George Byng, under the aegis of his uncle, Colonel Johnson, was appointed to a cadetship in the Tangier regiment. In less than four months he was made an ensign and in 1683 Lieutenant in the regiment. Because of these manoeuvres the Navy's commander in the Mediterranean appointed him a Lieutenant in the sea service on 23 February 1684.[3] He saw service in a number of vessels before being paid off in 1687, and at this point Byng went back to his regiment. After the Glorious Revolution in 1688 King James, the former Duke of York and Lord High Admiral, was deposed and William of Orange and his wife Mary, daughter of King James, were invited to take the throne. According to George Byng's own account he played a central part in bringing over a large part of the Navy to the side of William and Mary. However, at the time George Byng was only a Lieutenant and modern scholarship casts doubt on the claims in his unpublished autobiographical sketch.[4] Even so, the young George Byng was to benefit from this change in the monarchy. Under Admiral Russell, who was one of the mainsprings of the coup, George was to flourish in the sea service to such an extent that in 1690 he resigned his commission in the army to his brother and remained for the rest of his life in the Navy. His example shows how, at this time in the late seventeenth century and the early eighteenth century, sea officers could come and go with an ease which would be a surprise to later generations of officers.

Something of great significance also happened on 5 March 1690. George Byng married Margaret Masters at St Paul Covent Garden. Margaret Masters' family had been courtiers under Charles I and her father was a senior Law Officer, so the young George had made a good match. He and Margaret would go on to have eleven sons and four daughters.

When war broke out again in 1701 George Byng was destined for high office: he was destined to become the Earl of Pembroke, who was to be Lord High Admiral, according to his entry in the New Dictionary of National Biography, and this would have made George Byng a very powerful man indeed.[5] However this was thwarted by the rise of the Churchills, one of whom was to sit as an advisor to the Lord High Admiral, who was to no longer be the Earl of Pembroke, but to be Prince George of Denmark, consort to Queen Anne.

This left Byng out in the cold as far as high command was concerned and he was told in no uncertain terms that he either served as a Captain or he had to resign his commission: George was to wait until 1703 before he would get his flag as Rear Admiral of the Red and be sent to the Mediterranean. In that year George Byng was to take part, in command of the inshore squadron, in the capture of Gibraltar. In the following years Byng continued to carve out a very solid career at sea, including his part in checking the pretensions of the Stuarts from returning to Britain when he commanded ships off Dunkirk and then chased them all the way up to Scotland, something which his son John would mirror in the campaign of 1745–46.[6] Byng was appointed to the Board of Admiralty in 1709 and would remain there until 1714, and would return to the Board again in that same year under the new monarch, George I, and he would remain there until 1721. However, appointment to the Board of Admiralty did not preclude his serving at sea which he did in 1715, when again he went to sea to fend off the Stuart pretenders once more, this time during the rising inspired by the Earl of Mar.

In 1717 Byng was to take a squadron into the Baltic, in part inspired by the thought of some that the Swedish were looking to back the Stuarts. However, in reality he was there to stop the predation of privateers, which were there because much of North Europe and the Baltic States were at war. This was a huge danger to British Trade through the Baltic, which was vital to ship building as pitch, tar and deal boards, as well as pine masts, all came from this area. It was to be George Byng's next commands which would see his two sons, his eldest Pattee and his younger son John, go to sea with him. For George this would be his last command at sea and also his most successful.

John Byng was rising fourteen when he was entered on the books of the *Superb*, a 60 gun ship of the line.[7] Her commander was Streynsham Masters, his uncle John's mother's brother. Streynsham Masters had been brought into the Navy under the patronage of his brother-in-law, Sir George.[8] Sir George Byng was ordered to fit out a fleet in early 1718 which would bring about one of the least known naval battles of the eighteenth century and a war which would see old enemies in alliance.

After the conclusion of the War of the Spanish Succession, and the subsequent Treaty of Utrecht, Great Britain had undertaken certain obligations, one of which was as a guarantor of the Austrian Hapsburg land in Italy.[9]

The murky waters of diplomacy which found Great Britain and France in league with one another have exercised others.[10] It is sufficient to say that with the death of Louis XIV in 1715 a period of regency followed and with the active encouragement of the new principal Minister Cardinal Fleury relations between Great Britain and France improved.[11]

Britain too had a new monarch, the Electoral Prince of Hanover, who was to reign as George I.[12] This not only brought a Protestant to the throne, but tied Britain into continental politics ever more closely. One upshot was an influx of German ministers and a concomitant worry that Britain was being tied to continental concerns rather than following the 'Blue Water' strategy, which many of the Tories in Parliament had thought was best.[13]

This strategy would have seen Britain concentrating on her colonies, with less engagement on the continent of Europe. This would have been difficult for the new King to acquiesce in, as his patrimonial lands were in the heart of the Holy Roman Empire and he himself was steeped in the politics of that amorphous institution.[14] Whilst George and his ministers sought to conciliate the Tories in Parliament, Spain's new ruler, Philip V, grandson of Louis XIV of France, and his wife Elizabeth Farnese, were seeking to assert their rights over certain land which the Spanish Hapsburgs had held on the Italian littoral.[15] This would bring them into conflict with the Austrian Hapsburgs. One of the main areas of contention was over the Kingdom of Sicily. Britain too had an interest in the Mediterranean, as witnessed by John Byng's father, who had served under Admiral Herbert in the 1680's at Tangier and in the Mediterranean and subsequently in the War of the Spanish Succession.[16]

The British interest in the Mediterranean can be traced back further even than Sir George's career. In terms of commitment of ships of the Navy it was the War of the League of Augsburg, otherwise know as the Nine Years War, which brought about Britain's decision to keep a squadron of ships in the Mediterranean rather than in the Straits or at Tangier.[17] With this came the need for a dockyard or friendly port. It was this that made the capture of Gibraltar in 1703, and its possible use as base of operations, so significant. It was an operation in which John Byng's father, Sir George, was prominent[18]

However Gibraltar, whilst appearing to be the cork in the bottle, had few of the necessary advantages, apart from location, which a squadron needed. There were no docks and, although there was fresh water, it was insufficient to water a large squadron, hence the need to send British ships to the African coast to water.[19] It was only with the capture of Port Mahon in 1708 that such a base was acquired and it was under Sir George that this was developed as a British base of operations in the Mediterranean.[20] This was to be the most important overseas base for the Royal Navy for the next 49 years, a Hospital being built there in 1711.[21] Britain kept the island of Minorca after the Treaty of Utrecht and with it what has been called by one authority 'the ideal naval harbour of the eighteenth century'.[22]

It is against this labyrinthine background that the fifth son of Sir George and Lady Byng was to start his naval career. The fleet, of which the *Superb* was to be a part, was Britain's response to Spain's continued encroachment on Austrian land in Italy. Far from being a spent force, as is so often portrayed, Spain in the early part of the eighteenth century had undergone a transformation, and not just the dynastic change from Hapsburg to Bourbon.[23] Her Navy, which had been decimated in the previous war, was undergoing reconstruction, much of the new building taking place in Havana.

This in and of itself was a threat which Britain could not ignore. However at the same time that Spain was seeking to assert its rights in the Mediterranean there were also problems in the Baltic which meant that

Britain sent a large squadron into the Sound (the sea area between Denmark and Norway) in 1717.[24] There were domestic problems as well, with Robert Walpole helping to split the Whig party on the issue of intervention in the Mediterranean as well as in the Baltic – in the former case on the grounds that it might lead to war with Spain.[25] In this he was correct, although the nature of the war, as already alluded to, was most usual.[26]

However, when Spain landed troops on Sicily and subsequently expelled the Austrian garrison, British ministers acted: her interests were threatened by the possibility of Spanish naval forces controlling the access to Venice and Turkey. Daniel Defoe put it thus: 'if the present Spanish King sets up a superiority of his naval power, Sicily, in such a hand, would be like a chain drawn across the mouth of the Levant Sea'.[27] According to at least one revisionist account of the period, George I was feeling threatened from a number of quarters.[28] There were fears over Spain's rise in the Mediterranean; also that she might attack British Colonies in the Carolinas in America. George brought in the continental view of politics, viewing the rise of Russia and confrontation with Prussia and Sweden with some alarm. There was, in short, a fear of encirclement.

Thus it was that before a formal declaration of war Britain sent a powerful squadron into the Mediterranean to try and dissuade King Philip V from any further actions. On this occasion Sir George took not just one but two of his sons to sea with him; as well as John, who would be aboard the *Superb*, his eldest son, Pattee, would be aboard his flagship, the *Barfleur*.

Pattee had been born in 1699 and was to go on to be a Privy Councillor and a Member of Parliament, as well as a Treasurer of the Navy: he would later marry the fourth daughter of the Duke of Manchester.[29] Also aboard was Thomas Corbett, Byng's Secretary. He was to be used as an emissary to the Spanish and later would, through George Byng's patronage, become Assistant Secretary to the Admiralty Board and subsequently Secretary to the Board.

Byng entered the Mediterranean with orders to communicate with the Spanish. Part of those instructions are worth quoting:

> But in case the Spaniards do still insist with their ships of war and forces to attack the Kingdom of Naples, or other territories of the Emperor of Italy, or to land in any part of Italy, which can only be the design to invade the Emperor's dominions, against whom only they have declared war by invading Sardinia: or if they should endeavour to make themselves masters of the Kingdom of Sicily, which must be with a design to invade the Kingdom of Naples, in such you are, with all your power, to hinder and obstruct the same.[30]

He detached the *Superb* with a letter for the British Minister at the Spanish Court, James Stanhope. Part of Byng's instructions were that he was to take his orders from Stanhope, who was trying to keep the peace between Britain and Spain. Stanhope ordered Byng to show his instructions to the Spanish Court in the hope of deterring them.[31] The *Superb* carried not just the letter but Sir George Byng's brother-in-law, his secretary and his son John. Corbett, his secretary, was sent ashore with the letter and did not catch up with the fleet until after the battle off Cape Passaro.[32]

George Byng continued on towards the Straits of Messina, not waiting for Philip V's reply. By this time, 30 June, Spanish troops were already on the island of Sicily: upwards of 12,500 troops had helped to expel the Austrian garrison. Byng's view was that he would have to interdict the Spanish line of communications.[33] Byng continued toward the Straits, arriving off Cape Spartel on 8 July where he was rejoined by the *Superb*, and also by the *Rupert*, which he had previously detached and sent into Lisbon to gain intelligence of Spanish intentions. It was from the *Rupert* that Byng learnt of the Spanish movements, which included the stopping of merchant ships sailing from their port as well as the arming and fitting of ships of war.[34] Under his instructions George Byng was allowed to take under his command the squadron of Vice Admiral Charles Cornwallis, which had been operating off the coast of Tripoli. Thus reinforced he continued his voyage.

Stanhope, in consultation with the Earl of Stair, sent Byng instructions, dated 21 July 1718, both of them having now been disabused of the idea that the Spanish wanted peace. In these instructions Byng was to resist the capture of Sicily by force of arms if necessary. He arrived with another letter from the ministers at home stating that: 'you are not to amuse yourself by beginning to take any single ships, but you are, the first blow you strike, to endeavour to destroy their whole force … our trade … will be entirely lost, as it can be in time of war'.[35] He landed troops at Port Mahon to reinforce the garrison there on 25 July before sailing onward towards Naples in response to the Austrian Viceroy's call for assistance. The Spanish had made slow progress down the coast and the Viceroy wanted Byng to convoy German troops which had been hired to resist the Spanish onslaught; Byng embarked these troops on 6 August and landed them on Sicily on the ninth day of that month.[36]

Byng also sought to communicate with the commander of the Spanish force besieging the Citadel at Messina. The commander's response was that he had 'no power to treat with him'.[37] It was whilst all of this was going on that two scouts from the Spanish fleet, sent by Philip to support the troops operating on Sicily, were sighted. This was on 10 August. Byng sent some of his faster ships to keep contact with the Spanish and, in case the chase lasted throughout the night, which seemed likely, he organized what signals they were to make to keep in contact with the main body of the fleet.

It was on 11 August that the action took place between Byng's squadron and the twenty six ships of the Spanish fleet. This was not a line action and Byng had to signal a general chase, as the Spanish split into two groups, one going inshore, the other continuing in the offing.

Byng sent eight ships inshore, under Captain Watson of the *Canterbury*, to engage them. Byng also gave all flag officers instruction as to where to rendezvous if they became separated. The *Superb* was one of the first ships to come into action. It is unfortunate that, unlike his elder brother, who kept a journal, there is no first hand account of John Byng's impression of this action, which as it turned out was devastating to Spanish hopes of a resurgence of their sea power in the Mediterranean.[38] Simms sees Byng's exploit as part of a pre-emptive action by George I, both against the Spanish and the Austrians, in the former case to curb their power, in the latter to get them to sign up along with the Dutch, French and British, who were already in association to form the Quadruple Alliance.[39] Ragnhild Hatton in her biography of George I, also sees Byng's fleet as part of the German monarch's grand design, albeit not quite as black and white as Simms' version, to put pressure on both Charles VI of Austria, as well as Philip V of Spain.[40]

Byng knew that, notwithstanding his having won a stunning victory and having captured or burnt twenty Spanish vessels from ships of the line to transports, his work was not ended. The application of sea power meant the maintenance of a fleet across the lines of communications of the Spanish, as well as the authorisation of local British merchants to hire vessels to counter the Spanish privateers, which were fitted out in the wake of the Battle of Cape Passaro.[41]

In fact Byng remained in the Mediterranean until the end of 1718, and his reward, if such it was, was to wait on the King in Hanover, something Sir George found wearing to say the least.[42] The British squadron was not reduced in the Mediterranean until 1720.[43] The ending to this very strange war was a French invasion of Spain in 1720, which finally brought Philip V to the table. After his sojourn in Hanover Sir George returned to Great Britain and would not fly his flag again at sea. He would also be removed from the Board of Admiralty, only to return in 1727 as First Lord, a position he would retain until his death. George Byng was elevated to the English peerage on 9 September 1721 as Baron Byng of Southhill and 1st Viscount Torrington.[44]

There were, however, eerie foreshadowings of the relief of Minorca in 1756. The task was not wholly the same in as much as when Sir George sailed there was not a state of war between Britain and Spain, and in that his role was to apply maximum diplomatic pressure on the Spanish Court. Nonetheless, he was essentially there to use force to stop Spanish troops from occupying what was the territory of the Holy Roman Emperor in Italy. There could be only one way to do this if deterrence failed: force. He had to show resolution of purpose, and did not need to await instructions, notwithstanding that they had only to come from James Stanhope and not from ministers in England. In any event Byng was mostly at sea and out of communication with Stanhope.

What Sir George did was interpose his fleet between the Spanish troops besieging the fortress and so cut their lines of communication. At the same time he also sought to open negotiations with the Spanish commander in the field; however, as has already been alluded to, he was not willing to treat with Sir George.[45]

He also kept his fleet on station until such time as the pressure paid off. George Byng's correspondence shows quite clearly that the Spanish fleet was the main objective, once he knew that it was fitted out and at sea.[46] He concentrated his forces and used them to cut off the Spanish troops once he saw that diplomacy would not work. Sir George allowed his fleet to attack the enemy as they came up and had sufficient foresight that he arranged a rendezvous for the ships should they become separated from the fleet during the course of the action. It is true that there was clear political direction, notwithstanding Walpole's opposition, and that the fleet, whilst not fully mobilized, had kept quite a number of ships in commission for the squadron in the Soundings, which Byng had commanded the previous year.[47]

What lessons were learned by his son John are in the realm of speculation, in the same way as there is no knowing how much he, as against his elder brother Pattee, was aware of all of the diplomacy which was being carried out. If the young Byng wanted an object lesson in the use of sea power to thwart an invasion, his father's handling of the squadron in the Mediterranean in 1718 was it.

Once the action was over the British navy returned to what passed for a peacetime routine, given the occasional scares and Armaments which punctuate the next twenty years. John Byng was going to have to learn his trade as a young gentleman under instruction. The rules which now governed Byng's progress had been in place since the late seventeenth century.

The world which John Byng had entered was on the one hand familiar, via his father's service, yet once Byng was on the books of the *Superb*, the reality of life aboard must have come as something of a culture shock.[48] He would live with the other volunteers and whilst he would have the advantage that on this his first ship his uncle was in command, he would still be expected to learn the same things as the others. Modern scholarship has redrawn how the recruitment and training of officers was undertaken in the eighteenth century.[49] Whilst under instruction this was not a soft life, nor one which did not require a moderate amount of intelligence at the very least: a volunteer had to be able not just to run a log, but also to learn the intricacies of navigation from the sailing master, as well as all the other practical necessities which were involved in working a ship under sail.[50]

John Byng first went to sea in the second decade of the eighteenth century. Those with whom he sailed would have gained much, if not all, of their experience in the late seventeenth or early eighteenth century. As such they would have been constrained in their ability to navigate long distances by a lack of an accurate time piece. In a similar vein, they would have had only a rudimentary knowledge of the effects how to keep their crews healthy. All of this the young Byng would have absorbed in much the same way as an apprentice learnt his trade from his master.

The irony is that Byng's first commanding officer, Captain Masters, his maternal uncle, had not been destined for the sea, but rather the law. He was called to the Bar in 1699.[51] It was under his brother-in-law George Byng that Masters went to sea, and he was in the Mediterranean with George Byng and was wounded in the leg during the capture of Gibraltar in 1704, when he was appointed lieutenant. Masters had risen to be a post captain in 1710.[52] He was given command of one of the vessels during the Jacobite rebellion of 1715, after which Masters came home with the *Superb* in 1719 and did not serve at sea again. Masters made quite a large amount of money during his service; however, although there is no direct evidence of where the money came from, something can be adduced from the available evidence. He certainly shared in the *Superb's* Prize Money after the Battle of Passaro and as her commander he would have received 25 percent of the total value of any ship taken.

Whilst this says little of his knowledge of the sea, it indicates that he was an educated man who made money from prizes and invested it in land, as did most successful sea officers. How much effect this had on the young Byng is almost impossible to ascertain. Upon Masters' death his executors were able, as his will states, to sell land to the value of £7,000 without touching the main estate.[53]

All of this tends to the view that Byng's maternal uncle fitted the model of the early eighteenth-century sea officer who looked to gain advancement and money in equal measure.

What the young Byng thought of his early exposure to life at sea has not been passed down to posterity. The next step in Byng's career would come when he was examined for Lieutenant. Having entered the Navy at fourteen

Byng was in the middle of the age group of those who wanted to have the sea as their career: some might have been as young as eleven, others as relatively ancient as nineteen. It would take Byng five years of study before he was to present himself to be examined for what was the first true step into the world of the sea officer. Prior to the passing of an examination for Lieutenant, a 'young gentleman' could be on the books of various ships, probably as a Captains servant. Captains were allowed a certain number of places, depending on the size of their vessel, for followers to become young gentleman under instruction.[54]

Under the instructions instituted during the period of James II, a candidate for examination for Lieutenant should have been twenty-one years of age and have spent six years at sea in a number of ratings. When the young man was to be examined he was to present a certificate both of his service and his age. Older historians suggest that if he was examined at home, the porter at the Admiralty could supply the certificates for a 'payment'.[55]

Nicholas Rodger has totally undermined the view implicit in the Lloyd quote that progression in the Navy could be bought at a base. The young Byng would have to show that he could tie knots and answer the questions of the three Captains who were to examine him on seamanship.[56] Once Byng had passed for Lieutenant he would have been on a slow but steady upward curve which, with luck and some influence, would take him to Flag rank. However, although Byng passed for Lieutenant at the age of nineteen, it would not be until his twentieth year that he was given his first appointment to a ship. Only once that had happened would the clock of seniority start ticking.

Byng was to continue in the Mediterranean for most of his early service up to the point when he was made a Post Captain in 1727. After five years as a Lieutenant, this was at the age of twenty four, which was not all that young.

What has been impossible to ascertain from the records which are still extant was the influence of his father George, who, although no longer a member of the Board of Admiralty, was still a powerful figure in the service as an Admiral of the Fleet. Whether he had been able to exert that influence on his son's behalf cannot be established. However, this was almost certainly the case, as he would have wished to see his son gain a good start in the Navy and not have to spend a long time on half pay, which would be the lot of many of the officers during the period.

The Mediterranean had been central to British thinking since the 1690s, when the Fleet was first kept out over the winter of 1694–5.[57] From there it was not a huge leap to see that there would be the need to have a base of operations. First this would be Gibraltar, captured in 1704, then Minorca was taken in 1708 and would remain British until 1756. The Mediterranean was the place where Byng's father would accomplish his most notable achievements. The regulation of the trade in to and out of the Mediterranean had in fact been one of the tasks of the Navy since the 1670's when it was providing escorts for the trade to the Levant; the main opponent at this point was the Barbary Corsairs.[58] There would be a Royal Navy presence in that sea area for the next three hundred years. This was not founded on historical whim but hard politics, since in order to trade with the Mediterranean it was necessary to keep the Corsairs in check. However, there was an even bigger reason for a squadron, or fleet, to be in the Mediterranean, and that was to counteract the influence of France.

That is why it was important to control not just Gibraltar but also Minorca, which sat astride the sea lanes to France's most important port in the Mediterranean, the Naval arsenal Toulon. The worry throughout the eighteenth century was that the French navy would be able to combine the squadrons in the Atlantic ports with those from the Mediterranean and thus pose a direct threat to the British in home waters. There was of course the other salient fact that to counter French influence within the countries bordering the Mediterranean there was a need for a military, and specifically a naval presence in that sea.[59]

That is the reason why Byng was to spend most of his active service in and around the Mediterranean. For the most part the time he spent in the Mediterranean and cruising off the Iberian Peninsular was uneventful. He would have had the opportunity of getting acquainted with Minorca and Gibraltar, as well as ports such as Lisbon in Portugal. During the long peace which stretched from the Treaty of Utrecht in 1713 to the outbreak of War in 1739 there was little or no chance of gaining Prize money.

However, what Byng may have benefited from, once he became a Post Captain, was 'freight money'. This was money that captains of warships were allowed to charge for the carriage in their ship of bullion of any sort. In Byng's case the surviving records make it impossible to ascertain what he gained in this way, however as he was stationed between Minorca and Lisbon he probably would have carried specie for the garrison at Fort St Philip. It was customary to charge between one and two percent of the value of the bullion as payment, even if the money was being taken on government service, which pay for the troops would have been.

This should not be taken as guilt by association: there is no hard evidence that Byng received freight money. Nonetheless, it would be quite unusual, to say the least, that a Captain in his position would decline such opportunities as there undoubtedly were to gain his one or two percent. Now it can be seen why a posting to either Lisbon, where the merchant would freight specie, or the Mediterranean would be so sought after, and this lends weight to the argument already advanced that Byng's interests were being helped by his father, whether or not he was active on the Board of Admiralty.

In 1727 Byng was able to avoid service in the West Indies when the ship to which he was appointed was ordered there. Ordinarily this would have meant that Byng would have been ashore for some time, however he was almost immediately appointed to another vessel. Service in the West Indies was not popular in as much as there was a high mortality rate, as demonstrated in 1726 when a squadron under Admiral Hosier was decimated by yellow fever when he sailed to the West Indies on his way to blockade Spanish America. In the case of Hosier's squadron something like 4,000 officers and men, including the Admiral, died whilst on blockade of the Isthmus of Panama.

Something of the way that the young Captain Byng deported himself during these early years can be found in the correspondence between the British ministers in Portugal, Lord Trawley and the Duke of Newcastle. The first mention of Byng in this correspondence is on 16 June 1728, one year after he had become a Post Captain, when Trawley had requested that a Royal Navy ship pick up some intelligence which could not be entrusted to a letter. Captain Byng was more than happy to comply with this request.[60] All seemed well between the new Captain and the new minister, who would later become the absentee Governor of Minorca immediately prior to its fall. Trawley, by all accounts not the most pleasant of men, was soon writing to the Duke of Newcastle asking that he, rather than the Admiralty, might give orders to Byng. This letter saw Newcastle and the Board of Admiralty, together, it would seem, with Byng, for once united on a subject: the request was rejected, to the disquiet of the minister.[61]

The next letter from Trawley to Newcastle informed Newcastle that Byng could not find the Consul at Lagos from whence the intelligence information had been generated. Furthermore, on close investigation he had found little or no grounds for the Alarm which could not in the first instance be committed to paper. Byng had also looked into the predations of the Barbary Corsairs whilst he, Byng, was at Lagos.[62]

There it might have ended: the first meeting between Trawley and Byng seemed, on the face of it, to have gone quite well, but there was a worrying undertone. Allowing for the fact that these were official despatches between the minister and the Secretary of State, there are more than hints of strain between the two, both of whom seem to have taken a stance on the dignity and authority of their respective positions within government. This was to break out into the open with a complaint concerning Byng's refusal to acquiesce in some of the requests that Trawley made of him. However, this would take a full four years to ferment before the vitriolic Lord would once again vent his spleen over Byng's behaviour, this time in July 1732, and once again over the matter of precedence.[63] So bad were relations between the two men that Trawley asked that Byng not be allowed to return to the Lisbon station.

What this tells us about the young Byng is that he had enough self confidence to stand up to a man known for his outbursts, and that he also seems to have been as blunt as Trawley when faced with the question as to whether he would accede to the minister's request to take his notification of who was allowed aboard British ships, or whether he would await instructions from the Admiralty on the matter. On the face of it this all seems very petty, but perhaps it was a shy man's defence when faced with a bully.

What can be said with some degree of certainty is that after fourteen years in the Navy the young Byng was aware of the respect due to a sea officer and was not afraid to stand his ground.

This is how the young John Byng spent the years from 1727 to 1739. There would be no fleet actions and no great tests of command. This did not mean that all was right with the world – in fact far from it. However, with the exception of the Barbary Corsairs, there were no major disruptions to peace time activity within the Mediterranean.

The one area were there was still no settlement was with regard to Spain over access to its South American colonies. A settlement of sorts had been arrived at under the provision of the Treaty of Utrecht in 1713, one part of which gave Britain the contract for the *Asiento de negros*, which in plain language was the contract to supply slaves to the Spanish Empire. In technical terms the Spanish had abolished the trade in slaves, but not slave owning, and therefore third parties supplied them. As part of the general peace after the War of the Spanish Succession, Britain had been granted that contract, which meant that British merchants could trade legally with Spanish colonies, something which they had been doing illegally throughout the early eighteenth century.[64]

The Company which was set up to carry out this contract was the South Sea Company. The Company had the sole right to carry on trade with the Spanish colonies, and, like its counterpart the English East India Company, this put them in a very powerful position and those who invested in the Company were amongst the most prominent men in Britain. The dispute was mainly about the refusal of the Spanish to honour their treaty obligations and the relative inefficiency of their bureaucracy. However the situation was made far worse by the blatant illegal trade which the South Sea Company and its agents indulged in, and the fact that because so many prominent people had investments in the Company it was politically very powerful.[65]

This meant that it was difficult for Robert Walpole to come up with a solution which was to the liking of the South Sea Company and its investors. Negotiations dragged on throughout the period 1737–39 and it was thought at one point that a solution had been found. However, in the end, and much against his will, Walpole was persuaded that the use of force against the Spanish in the Americas was necessary, yet there was a great concern that there should not be a war in Europe if that was at all possible.[66]

One incident that came to symbolize this dispute more than any other was the plight of Captain Jenkins and his ear, which had been cut off. Under the Treaty of Seville of 1729, which had ended the quasi war with Spain between 1726 and 1729, Spanish warships had the right to stop and search British vessels off their colonies. This war had also precipitated the sending of the unfortunate Admiral Hosier to Panama in 1727.

It was not just regular warships which undertook these duties: the *guarda costas* were in fact licensed by the Spanish authority to stop British shipping in the West Indies and search them for contraband. The *Guard Costa* were the Spanish equivalent of British privateers, licensed by the state but with the ships, crew and everything else supplied by private individuals hoping to make a profit from captured enemy ships. However, as with so much else concerning this dispute, the lines were not clearly drawn between those who had a royal warrant to stop and seize vessels from Spain's colonies and those who were no more or less than pirates. The predations of the *guarda costa* were a major problem and it was here that Captain Jenkins comes into view. In 1731 his ship was spotted by the *guarda costa*, who not only illegally stopped his vessel but also, in a cruel and vicious act, cut off one of his ears.[67] However it was not until 1738, as part of the heightened tension of that period, that Jenkins was called to the Bar of the House of Commons to recount his ordeal and according to some accounts flourish the severed ear in a jar, presumably to give weight to his testimony. As Philip Woodfine has shown, at the time of the incident in 1731 there is virtually no published record of the event and certainly none of the London papers even mention it. However, as Woodfine goes on to point out, Jenkins and his ear became totemic of the unreasonable and barbaric attitude of Spain and the incident helped to play to the growing public outcry, orchestrated by the South Sea Company against Walpole and his pacific policies.[68] However, the war which was declared in October 1739 would not plunge Byng and the Navy into a large scale war with all of Britain's old foes: it would, for the main, be a war fought thousands of miles away and one in which at first Captain Byng took little or no part.

Chapter Two

A Most Unsatisfactory War

The situation as the war with Spain entered its first full year was a strange one: there was a full-blown assault, under Admiral Vernon, going ahead against Spain's colonies and manoeuvres in Europe and the Mediterranean. In effect, what the British were seeking to do was to stop Spain from concentrating its forces and sending them out to the West Indies; to this end Admiral Haddock, who had been commanding in the Mediterranean, was sent new orders.[1] As was often the case at the start of many of the eighteenth century wars, the British ministry was seeking to find out what the enemy's intentions were. In this case the concern was the possible conjunction of the squadrons at Cadiz and Ferrol, and if so were these combined squadrons going to go to the West Indies or into the Mediterranean to disrupt British trade and threaten Minorca.[2] Haddock was sent at least two sets of contradictory orders dependent upon circumstances. The effect on Byng was that in October of 1740 he was ordered to take three other ships under his command and keep a watch off the port of Cadiz.[3] The ministry's handling of the opening of the war became a matter of hot debate within parliament, to the extent that some members of the House called for an enquiry.[4]

Byng's small squadron off Cadiz was made up of two heavy ships and one fireship. He was to watch the movements of the Spanish and report them to his Commander-in-Chief, Admiral Haddock. Herbert Richmond is of the opinion that Byng's prolix style of writing on many subjects betrays an inbred fatalism which was seen throughout his career in the senior ranks of the service.[5] This is too harsh: Byng did carry out what he was ordered to do, notwithstanding what he wrote and the style in which he wrote it.

As the War in Europe and the Mediterranean went nowhere, Byng stayed in the Mediterranean and took command of five more ships, as Admiral Haddock sought to keep the Spanish and French from joining up – something he feared might happen and thus threaten Britain's navy with an overwhelming force. The Admiral in the Mediterranean and the ministry at home did not know that France had no intention in 1741 of starting a general war.[6] Byng remained in position and at one point in October 1741 gave chase to the Spanish as they left Cadiz. However, he and the rest of the ships could not catch up with them: this would be as close as he would come to another general action until the next war.[7]

However Byng was not to stay in the Mediterranean. In 1742, for the one and only time, he was to cross the Atlantic and take charge of the Newfoundland fisheries. This was an important step up in his naval career, as he would also be made Governor of Newfoundland for the duration of his stay. This allowed some opportunity to make money, as a later Governor, George Rodney, was to show.[8]

During the time that Byng was in Newfoundland he did his best to regulate the trade and, within reason, stamp out the obvious abuse which could occur when there was such a lucrative trade being carried on by a limited number of people. As was the case with such appointments it was only for one season and in 1743 Byng was back in home waters, this time as part of the channel squadron in command of the 50 gun ship *Winchester*. In 1744 he was appointed to a second rate ship of the line, the *Saint George*. She was a ninety gun ship, and Byng was to be on very familiar ground when in command of her: she was to be part of the convoy for the trade that was going to Lisbon and thence into the Mediterranean.

This gives ample evidence that Trawley's protestation that Byng should never be allowed back on the Lisbon station had not been heeded at the Admiralty.[9] Byng by this time had spent the whole of his adult life in the navy and, unlike many of his contemporaries, a good proportion of those twenty seven years had been at sea rather than on half pay.[10] The next step in his career would be when he was given his flag and moved from Post Captain to Rear Admiral.

Byng was promoted to Rear Admiral, by seniority, in March of 1745, and proceeded to take part in the maritime aspect of the campaign to defeat Charles Edward Stuart and the rising in Scotland and the North of Britain. The background to these events was that by 1745 Britain was at war with France once more and, during the course of a long campaign on the continent of Europe, France was prepared, for the last time, to use the threat of the Stuart restoration as a weapon to destabilize the British.[11]

What has become know in historical shorthand as 'The '45' evoked a large response from the Navy and Byng would play a central role in that effort. At first Admiral Byng was to be under the orders of one of the most colourful and insightful British Admirals of the mid-eighteenth century, Edward Vernon.

It would be Vernon's task to stop the French from sending aid to the Jacobites and to this end he placed Byng in command of a squadron which would try and blockade the Channel ports in Flanders. In this Vernon and John Byng would be undertaking the same task that George Byng had done almost forty years before in 1708.[12] For the blockade Byng was giving a certain amount of leeway as the plan evolved and it was decided that Byng should be sent to cruise off Dunkirk and watch for any vessels running into the North Sea and hence to Scotland.[13] Byng was ordered to keep up a regular correspondence with General Wade and the other General officers in the Highlands. As Richmond points out, once Byng arrived off Scotland he received orders from both the Generals and the Duke of Cumberland, and the Sate Paper shows that there was a continuing stream of letters back and forth on matters both great and small.[14] This is a very good point to look at the career of Byng: his actions must be seen as an unqualified success as he and his small squadron tracked the movements of Charles Stuart and sought to cut off any means of reinforcement from France by sea.[15] Much of what appears in this correspondence is information concerning the location of the Jacobites, what they might have been doing on the coast, and how Byng's squadron might disrupt that.

Byng had 18 vessels with him off Scotland as he looked to restrict the movements of the supporters of Charles Edward Stuart. Off Edinburgh he had two fifty-gun ships, two forty-four gun ships and three smaller vessels. Sailing between Edinburgh and the north of Scotland there were a further five vessels, and off the west coast there were four vessels. In addition to these there were one or two vessels which were as far south as Hull.[16] This was not necessarily the largest force in the navy, however it showed beyond a shadow of a doubt that Byng was more than capable of operating in close co-operation with the Army and, more to the point, was able deal with the highest ranks, for example the Duke of Cumberland, with little or no problem.[17]

It was to be on Culloden Moor that the fate of the Stuarts was to be finally settled, yet Admiral Byng had played a not insignificant part in stopping what had, at the start, been quite a threat to the House of Hanover.

Whilst Byng was going about his business off Dunkirk other matters which were to affect both him and many other sea officers were taking place off Toulon. In February of that year the British fleet under Admiral Thomas Mathews and his deputy Richard Lestock fought an inclusive action against the Franco-Spanish fleet. Whilst the van under Admiral Rowley and the centre under Admiral Mathews came into action, Admiral Lestock held back. What lay behind this miscarried action was both personal disagreement, concerning the promotion of Lestock, and, much more importantly, the quality of the Sailing and Fighting instructions. In these there was a set of instructions on how to form the line of battle, discussed later in connection with the action off Minorca in 1756.

The Navy in this war had not been all that successful and in fact there was discontent with it. There were just a few incidents which were to lift this gloom: one would be the return of Captain Anson in the *Centurion* having attacked and taken the Manila Galleon, but little else up to the operations off Scotland in 1745, which were successful but unspectacular.[18] What happened was that the battle was not the end of the matter and that the political nation took an interest in what was happening with the Navy, hence its being brought before Parliament.

The arguments between the two Admirals was every bit as vicious as that which would engulf Byng in the next war and Keppel in the American Revolutionary War.[19] Like the subsequent debacles, this one was to end up being examined on the Floor of the House of Commons over a great many days. However, unlike the others which have already been mentioned, there seems to have been less party politics with this examination, at least in the first instance.[20] There seems to have been high expectation by supporters of both Admiral Mathews and Lestock as to what the results might be of all of this Parliamentary activity.

All of this political activity led to questioning of the running of the war, and this in turn led to a great deal of time being spent in Parliament not just discussing the action but holding an inquiry into the events leading up to it as well. The way this was done was by the House as a whole sitting as a committee. They interrogated most of the participants at the Bar of the House, some of whom turned out to be less articulate than others. In particular, Admiral Mathews and some of his supporters performed badly during this questioning which undermined his case.[21] All of this Parliamentary time ended with the committee making an address to the King for a court martial to be held on both officers. In fact, there were to be at least eleven officers court martialled after the action, excluding the two Admirals. In the end several officers were found guilty of neglect and were dismissed from the service, but many were restored to the service. One of these was Captain Temple West, who would be second in command of the squadron which Byng took out to the Mediterranean.[22]

Byng's part in this affair was that he would sit on the Court which tried Admiral Lestock, which was held aboard the *Prince of Orange* moored at the Nore. There were three Admirals and fourteen Captains who sat on this Court: the number would not be reduced to thirteen in total until after the Act of 1749, which changed the system as well as the sentences which the Court could deliver. The Lestock trial started on the 6 May 1746, and after all of the evidence had been heard the Court was unanimous in its decision to acquit Admiral Lestock.[23] It would be October when the last court martial was held, that of Admiral Mathews. He was blamed by Admiral Lestock and in the end Admiral Mathews was the officer dismissed from the service for breach of duty. It is unlikely that these verdicts altered how Byng and other officers thought about the Sailing and Fighting instructions. What did happen was that after the war a new Act was passed in 1749 which reduced the scope for alternate punishments to be handed out for neglect: there would now be only one – the death sentence.

Byng was next to be appointed to the Mediterranean as Second in Command to Admiral Medley. He was ordered to sail in December 1746 but did not sail until February 1747 with four ships as reinforcements for Medley.[24] In 1747 Byng operated off the Lerins Islands with a small squadron and would subsequently take over command of the Mediterranean squadron. He would see out the end of the war in the Mediterranean, not sailing home until July 1748.[25]

Byng has received heavy criticism for this part of his service; his letters home are seen as doleful and negative. He was also supposed to have put his favourites in the best cruising grounds, to help them to capture prizes. He entered the war in the Mediterranean when it was a relatively quiet period, and from mid 1747 the war was in effect running down in that area. Byng was ordered to send ships home yet was expected to still carry out his original orders, which he did quite successfully.

All seemed set fair in the period between 1748 and 1755. A great deal changed at home. He bought the land for what was to be his new country house at Wrotham Park, and he would have a change in his domestic situation: he met Mrs Hickson, a widow whom he took as his mistress. Up to this point Byng had been bachelor for all his life. He was promoted to Vice Admiral of the Red and elected to Parliament for Rochester in Kent. He had money and a position. Meanwhile, across the Atlantic in the Ohio Valley violence was breaking out between English and French settlers as they pushed further into the hinterland of America; the seeds of the next war were already being sown.

Chapter Three

Blue Water and Fog

On 3 May 1755 three squadrons of ships weighed and sailed from harbour: aboard were troops and a new Governor General of Canada.[1] Such movements were not unknown during the period of peace which followed the signing of the treaty of Aix La Chappelle in 1748.[2] One of the three squadrons was to escort the others some six hundred miles out into the Atlantic before the six ships which made up this detachment would return to harbour, leaving the rest to make their way across to the Banks of Newfoundland.[3] Seven days earlier, on 27 April, another squadron, numbering eleven ships had made their way out into the Atlantic, and, as with the other two squadrons, their landfall was also to be Newfoundland.[4]

The two groups of ships were of differing numbers and force: those which sailed on 3 May numbered thirteen ships of the line, after the detachment of their escort, as against the eleven which had sailed in April.

There was a difference too in their armament: of the thirteen ships only four were fully armed, the other nine carried most of their great guns in their holds, a practice called *en flûte*. In place of guns these ships carried troops to reinforce the overseas garrison. All of the earlier eleven ships of the line were fully manned and armed.[5]

These two squadrons were to meet on 10 June 1755; or rather, parts of both squadrons would meet, off Newfoundland's Grand Banks.

The two squadrons were under command of the French Admiral de la Motte, who was to carry troops to the French colonies in Canada along with a new Governor General.[6] The other squadron was under the command of Vice Admiral Edward Boscawen.[7]

What happened next was less of a fleet action and more of a skirmish; Boscawen's ships found just three of the French vessels, as the others had been scattered by stormy weather on the crossing, then been shrouded in fog, for which the Grand Banks were renowned. The *Alcide*, the *Lys* and the *Dauphin-Royal* were engaged by, amongst others, the *Dunkirk*. The British ship was commanded by Richard Howe, who informed his opposite number that France and Britain were still at peace before he opened fire. What followed was a short sharp action in which the *Alcide* and the *Lys* were captured. Aboard the latter was ten of the fifty two companies of infantry which were bound for Quebec.[8] The *Dauphin-Royal* escaped and on 12 June more of the French ships sailed safely into the principal French base in Canada at Louisburg. Along with the ships came another twenty-six infantry companies to reinforce the defences of French Canada.[9]

What happened off Newfoundland would have a profound effect on Britain, France and, although he did not know it at the time, John Byng. One of Byng's contemporaries summed it up thus: 'It gives me much concern that so little has been done, since any thing has been done at all' wrote Hardwicke to Lord Anson on 14 July 1755 after hearing reports of the action.[10] What had caused these ships to be ordered to Newfoundland's Grand Banks and who had given them permission to attack the French?

In 1748 with the peace of Aix la Chappelle, Britain had been forced to confront the dichotomy in British policy between those who believed in colonial acquisition and those who thought that Britain's best interest was served by seeking to keep the balance of power on the continent of Europe in equilibrium.[11] One of the things which had happened during the War of the Austrian Succession was that a large portion of what is now Belgium and the Netherlands passed effectively under French control. This forced ministers to face up to where Britain's interests lay, and according to one modern historian it was in Europe that Britain had to find an accommodation with the French, otherwise they would be in control of the coast from Zealand to Bretagne.[12] This would leave France in control of some of the most important coastal and river access to central Europe.

What would have to be surrendered would be some of Britain's overseas gains made during the last war. The most important of these would be Cape Breton in Canada and the fortress and port of Louisburg. The Earl of Sandwich as well as the First Lord of the Admiralty, Bedford, protested over this in the strongest terms. They had seen the attack on France's overseas colonies as vital both to increase Britain's overseas possessions as well as securing those which she already had. The most important of these would be the thirteen colonies in America. These were, and had been, under threat from French Canada, as well as the French possessions in Florida and the Mississippi.[13]

Louisburg had been attacked or threatened both in the War of the Spanish Succession as well as in the late war. Now that it was in British possession it was not to be given up lightly; it was seen as one of the blocks to the final peace and engendered an impassioned debate within the ministry as well as amongst opposition politicians.[14] Lord Chesterfield told Newcastle:

I was aware at first of the difficulties it would create, and, when I heard people bawling and huzzaing for its being taken, I wished it in their throats. But know I think you have no option left, and you might as much easier give up Gibraltar and Minorca.[15]

In the end Louisburg was handed back and French troops withdrew from the Netherlands and Brabant, though this did not sit well, as one popular ballad gave voice:

If Britain's sons all Gallic arts despise.
Why listen we at aix to Gallic Lies ?
If on our Navy Heaven confers success.
Why this long quibbling, and this fine address?[16]

The peace was at best temporary and the underlying issues would be revisited again in the short to medium term. Henry Fox, the Secretary of War at the time, summed up the ministry's point of view: ' because our conquests at sea, or in America, would in the end signify nothing if, while we were busied about them, the French should make themselves masters of the continent of Europe'.[17] This is why the two squadrons were off the Grand Banks on that foggy June day. That and the fact that tensions between Britain and France in the Ohio Valley were causing friction. This a loose word for fighting in the wilderness which was, in theory, the preserve of the Native Americans and fur trappers.[18] The peace was neither final nor was it satisfactory for either France or Britain. At sea it was Boscawen who fired the opening salvo of what became known subsequently as the Seven Years War: on land the fate of General Braddock caused consternation and concern in equal measure when he was defeated on the Monongahela River in 1755.[19]

The mood seven years after the Peace of Aix was caught by the Duke of Newcastle: 'They are building forts endeavouring *a la sourdine* to confirm our great valuable and extensive dominions in North America to a bare *liziere* of country towards the sea'.[20] This very nicely summarized the problem for British ministers in what turned out to be a short period of peace. The increasing incursion of the French and their allied Native Americans down the Ohio Valley, and the new chain of fortifications which followed in their wake, was a huge source of worry and increased the tensions which had been simmering since the last War. This is why Braddock had been sent, and why the companies of infantry aboard the French ships were in many ways more important than the ships themselves.

It also brought once again into sharp relief the dilemma of whether British ministers should seek to check French ambitions at home or abroad.

It seemed nothing short of war would settle this but whether this was to be a Blue Water campaign, in which colonies and overseas factories were to be the target was as yet unclear. This was one of the problems which faced the King's ministers in 1755: how to stem French aggression without precipitating a general European war. In the ensuing brinkmanship Braddock, Boscawen and Motte were the opening gambit.

However both British moves failed in their primary objectives; the backwoods were still the preserve of the French and their allies and most of the reinforcements which the French sent had got through.

Boscawen's instructions, whilst allowing him to take the ships at sea to blockade Louisburg, did not allow for an assault on the port. It is to be doubted whether such an attack, had it been allowed, would have been successful without the troops and all the appurtenances of siege warfare which had had to be used last time that it was taken. The prospects of a blockade of Louisburg were summed up by Boscawen thus: 'the dismal prospect of floating islands of ice sufficient to terrifie the most daring seaman'.[21] He sailed off the Isle Royale and was joined on 21 June by six more ships of the line which had come from across the Atlantic, and by the beginning of August two more vessels, frigates, sent from Virginia had joined his squadron.[22] Keeping station off Louisburg was not easy, however Boscawen could at least make use of the British yard at Halifax for supplies. Nonetheless his expanded squadron, or more particularly the seamen, were starting to suffer, something which was to have a direct impact on what the Royal Navy could or could not do as 1755 drew to a close and plans were made on both sides of the channel for the coming year.[23] Just at year's end Vice Admiral Edward Hawke sailed for the Bay of Biscay with sixteen ships of the line, his instructions, after intense debate, allowed him, like Boscawen, to take ships of the line but not merchant vessels. However, once Hawke had sailed his instructions were changed , and he was now allowed to capture privateers and merchant vessels.[24] In total the Royal Navy captured some 300 ships and their cargoes during 1755, worth, according to one historian, 30 million livres.[25] Along with the ships and the cargo were 7,500 seamen, all of whom were brought back to Britain.[26]

What happened in Britain was that King George II sought to gain protection for his patrimony lands in Hanover. Under the Act of Settlement the Monarch could not use armies or navies except in defence of Britain and its land and territories, not of those which were, as with George and Hanover, his or her personal fiefdom.

The political outlook throughout 1755 had been grim and George, notwithstanding his British ministers' misgivings, had made his annual trip to Hanover and whilst he was there had arranged to step up its defences.[27]

France, through their resident Minister in Britain, had made it clear that if open war came about it would not be limited to the colonies.[28] As such Hanover would be a target and George increased the size of its army by 8,000 to 29,000, as well as signing agreements with other Electors to supply troops on payment of a subsidy.[29]

In France King Louis XV also had been meeting with his ministers, yet in this case it was more as to when and where France might strike. The main point under discussion was how to offset any British gains in the Americas with French gains in Europe which could then be negotiated away at the subsequent peace. Also under discussion was whether France's new ally, Fredrick II of Prussia, should strike at Hanover as a pre-emptive move. Louis decided against this but attacks against the Austrian Netherlands, much of which had been occupied by France in the preceding war, were discussed, although the King decided that hostilities would be signalled to the Austrians by a formal declaration of War.[30] But war was not coming: it had already begun. The actions of Braddock and Boscawen, had set the seal on it. At the start of 1756 Great Britain had some 60,000 soldiers, most of which were needed either in the Americas or in India. By the same date Louis' army numbered some 220,000 regulars and 60,000 militia, most of whom were to operate on the continent of Europe in the war.[31]

The French Navy, despite the set back off the Grand Banks, and the captured seamen already alluded to, ended 1755 increasing in strength, with three new ships of the line launched, one 74 and two 64's, and nine ships of the line under construction as the year ended. There were 57 ships of the French Navy either at sea, in port or undergoing repairs.[32] All of the ships in service in 1755 took 7,500 officers and men to send them sea. For France to equip a fleet of ships for service required the King to allocate some 17.5 million livres, to the Navy for the coming year of 1756, which would equate to the equivalent of 6 million pounds at the time. This would allow the French to fit out some 45 ships of the line for future operations. Overall the King's, and by implication France's, finances were in a good state: the annual income was 260 million livres over the previous five years. Some estimate that France could have raised 120 million livres in extra revenue.[33] In terms of financial muscle the French Navy entered 1756 in good shape.

What of the British Navy as the year came to an end? From late in the year the Royal Navy was getting prepared for war and by October there were 77 ships in commission. Fifteen of these were under Boscawen off Louisburg and would not return from Canadian waters until November. There were twenty four ships, most of them of the line, cruising in home waters, and there were another twenty four being fitted for service in home ports.[34] In all some forty ships were in home waters whose sole purpose was the defence of trade and of the kingdom.[35]

This in itself was a major achievement for the ministry, as towards the end of the last war there had been problems with the large number of ships which needed repairing and refitting.[36] Much of this work was caused not just by the exigency of war but as a result of how timber was stored in the Dockyards.

This meant that by 1749–51 there were less than thirty ships of the line that the Royal Navy could call upon in time of war. The green, unseasoned wood promoted rot and fungus, which meant that the average life span of a wooden ship before a great repair (i.e. a major refit) was needed was reduced from an average 12–17 years to less than ten. Given that the Royal Dockyards could only refit between five and seven ships a year and that there were above thirty ships in need of attention, the scale of the problem can be surmised.[37] Anson carried through some reorganisation of the Royal Dockyards and placed new orders with private yards, thus leaving the Royal Yards free to concentrate on refitting and repairing ships. Part of the reform was to dismiss some of the artificers of the yards, perversely allowing the Navy Board to improve its credit, and it was this credit which was so vital to the working of the Navy in 1755–56, as what had started as a punitive expedition translated into war.[38]

Byng took over cruising in the Bay of Biscay in October with seventeen ships of the line. Numbers were important in every war in the eighteenth century, as it was necessary to find the balance of how many ships were available for the various services the Royal Navy would be called upon to perform. In 1755 much of the Royal Navy was already fitted and much of it manned and ready for service. However, as November moved into December more ships came home and most went into dock: those which had been with Boscawen came into port and had lost nearly 2,000 dead.[39]

Manning was a perennial problem on both sides of the English Channel. The death of 2,000 men from Boscawen's squadrons was a huge blow at the start of a war.[40] According to one source the pool from which the Royal Navy could draw was approximately eighty thousand seamen, whilst on the French side their Royal Navy had some fifty two thousands seamen in their classes.[41] At least in theory, the French system allowed the Navy to know how many men it could draw upon whereas Britain, despite the attempt in the early seventeen hundreds to create a register, which failed, was forced to rely on the press gang. This was much abused both at the time and subsequently by some historians, yet it was a vital tool for manning the Navy. On the other hand recruitment was only one aspect, since preserving the health of the crews was as important and the longer the ships were overseas and away from the well-developed network of bases the unhealthier men could get. This seems to have been the case with Boscawen's crew off Louisburg, and hence the high mortality rate aboard his squadron.

With this gathering of forces came a new phase in the war. Where would the French strike next: on the continent of Europe, or in the Americas, or, as at the start of the previous war, would hostilities be carried out at sea, as the British already were? Invasion was something which, even if not considered as practical, would, for the French, keep the ministry in Britain on its guard and divert both men and ships away from the Americas. All of this comes down to what each side knew about the other's intentions. British ministers seem to have had a steady stream of information about which ships were fitting out in what port in France. Chancellor Hardwicke's papers contain hundreds of such reports.[42]

Throughout August reports were being received about a build up of activity in the French Mediterranean ports, intelligence which came from consuls in friendly countries throughout the region.[43] One such was received on 6 August 1755: 'Orders are sent to Toulon to equip with all expedition all new ships there and to get the old ones in condition for the same purpose... Many say, tho' it is only conjecture, that they are intended for Gibraltar'.[44]

This of course does not prove that the French had any plans for Gibraltar or any other place within the Mediterranean, but when taken with the comments of the French Minister to George II which have already been alluded to, that any war would not be confined to the colonies, it should have at least put the ministry on the alert. On 30 August they received from the British Minister in Turin, the Earl of Bristol, a despatch dated to the sixteenth of that month:

> It is said that a body of 20,000 men are preparing to form a camp at Valence in Dauphine; some that it is to be a corps of observation, which is intended to be ready on all occasions.[45]

Any such force mustered in the south-east of France would be in an excellent position to embark at either Toulon or Marseilles on the French Mediterranean coast. Another dispatch, this time from Bern, confirmed what the Earl of Bristol had reported, albeit with some modification, in as much that there was a camp at Valence but that not all of the infantry were being brought up to full strength.[46] On 16 September a despatch dated 25 August from Nice gave more news of the build up of French troops and the preparations at Toulon: 'The French are augmenting their land forces and are actually recruiting in Languedoc and Provence: last post orders came to Toulon to fit out 16 sail of men-of-war'.[47] Others spoke of the French seeking to buy three ships of the line from the Genoese, as a well as a host of other details. What they all seem to point to was that France was looking to mobilize as much of its navy as it could and that there was a build up of troops in the south-east of the country.[48] By late September more information of the same kind was being received from consuls around the Mediterranean, which suggested that ships at Toulon were being fitted out.[49]

This was important for two reasons. First of all British ministries throughout the eighteenth century were worried that the Toulon, Rochefort and Brest squadrons would join up and sail into the English channel, a move which would restrict trade and possibly presage an attempt, if there was news of troop concentrations in northern France, of an invasion.

The second thing which the ministry and their Naval and Military advisers had to look to, if the French were manning their Toulon squadrons, was a possible attack on one of the two bases, Gibraltar or Minorca. These two were important to Britain as they allowed the Royal Navy to keep ships in the Mediterranean not just victualled and watered but also repaired, using the dockyard in Minorca at Port Mahon.[50] They were also potentially vulnerable to attack from French forces. However, both Gibraltar and Port Mahon were neglected in the period after the War of the Austrian Succession. In both cases the garrisons were allowed to dwindle and most of the senior military officers were on leave of absence in Britain. Furthermore, there was often difficulty in getting skilled dockyard workers to go overseas to either Gibraltar or Port Mahon.[51] James Lind put it most succinctly when he stated that Port Mahon was 'by much the most valuable' when compared against the merits of Gibraltar.[52] Indeed it has been called 'the ideal naval harbour of the eighteenth century'.[53] This was most certainly the case as Europe tumbled towards war in 1755.

Britain had kept ships in the Mediterranean since 1694, half way through the War of the League of Augsburg. At that time Lisbon was where they were victualled and minor repairs could be made. It was, as has already been mentioned, the following war which gave the Royal Navy the two bases which it needed to keep a close watch on what the French squadrons in the Mediterranean were doing and, importantly, to stop them from leaving undetected and hence form a dangerous combination with the French squadrons on the Atlantic coast. How the ministry reacted to the information which was coming in would be vital. There were only so many ships, despite the large overall number, which could be detached from duty at home and sent overseas on operations.

This first assessment would in the end rest on the experience and judgement of one man, Anson. George Anson had had a successful career up until this point which included his famous voyage of circumnavigation between 1740 and 1744. Additionally, he had fought an action in 1747, already alluded to, off Cape Finisterre.[54] Furthermore, he had extensive experience at the Admiralty, and by 1755 was in all but name head of the service. He was also married to Elizabeth Hardwicke, daughter of the Lord Chancellor, and so connected to one of the most important political families.[55] Finally, he was independently wealthy, much of this due to the capture of a Plate Fleet ship on his voyage of circumnavigation.[56]

How then did Anson look at the situation in 1755, when there was much intelligence which said there was a build up of forces in the Mediterranean? There was also information which purported to show a similar build up in Northern France. This might presage the much-feared invasion. One innovation in which Anson was intimately involved was the creation of the Western Squadron. This was formed by bringing all the principal squadrons operating in home waters to cruise in the Western approaches and the Bay of Biscay, thus preventing a conjunction of the French squadrons.[57] Whilst not the sole inspiration for the Western Squadron, Anson had proposed the conjunction of the home squadrons in July 1746, backed by Sandwich, Bedford and Admiral Vernon, all of whom had had similar thoughts on this matter. It was this squadron, and the need to have sufficient ships for it, which was to weigh heavily on Anson in the closing months of 1755.[58] Admiral Warren described Anson and the Western Squadron thus: 'No service had ever been so agreeable to him as this cruise under Anson ... with respect to action he had learned more from him than in all the time at sea before'.[59]

In December of that year the important thing was the number of ships which could be brought into service. There is much information on these numbers, however some of it was drawn up in the wake of what happened in May 1756 and therefore has to be treated with some scepticism.[60] In bald figures, there were eighty-three ships in commission at the end of the year. Of these, eleven were in the Plantations, three were in the Mediterranean, four in the East Indies, fourteen cruising in home waters and fifty-one fitting out in home ports.[61]

The salient point is the number which was available in home waters, which, if those cruising are aggregated with those fitting out, totalled 65 vessels of all rates. This number was more than enough to have a powerful Western Squadron on station. What should also be noted is that even allowing for the increased tension between Britain and France, there were just three ships stationed in the Mediterranean. It was here that any major reinforcement might be needed and it would be on the advice of Anson, in consultation with the Duke of Newcastle the leader of the government, and the King that any such decision would be made. The King was no mere cipher in these discussions; he had his views and they were not just politely listened to and ignored. He had paid out of his own funds for the defence of Hanover and as an Electoral Prince held some sway, although how much is a moot point, in the Holy Roman Empire.[62] He, Newcastle and Anson were all in agreement as to what was the most pressing danger, and it was not in the Mediterranean.

Some of the reasons why this was thought to be the case can be gleaned from the intelligence received from the northern ports of ships being fitted out and of troop movements, as well as the rumours that Prince Charles Edward Stuart the Young Pretender was to lead this force. As summed up in one report received by the ministry early in 1756, the threat of invasions would: 'alarm the nation, distress our credit and prevent our transport being sent abroad'.[63] Wild rumours, common in most wars in this period, were that there were hundreds of transports ready to sail, with smugglers ready to pilot these ships to land their troops from Kent to Hampshire.[64]

There were said to be twenty-eight squadrons of cavalry and upwards of one hundred and eighteen battalions of infantry camped near the coast ready to be embarked for this grand scheme.[65] Such was the nature of the material which the King and his principal misters had to work on at the beginning of 1756. The forces kept in Britain were small by comparison with those reported by informants on the continent. There were approximately 13,000 foot soldiers and some 4,000 dragoons, plus the foot and horse guards.

Thus what they decided was that at the beginning of 1756 the Western Squadron and home defence would take priority over any possible French action in the Mediterranean. This meant that any squadron sent to reinforce ships already out there would have to wait for ships to be brought forward out of reserve or for vessels to return from other duties. The crux of the argument was to place the maximum force to the maximum good for the country and its trade, for without a secure trade there would be no secure credit and credit is what most British eighteenth-century wars were fought on. The Mediterranean, and the French build up there, would have to wait.

There was a small squadron of seven vessels in the Mediterranean, reduced to three at one point. The three largest vessels were one ship of sixty guns and two of fifty guns, more a squadron of observation than a serious military force. These vessels were under the command of the Hon. George Edgcumbe. His role was not just keeping a watch on what the French navy were doing at Toulon, but also keeping British trade free from interference.

There was no prospect that this force could take the offensive, and certainly there was no possibility of it standing in the way of a fully-fitted-out Toulon squadron. It is easy with hindsight to castigate ministers for decisions made, but it is ironic that what the ministry feared, as much as the actual or potential invasion, was the effects of the threat of an invasion on the public: panic, and the possible undermining of British credit at home and abroad. The irony is all the greater in that one of the weapons used by the ministry after the fact would be public sentiment and the fear of invasion following Byng's action in 1756. The public could be manipulated through the local and national press; however this was not something which was easy to control: once the rumours were spread in print and took on a life of their own.

Despite the comings and goings of French politics, which saw ministers and court favourites seeking to outflank one another, there was steady if uneven progress in fitting out ships at Toulon. Admiral La Galissonnière was appointed to command the squadron and his military counterpart would be the Duc de Richelieu.

It would be early in March that things came to a head as to whether or not to reinforce the squadron out in the Mediterranean. Things moved in quick succession.

The Secretary of War, Barrington, ordered all absentee officers of the garrisons at Gibraltar and Minorca to return to their post and asked the Admiralty to provide transport for these officers on 8 March.[66]

At the same time the Admiralty looked to send out a squadron to the Mediterranean to reinforce Edgcumbe, and the man who was to command was the senior Vice Admiral of the Blue, John Byng. Byng had completed his late-season cruise without incident and had had a large amount of experience of this potential theatre of war, including a time as Commander in Chief, at the close of the last war.[67] This contradicts later historians, who as a result have to down play what went on in 1747, even suggesting that the Admiralty had plenty of information on why Byng was inadequate to hold high command, some of which has been discussed in preceding chapters.[68]

9 March was the day that the Duke of Newcastle called for a meeting of the inner cabinet, a discreet group of ministers who de facto ran the government. Included amongst those who attended was the Lord Chancellor, Hardwicke, the Lord President of the Seal, Lord Granville, George Anson, the Secretary of State for the Southern Department, Henry Fox, as well as the Earl of Holderness, Secretary of State for the Northern Department and lastly Sir Thomas Robinson MP, Master of the Wardrobe and a former diplomat.[69]

The agenda made out by the Duke read as follows: 'Advice from Spain – Port Mahon, Squadron for the Mediterranean, Cressener's intelligence – Port Mahon, Canada–8000 man-invasion'.[70]

The information that was before them was from a wide range of sources, including Edgcumbe, all of which pointed to the fact that an attempt was to be made on Minorca.[71] Cressener was a Frenchman who now appears to have had contacts at Versailles. His view was that France was seeking the help of Spain in the coming war, a situation which would be very difficult for Britain if it came to pass. The result of these deliberations was that Newcastle and his senior colleagues declared that: 'Their Lordships are humbly of the opinion that as strong a squadron as can be spared from hence be got ready to send into the Mediterranean'.[72] Byng's orders were drawn up two days later, dated 11 March 1756.[73]

This was a major change from what Newcastle and the King had decided at the end of 1755 and was to have major implications for the Admiralty, which had to perform its usual trick of operating in more places than there were ships to send. Byng was sent another letter from the Admiralty dated 17 March, informing him that he had been appointed Admiral of the Blue.[74] He was as near the top of his profession as he could have hoped to have been at this time in his career.

Byng arrived at Portsmouth on 20 March, which has in some quarters drawn the adverse comment that he was not treating his instructions with sufficient urgency. Yet he, as most sea officers, had to see to his affairs and close up not one but two houses; his main residence in Berkley Square and his new home at Wrotham Park, which in March 1756 was still under construction. Once at Portsmouth Byng was to fly his flag aboard the *Ramillies* of 90 guns. There were to be nine other vessels making up his squadron. These were: *Culloden* 74 guns, *Buckingham* 68 guns, *Lancaster* 66 guns, *Intrepid*, *Revenge*, *Captain* and *Trident* all 64 guns and *Kingston* and *Defiance*, both 60 guns. As well as these Byng was to take under his command the ships which were already out there under the command of Edgcumbe. It should be remembered that towards the end of the last war there had been 27 ships of the line in the Mediterranean, although Byng in his sojourn as Commander In Chief towards the end of that conflict commanded a much reduced number as the war came to an end.

All of the ships bar one were at Portsmouth; the *Intrepid* was at the Nore and had to come round the coast to Spithead. The *Intrepid* was short of men and was making water: also her commander, James Young, had not been notified that his ship was be used on overseas service and as a result was short of stores.[75] On his arrival Byng found that his squadron was short of men. This was not an unusual occurrence, as finding of crews at the start of the campaigning season was a perennial problem for the Royal Navy throughout the eighteenth century. To man all of the ships to full complement would take 4,245 men according to contemporary figures.[76] When Byng took command there were seventeen ships ready for sea service, ten fitting out in the Royal Dockyards and one for Harbour service. Their total complement, if fully manned, would have been 14, 640 but of these only 9,891 were on the ships books.[77] But of that number of 9,891 borne on the books only 7,349 were actually mustered, some 2,543 short of those thought to be aboard.[78] Some of these may have been sent ashore to hospital, others may have died since the last muster, as was seen with Boscawen's squadron which lost nearly 2,000 men by its return from Newfoundland.[79] The problem was not unique but it does seem that the Admiralty and by implication the First Sea Lord, Anson, had been caught out by the start of the war.

That this always took place, and would continue to do so, was not the point: Anson had rightly put his faith in the Western Squadron as a defence against invasion. However, it does seem that in this balancing act Anson underestimated the threat from the French to Minorca at the start of the year, and for this he and his colleagues must take responsibility.

For Byng the problem was how to find some 722 men that his squadron needed.[80] The usual procedure under normal circumstances would be for men to be turned over from ships in the harbour to those fitting out for immediate service. In fact, to turn crews over from one ship to another was technically against the regulations, but as with many such regulations it was more honoured in the breach than the observance.

However, Byng was not able to use this method, and was in fact ordered by the Admiralty not to take crews from the six ships at Portsmouth under the command of Captain Keppel, as these ships were ordered to be sent to sea to intercept a convoy off the French coast.[81] Another vessel which the Admiralty ordered Byng to help fit out, despite her not being part of his squadron, was the *Stirling Castle*.

For Byng this was another delay, since his squadron now lost 290 men from the total of 722 to another ship to help them get to sea, which was inimical to his completing his force and being ready to set sail.[82] Byng's own flagship the *Ramillies* was 222 men short of a full complement, as many of these had been lent to ships which were already at sea and therefore unlikely to be returned in a short time. It was not a situation which most Admirals would accept with any equanimity. Eventually, the Admiralty relented and allowed Byng to take men from the other ships at Portsmouth, and he was also told that he could have the men who were coming in on the pressing tenders, though many of these were landsmen and therefore not what Byng would have wanted to complete his crews.[83]

On 24 March the Admiralty wrote to Byng to hurry him to sea: he was to use the 'utmost diligence in getting everything in greatest forwardness for sailing that is possible'.[84] To add insult to injury, Byng was ordered to put his marine contingent aboard other ships in the harbour. He was to substitute for them men from Lord Bertie's regiment. This included 35 officers and 688 rank and file.[85] Lord Barrington wrote the orders for the regiment to replace the marines aboard Byng's ships and also wrote to the Governor of Gibraltar to say that Bertie's regiment was to be exchanged, when Byng arrived there, for a battalion of troops already stationed there. This order was to cause great confusion, which given the task the squadron was to undertake was quite unnecessary. Barrington added to the confusion by writing a second letter which was to be delivered by hand to General Stuart to the effect that Bertie's regiment was to be landed, but the battalion of troops under his command were only to be put aboard Byng's ships if Minorca was threatened. To make matters worse, he did not say that the second letter superseded the first, and this would make things very messy when Byng arrived at the Rock. The first of these letters was dated 21 March, the second the twenty eighth day of the same month.[86] In such situations clarity is called for yet it was lacking in the swapping out of the marines for a foot regiment and also to some extent in the contradictory orders that Byng was to receive with regards to manning his squadron.

As well as Bertie's regiment, Byng's squadron were to take those officers and men who were missing from the garrisons at Gibraltar and Minorca. This included 30 officers, 32 recruits and 8 deserters for Minorca, and 15 officers and 41 other ranks for Gibraltar.[87] Amongst those who was absent from his post on Minorca was Lord Trawley, with whom Byng had had such frosty relations in the 1730's when Byng was a junior Post Captain and Trawley was the newly appointed minister in Portugal.[88] Now Byng was close to the top of his profession and Trawley was being prompted to go back to his post, receiving a letter from the Duke of Newcastle to that end and to which he responded from his home in Blackheath.[89] In a strange twist of fate the two men were once again thrown together, albeit that Trawley was, for the most part, noticeable for his absence.

The ships at Spithead, all of Byng's squadron bar the *Intrepid*, which was still taking on stores, moved out to St Helens Roads, and all the while he was looking to fill his missing men from any ships he could. The Admiralty gave him permission to take men from the *Stirling Castle*, which they had forbidden him from doing previously, and said that as the *Ludlow Castle* was due in port soon he could recall the 199 men that had been lent to her.[90]

Another matter which has, in some quarters, been made much of and something that Byng was to bring up was the number and weight of guns which his squadron had. At least three of his ships had had to exchange one tier of guns: *Kingston* carried 12pdrs instead of 24pdrs on the upper deck and *Trident* had to exchange her 32pdr lower deck guns for 24pdrs. Two others of his squadron, *Captain* and *Revenge*, were cut down 70 gun ships, a design which made notoriously bad sailors and were over-gunned for their size.[91] Another of his squadron which has already been mentioned was the *Intrepid*, which had just undergone a medium repair at Chatham costing over £5,000 pounds, and was making water through her lee ports in any kind of seaway.[92] Whilst this would be of concern to any flag officer, it was not an unusual circumstance for many an eighteenth century admiral to find himself in. You fought with what the Navy had, although there was still the large question as to how well the ships which had been kept in ordinary had been looked after.

All the correspondence which passed to and fro was nothing out of the usual for an Admiral trying to get his squadron to sea as expeditiously as possible. Amidst this plethora of correspondence Byng also sought to have a frigate attached to his squadron for the express purpose of repeating signals. It was standard procedure to have a frigate, or other small vessel, stand on the disengaged side of a squadron during a battle and act as a repeater for any signals made by the Commander in Chief. There were several frigates in Portsmouth at the time fitting out for service, however the Admiralty had other duties for them and his request was turned down.[93] Byng also sought, but did not receive, a special commission as Commander-in-Chief of the Mediterranean; this would have allowed him to appoint officers to vacancies without final Admiralty sanction, something the Admiralty was loathe to do. By 1 April Byng was in receipt of another letter from their lordships urging him to get to sea with all dispatch.[94]

His instructions dated 30 March state quite clearly within the first paragraph that the main purpose of the squadron was to see to the threat posed by the French to Minorca: 'upon the several advices which have been received relating to the supposed intention of the French to attack the Island of Minorca, a squadron of ten ships of the line do forthwith sail to the Mediterranean'.[95]

As well as covering the possibility, as the ministry saw it, of a threat to Minorca, the orders from the Admiralty, under the authority of Fox, Secretary of State for the Southern Department, also sought to cover the possibility that the French might sail their squadron out of the Mediterranean and across the Atlantic to Louisburg with more reinforcements. In this case Byng was to detach Rear Admiral Temple West with a sufficient force follow them across to Newfoundland and once there West was to take under his command the Royal Navy vessels already positioned there.[96]

However, if no such intelligence was found of the French leaving for Newfoundland Byng was 'then to go on, without a moment's loss of time, to Minorca'.[97] The orders continued: 'if you find any attack made upon that island by the French you are to use all possible means in your power for its relief'.[98] They go on to set out what Byng ought to do should the Toulon squadron not have sailed at all. In this case he was to place his squadron in the best position to blockade them, a sub-clause enjoined Byng to protect both Gibraltar and Minorca from any attempts against them by the French.[99]

It would not be until 6 April that Byng could finally sail for the Mediterranean, which was partly due to poor weather and partly because he was getting the boats of the squadron to complete the *Intrepid's* stores. The entry in his journal puts it most succinctly: 'The squadron weighed ... and stood out to sea'.[100]

As Byng put to sea the French presented a clear and present danger to Minorca. Admiral La Galissonnière and the Duc de Richelieu were seeking to put together a force which would indeed be used make an attack on Minorca. The forces mustered were not inconsiderable. Not including the warships to transport the Duc's force, it would comprise fifty transport vessels and one hundred and thirty transport ships. All of this was needed to convey fifteen thousand troops, approximately half of what had been mentioned in the consul's reports alluded to earlier, which equate to twenty-five battalions plus one battalion of artillery, the latter essential if siege operations were to be undertaken.[101] As well as manning the transports the French had to find enough men to fill the crews of the twelve ships of the line and five frigates which would form the escort under La Galissonnière's command. His instructions were to protect the convoy carrying the troops and artillery train and to keep the sea lanes open so that supplies could be got to French forces once they had landed. Any engagement with the British would have to be seen in this context; La Galissonnière only needed a tactical draw in any battle to gain a strategic victory.[102] However, like the British, the French suffered from under-manning and sickness aboard their Mediterranean squadron, and within a month of sailing La Galissonnière's squadron had lost 41 dead and had a further 233 sick.[103] In the end La Galissonnière sailed on 12 April with his convoy of troops and their attendant transports, some six days after Byng sailed from Portsmouth.

The voyage to Minorca from Toulon was much shorter than Byng's, as Byng's involved crossing the Bay of Biscay, which in April was never a straight forward task, before sailing into the Straits of Gibraltar and, as Byng thought, disembarking one regiment of troops and taking on a separate battalion. Byng's voyage to the Straits was very slow, although this had nothing to do with Byng and everything to do with the contrary winds, and it took twenty-six days to get into the Straits.

Whilst the distance was short the French did not have plain sailing: they too had problems with the weather and they had to take shelter in the lee of Hyères. It would be two days before the whole armada could get under way again for while the wind was in the south-west the ships could make little or no headway.[104] Even then the winds were not all that kind to La Galissonnière, as he and his ships had to beat to windward to gain landfall at Minorca and when they did so it was on the west coast opposite Ciudadela. All the while both he and the Duc de Richelieu were worried lest a British squadron should catch them in open waters. As it was, after a council of war the French decided to land where they were and march their troops and artillery more than 30 miles to invest Fort St Philip, which controlled Mahon Harbour.[105]

What the French found on the Island of Minorca was a small British force of some 2,500 rank and file, including Rich's regiment, which had been stationed at Ciudadela. However, on news of the arrival of the overwhelming French force , they had withdrawn towards Fort St Philip. In Port Mahon itself Captain Edgcumbe still had his small squadron, the *Deptford*, the *Princess Louisa*, the *Portland* and the *Chesterfield*, plus two smaller craft, the *Proserpine* and the *Dolphin*. There was no possibility that Edgcumbe could meet his French opposite number in open water and disrupt the landing and he therefore moored his largest vessels bow-to-stern across the Harbour entrance in the hope of frustrating an open attack on the harbour. He also had some of the ships' smaller guns landed to help with the defence.[106] However, within days Edgcumbe called a council of war with his Captains as to whether his ships could do any material good by remaining in position within Port Mahon. They unanimously decided that they could not and to the contrary that the Kings service would suffer by their loss if they remained. This resolution was taken to General Blakeney, who in the absence of Lord Trawley was in command of Fort St Philip. His own council of war was all for the sailors coming ashore and supplementing the troops in the defence of the Fort and the port. However, the sea officers were against this and resolved to sail, which, given that the Admiralty had thought that Edgcumbe's squadron would be taken under Byng's command when he arrived, was remarkably fortuitous.[107] La Galissonnière did not seek to intercept this small flotilla: his main objective was to support the Duc in his assault on the island, and, in truth, Edgcumbe's squadron was no threat to his fleet.

Once the French had landed they had to move all of the stores across the island. These included 1000 barrels of powder, twelve 36pdrs, twenty four 14pdrs, eight 12pdrs, eight 12inch and six 8inch mortars, plus 300 tents and something like 6,000 rations of hay and 2,500 oxen.[108] This gives some idea of the sheer scale of the French operations against Fort St Philip, and also just what a tempting target the supply convoy to sustain this operation would be if caught in the open sea by a British squadron.

What then of the British squadron sent to relieve what was no longer a prospective attack but a reality? As Byng's squadron came into Gibraltar he carried not just the recruits and officers for the garrisons on Minorca and Gibraltar, he also had aboard some of their families.[109] Amongst those who were taken aboard were the Earl of Effingham and General Stuart as well as their families and attendants. The Earl and Countess went aboard the *Revenge* and the General aboard the *Culloden*. Together with the officers there were forty two women and children belonging to Bertie's regiment aboard the squadron which arrived on 2 May.[110] It may seem strange that families would be sent out for what might be a relief of a fortress under siege. However, it was the norm that a certain number of army wives would literally be camp followers and this was certainly so in this case.

What met Byng when he got there was not to his liking as the Dockyard was 'ruinous and tumbling down'.[111] According to a list which dockyard officers gave to Byng when he arrived on 1 May there was a boathouse, a pitch house, a smith's shop and a cable shed, as well as a careening quay and capstans.[112] The list continues on to say that 'in case it might be necessity to careen or caulk any of His Majesty's ships, there is neither floating stages for that service, or boats for the officers to attend their respective duties'.[113] If Byng had been worried about the preparedness of his squadron, what he found at Gibraltar did not help. When he had last been in the Mediterranean, at the end of the previous war, Gibraltar and Minorca were comparatively speaking in a fairly sound state, and what met him now nine years later was not good at all. He found that such ships stores that were there were not in a fit state to be used to supply those ships which were in need of them. This was owing to the lack of sheds to protect them from the ravages of the Mediterranean climate.[114] The description of stores mouldering on the quay may be a slight exaggeration, however it is indicative of the state of both Gibraltar and Minorca in early 1756.[115]

To add to the material woes, the supply of fresh water at Gibraltar was, and throughout this period continued to be, a problem, often requiring ships to be sent to the African coast to take on water. As yet Byng did not need the services of the careening quay but if he saw action with the French he would need one uncontested base to carry out any repairs which might be needed. When Byng's squadron hove to in the Bay, he sent an order to all of his Captains to survey what stores they had aboard and determine what state they were in. Most of the ships seemed to have been in a fair state as far as both wet and dry stores was concerned.

One of the myths surrounding Byng is that all of his ships were rotten or worn out, as well as undermanned. At this point it is worth looking briefly at this point as it is of some relevance to what was to transpire. [116]

Byng's flagship, the *Ramillies*, was, according to previous works on this subject, the former *Royal Katherine*, a ship put into service in 1664, four years after the restoration of King Charles II in 1660.[117] She was supposed to have undergone two major rebuilds, one in 1702 and the other in 1742, and after the first rebuild she was renamed *Ramillies*.[118] However, modern research has shown that many so-called rebuilds were not ships taken to pieces and some part of the old ships worked into the new vessels; on the contrary they were new vessels from the keels on upward and the only thing they had in common with the old ships was the name.[119] In the case of the *Royal Katherine*, she was rebuilt at Portsmouth Dockyard in 1703 and renamed *Ramillies* in 1706, but was in fact broken up in 1741.[120] Byng's flagship was not built until eight years after the old *Ramillies* was broken up. Originally ordered on 29 July 1739, her keel was laid down on 22 February 1742 and she was not launched until 8 February 1749.[121] When Byng took her to the Mediterranean in April–May 1756 she was seven years old and from the length of time she stood in frame was a well-seasoned ship.[122]

What of the other ships in his squadron? Rear Admiral Temple West's ship the *Buckingham* had been ordered 25 October 1745, laid down 26 January 1747 and launched 30 April 1751, making her five years old.[123] The *Defiance* had been built at Deptford, laid down 22 March 1743 and launched 12 October 1744, making her twelve years old.[124] The *Culloden* was laid down 23 May 1745 and launched 9 September 1747.[125] This made her just nine years old when she joined Byng's squadron. The *Lancaster* was laid down 4 February 1744 and launched 22 April 1749, making her seven years old.[126] The *Captain* was laid down 20 February 1740 and launched 14 March 1743, making her one of the oldest vessels in the squadron.[127] The *Princess Louisa* was laid down 20 March 1743 and launched 1 January 1744.[128] The *Portland* was laid down 29 April 1743 and launched 11 October 1744. The *Portland*, the *Captain* and the *Princess Louisa* were all around ten to twelve years old and were all built in response to the previous war, and, whilst not brand new, neither were they totally worn out.[129] The *Revenge* was built at Deptford Dockyard, laid down 24 May 1740 and launched 25 May 1742. The *Intrepid* had been built at Toulon in 1740 and she had been captured 3 May 1747 by Anson at the Battle of Finisterre.[130] Such ships were often treated as suspect, certainly by Dockyard Officers, but many such ships served in the Royal Navy with distinction.

It has already been mentioned that two ships of the squadron, the *Kingston* and the *Trident*, had to swap some of their guns for lighter pieces, but in terms of age and general condition, from the evidence which survives, and not withstanding the *Intrepid's* leaking ports, the squadron was no worse or better than the one which Boscawen took to Newfoundland in 1755. The start of wars usually found the Royal Navy somewhat ring-rusty, suffering from the natural phenomena of financial cuts to reduce the national debt when the peace came, and the consequent lack of maintenance when ships were in ordinary between commissions. This often took several years of war to overcome and for the fleet to be in a good fighting condition.

Of the other matters waiting for Byng when he arrived, the most important was neither the state of the Dockyard nor of his ships: it was the news that the French had landed on the Island of Minorca. The question now was what would he do next?

Chapter Four

Rock of Contention

What Byng found at Gibraltar, as well as the disarray at the Dockyards was news that the French had landed on Minorca. Captain Edgcumbe, along with three of his small squadron, the *Princess Louisa*, the *Deptford* and the *Fortune* were there.[1] This was no longer to be a straight-forward operation where Byng would land reinforcements on the island and cruise outside Toulon to prevent any hostile movements by the French: the French had landed, and in some force. Knowing what was at stake the main task would be to lend succour to the garrison on Minorca. This would be a testing time for all of those involved and like many joint operations would in large measure depend on the co-operation of the Navy and the Army for a successful outcome to be achieved.[2] Conjoint operations had not always been the happiest experience in the eighteenth century where the Army and the Royal Navy had been concerned. At the start of the preceding war Admiral Vernon, not the quietest of souls, led an expedition to attack Spanish possessions in South America. Whilst he met with some success, the campaign also highlighted the difficulties inherent in such operations.[3] Byng was now going to have to negotiate this tricky situation. It was not something for which his previous commands had given him a great deal of experience. He was used to commanding his own forces without any division of command, and for this operation to be a success he was going to have to co-operate closely with his military colleagues. Some of this would be down to personal characteristics: Byng could be prickly if he thought his personal or service authority, not always one and the same, were being threatened. Some would be down to the orders all of them had received from their respective commands; Barrington for the Army, and Anson and the Board of Admiralty for the Navy.

As was touched on already, Barrington, as Secretary of War, had written contradictory letters to General Fowke, the Governor of Gibraltar.[4] Before Byng sailed there had been some confusion, with Barrington's orders that Bertie's regiment be landed and exchanged for a battalion from Gibraltar causing the Admiralty to object to Bertie's regiment being sent onboard Byng's squadron in the place of the marines and to act as part of the ships company. If they were exchanged at Gibraltar there would be no extra men aboard to send to the garrison in Minorca, it would merely be a swap of like for like. If the orders were allowed to stand, Byng's ships would be even more short of their complement.[5]

Therein lay part of the conundrum: the garrison at Gibraltar needed four battalions as a minimum, and exactly that number was there. How, then, would it be possible to detach one to send with Byng if the need arose?[6] Fowke's orders were couched in fairly broad terms and the fact that Barrington wrote to him on more than one occasion did not add to the clarity of the confused situation that the flag and general officers found themselves in during May 1756.[7] Fowke's last orders from Barrington, dated 28 March, give a flavour of how broadly they were drawn and to some extent had to be: 'I am commanded to acquaint you, that it is his Majesty's pleasure, in case you shall apprehend that the French threaten an attempt upon Minorca, that you make a detachment from the troops in your garrison equal to a battalion, commanded by a Lieutenant Colonel and a Major, for the relief of that place, to be put on board the fleet at the disposition of the Admiral'.[8]

There has been much debate as to whether, had Fowke been given greater autonomy, he might have acted differently, but the fact is that it was a general rule that orders given to overseas commander, unless on specific operation, had to be drawn widely. It was expected that they would interpreted in a positive way for the furtherance of the King's interests.[9]

What happened next was something akin to a Greek tragedy. The surviving evidence shows that Fowke had under his command 2,700 rank and file. For there to be sufficient men for garrison duty, there was a need for 839 men per relief, and three such reliefs were needed if the fortification were to be properly manned.[10] This would mean that in an ideal world Fowke would have needed 2,517 for garrison duty at Gibraltar. If he followed the spirit of his orders he would have to detach a battalion of 700 men, which would then go with Admiral Byng as part of the force for the relief of Minorca.[11] If that were done, Fowke could not maintain the minimum garrison at Gibraltar. What then could Fowke do when faced with the series of contradictions: there was intelligence that the French had in fact landed, brought to him by Edgcumbe; and there were the seemingly contradictory orders from the Secretary of War; and there were the ineluctable constraints of the mathematics of garrisoning his post. He decided to form a committee, or, more properly, to take advice from specialist engineers as to whether Fort St Philip could hold out against the besieging French forces.[12] Those charged with this task were Major James Mace of the Artillery, who had come out with Byng's squadron, as well as Captain Alexander Leith of the Artillery, and Archibald Patoun from the Corps of Engineers.[13] They were tasked with giving an opinion as to whether, given their knowledge of the situation and the fortifications at Fort St Philip, the garrison on Minorca could hold out long enough for a relief to arrive.[14]

The opinion when it came was that it would be difficult in the extreme to land reinforcements for the relief of the garrison. It would be dangerous if not impossible to land such reinforcements if the French had set up batteries on either side of the harbour entrance, and that the sally port through which troops would have to enter were both exposed and could only take one ship's boat-load of troops at a time, so all the rest would be exposed to enemy attack whilst waiting their turn.[15]

The day after these officers delivered their view of the situation Fowke convened a Council of War. Present were Colonel Joseph Dussaux and Lieutenant Colonels J. Grey, Charles Colville, John Crauford and Robert Scott. Also invited to attend were General Stuart, Colonel Cornwallis , Lord Effingham and Lord Bertie, all of whom had sailed with Byng from Portsmouth. Fowke laid before these officers the differing versions of the instructions he had received from Secretary of War Barrington, a copy of Byng's instructions and the opinion of the three officers – plus the latest news from Minorca.[16] What followed has been debated for the last two hundred and fifty years, both in pamphlets and serious works of history.[17]

Their resolution is worthy of some examination, as it sets the tone for what was to follow and gives at least some idea of the state of mind of those in command at this point. Much of what happened subsequently hinges on trying to understand why the Council of War came to the decision it did, and to whether Fowke should have called one into being in the first place.[18]

What transpired at this Council of War was recorded in the advices which was recorded in the first paragraph, and went to the heart of the matter and ran as follows:

> It Appears from Advice received by the Admiral Byng and Lieut-Gen Fowke that on the 18th of April last the French force were landed on the Island of Minorca ... and that His Majesty's troops on the said island had retired into the fortifications of St Philip's Castle, the Council also took into consideration the situation of His Majesty's garrisons in the Mediterranean ... of the opinion that a sending detachment equal to a battalion would evidently weakening the garrison of Gibraltar, and be no way effectual for the relief of Minorca.[19]

The advice continued to give the reasons why part of both of Byng's and Fowke's orders should not be carried into effect.

The reasons given were self-fulfilling. Number one on the list was a reprise of what had been in the report of the engineers, viz that these men knew what the fortifications were like, and that the situation once they were invested would make it almost impossible for any reinforcements to be landed successfully, and that to have had any real effect the troops should have been landed before the French arrived.[20]

This council also looked into the state of the two respective squadrons; they thought that, as Byng's squadron was not overwhelmingly larger, and was in fact in all probability weaker than the French, that this operation was flawed.[21] Given that they had only sketchy information of the true strength of the French, this was a truly devastating conclusion. This second article explains in some detail, including the manning issue which had so troubled Byng before he had sailed from Great Britain, the reason why it would not be wise for any engagement between the British and the French, given that there was little chance of succour being given to the garrison in Gibraltar should it also be placed under threat.[22]

This, on the face of it, runs totally contrary to what the ministry at home had wanted to happen. What is difficult at this distance is to reconstruct the thought processes behind these findings. The obvious – but dangerous – conclusion would be that this was just what Fowke and Byng wanted; a cloak for two defeatists to hide behind. But however seductive this might seem, were there real fears for Gibraltar?

There had been some suggestion in the material sent to London from consuls in the Mediterranean that France was making some advances to the Court of Spain to bring them into the war against Great Britain.[23] This would indeed be a cause of great concern to ministers, as a junction of the two fleets and an attack on Gibraltar would stretch British resources.[24] However tempting it might be to accept this theory, there was more evidence coming from the consuls and intelligence agencies that any attempts would be made either against Minorca or across the Atlantic against Newfoundland, rather than an assault on Gibraltar.[25]

But still there is the question of why, in the preceding war, Byng had shown his mettle by following the French from off Dunkirk to the north of Scotland, much as his father had done in 1708. Albeit that he had orders to do so, he did not shrink from following them and, as has already been seen, act in concord with the general officers tasked with crushing the invasion.[26] Why did he now give way to others remains the question. He does not seem to have been the type of man who would be overawed by others' authority: on the contrary, he was quick to defend his and the Navy's authority if he thought it was being questioned. Notwithstanding his actions in the previous war, later historians see in him a lack of resolution.[27] Yet this does not seem to have been the case previously, as he was diligent in his duties and, whilst affecting a somewhat self deprecating air, did not shy away from responsibility or action. Why then did he on this occasion seem to have gone along with those reports which had been presented by Major Mace and the other experts from the engineers and artillery? There seems to be no clear reason for his action at this point. Was it, as some historians say, that whilst he did not lack personal courage, what he did lack was the moral courage to take the big decisions?[28] In fact, the most excoriating condemnation comes from Sir Julian Corbett, writing thus: 'He was not a man for a doubtful enterprise where so much must turn on a capacity for prompt resolution and fearlessness of responsibility ... a man who met failure half way ... although personally brave was three parts beaten before he began.'[29] But as has been mentioned already, he had followed the French from Dunkirk to the north of Scotland.[30] His activities in Scotland did not attract criticism and his first cruise of the new war, carried on very late in the season, also did not bring the opprobrium which it might be thought would have come if Corbett's comments were an accurate reflection of the man.

What this conclave did was hand the initiative well and truly to the French. George Byng had faced a similar, but not congruent, situation in 1718. The Spanish had landed on Sicily and had already, by the time of his arrival, invested the fortress of Messina.[31] In that instance he sought to confront the Spanish on the high sea and interdict their lines of communication as well as seek, in the unique situation of the triple alliance, to negotiate with the Spanish field commander.[32] The main point here, and one that has been used against Byng previously, is that he failed to grasp the gravity of the situation and act in a dceptive manner.[33] What John Byng missed was the much broader strategic point that, notwithstanding the large number of troops that the French had landed, they were most vulnerable at sea on their lines of communications. An attack on the transports would have placed them in a very difficult position. What else Byng might have done will be looked at later; sufficient to say that at the very least he misread the situation before him and that there was the possibility, even with an equality of forces with the French, to significantly affect their operations.

It is also doubtful whether what the engineers said was true. The French under La Galissonnière could not get into the harbour at Mahon without great difficulty, the entrance being just 228 yards across, and they also knew that Edgcumbe had landed both guns and marines to help in the defence of the port.[34] The French would have to detach ships from where they had landed to assault Port Mahon and in doing so leave themselves open to an attack by an English squadron. Certainly, at least one historian has thought that any such French attack would be doomed to failure and would, as a direct consequence, leave the way open for Byng's small ships to interdict the French lines of communication.[35]

Although this is getting slightly ahead of the game, it is most certainly germane to ask why Fowke had sought such a council. His orders were, as has been seen, not of the clearest, yet Fowke cannot have been under any doubt what the main thrust of those orders were; the safety of Minorca and secondly, and only secondly, his command at Gibraltar.[36]

It is true that he needed four battalions for his reliefs at the Garrison and this has already been explored.[37] However once Edgcumbe arrived with definitive intelligence of what was really transpiring, Fowke should have been under no illusion as to where his duty lay. He could and should have followed the spirit of the orders and sent the troops. Subsequently, he was criticized in print, on some points this being withering criticism: 'whether a great part of the members of the Council of War were not under express orders to go to Mahon, and whether the eldest Lieutenant Colonel of the Garrison was not of them?[38] Once the dust had settled and the inquisition was underway as to why things had gone the way they had, George II said of him 'that if he was unfit to serve for one year, he is certainly so for ever'.[39] This comment was made after Fowke had been cashiered and had lost his regiment, a fact important in the eighteenth century as full Colonels were Colonel proprietors and in effect they owned the right to appoint officers and received government grants for uniforms and pay, which could be very lucrative.[40]

Byng also seems to have acted with less vigour than the situation required. Byng wrote a letter on 4 May which gives some idea of his state of mind just before he sailed from Gibraltar: 'If I had been so happy as to have arrived at Mahon before the French had landed, I flatter myself, I would have prevented their getting a footing on the island'.[41] He went on to say that the French had too much materiel and too many men for there to have been any realistic chance of a relief being successful.[42] However, he was determined to go to Minorca himself, saying: 'I am determined to sail to Minorca with the squadron, where I shall be a better judge of the situation of affairs there, and will give General Blakeney all the assistance he may require'.[43] This seems to run contrary to what had been decided within the Council of War, and Byng goes on to explain why the full complement of troops were not to be sent with his squadron.[44] In fact, Fowke gave Byng a detachment of seven officers and 260 men of other ranks.[45] They where embarked aboard the squadron on 7 May. This was less than half of the full battalion, but as was shown in the last chapter was almost exactly what would have been left from the 2,700 troops once Fowke had retained enough troops for the three full reliefs he thought a necessity at Gibraltar. All Byng had to do now was to wait for the arrival of four ships of his squadron, the *Chesterfield*, the *Portland*, the *Dolphin* and the *Experiment*. This would leave just one vessel not with Byng, the *Phoenix*, under his old friend Hervey, who at that moment was at Leghorn to gain what information he could as the situation unfolded.[46] It would not be until 8 May that Byng had carried out watering and such minor repairs as were necessary and his squadron stood out of the Bay of Gibraltar to the east in a freshening gale. What would he find when he arrived off the Island of Minorca?

The French had continued to invest Fort St Philip, undisturbed by any British activity. General Blakeney was unable to carry out the usual preparations for those who were undergoing a siege, for example by ripping up roads, because he had insufficient numbers of troops to carry out the task.[47] By 18 April the Duc de Richelieu had taken possession of Fornelles on the east coast of the island and by 20 April the marshal had divided his forces to block up Blakeney in Fort St Philip. In fact, Blakeney had decided that a withdrawal into the fort was the only possible response to the situation as it seemed to him. Blakeney, again because of the lack of troops, was unable to pull down housing around the fort, a usual precaution which stopped the besieger gaining lodgement under cover close to the fort.[48] The geology of the island also hampered the French in their assault upon the fort in that the ground was so hard that it was difficult if not impossible to dig approaches and trenches in the normal way that a besieger would do.[49] Blakeney on the other had was hampered in his preparation by the officers of the garrison being absent, some of whom were at that moment with Byng.[50] The circumference of the works was something approaching one mile, which meant that with the limited number of defenders and the lack of officers, General Blakeney remained in the castle at the centre and his aides-de-camp brought such intelligence as they could glean to him there. Another thing which made this defence more passive than perhaps it might otherwise have been was the decision by the British not to sally out from the fortress and try and disrupt the French as they sought to set up batteries and siege works, something which was not unusual in siege warfare especially on the continent.[51] This again was down to the small size of the garrison.

The French opened their attack by erecting batteries at Cape Mola on the opposite side of the harbour, later siting the mortar batteries much closer to Fort St Philip, which fired , according to contemporary accounts, 'with great fury' at the citadel.[52] In fact, given the overwhelming number both in terms of men and guns which could be brought to bear against them it was only a matter of time before Blakeney would have to capitulate, if succour did not arrive in a timely fashion.

Augustus Hervey in the *Phoenix* was also making his way to join up with Admiral Byng's squadron after he had managed to elude the French ship the *Gracieuse*. Byng had sent the *Experiment* towards Palma for intelligence of the French, and she had been spotted by the *Gracieuse*, who had shortly thereafter sighted the rest of Byng's squadron and had born away to warn the French command that Byng was in the offing.[53]

Hervey rejoined the fleet, greeting the flagships with a thirteen gun salute which the *Ramillies* returned.[54] The voyage from Gibraltar had been every bit as tedious as had Byng's out from England, with light airs making progress painfully slow. On the evening of 18 May the wind started up to the extent that topsails and topgallants were reefed as the wind looked to freshen into a full gale blowing from the north east.[55]

By now, Byng's squadron was nearing Minorca and what Byng had to do was gain intelligence as to whether Fort St Philip was in British hands and, dependent upon that, render what assistance, if any, he could to General Blakeney. As well as what was happening on shore, Byng had to be mindful that the French squadron under Admiral La Galissonnière could not be far away and he must prepare his ships for a possible fleet action against them.

To gain intelligence of what the situation was ashore, and also to lookout for the French, Byng detached three frigates, which were to be placed under the overall command of his protégée Hervey. They were to look into the entrance of Port Mahon and endeavour to land a letter from Byng which was addressed to General Blakeney.[56] All of this was to be undertaken early in the morning. The letter from Byng to Blakeney arrived aboard the *Phoenix*, according to one source, at 4am and it would take Hervey and his little flotilla nearly four hours to work their way inshore – at which point the wind dropped.[57] Given how close the *Phoenix* had got inshore, this meant that Hervey ordered the ship's boats to tow her off shore before the fluky wind then sprang up again, allowing the ships to come within sight of Fort St Philip.[58]

What Hervey saw was that the Union Flag still flew over Fort St Philip, and that the fort was under fire from the siege batteries erected by the French across the harbour, as well as inland.[59] He had the signal hoisted to communicate with the garrison and awaited a response, which was not forthcoming. He then made the signal to Byng, who was waiting in the offing, by firing one gun and clewing up his fore-topgallant. This was to signal that Hervey could see that Fort St Philip was being attacked.[60]

Byng's squadron out at sea had also lost the wind, so did not get into sight of Fort St Philip until nearly 10am and allow them also to record the fact that the fort was under fire from the French.[61] There seemed to be no response at first from the garrison, perhaps unsurprising given the bombardment that they were under. In fact it was recorded that some at least thought that the appearance of Hervey's flotilla was a ruse by the French.[62] There was some activity within the fort, despite little outward sign. One officer, Robert Boyd, recognized the signal for what it was and sought permission to row out and make contact. However, he was stopped from doing so until Lieutenant Colonel Jefferies had brought the matter up at a Council of War which was to be held in the afternoon. Given that Hervey's flotilla was sighted around about 10am, this was an unconscionable loss of time.[63]

It is true that the fort had been hit by a number of shells fired from the French mortar batteries, some of which had done great execution amongst the defenders, nonetheless why Jefferies did not communicate with General Blakeney, who was by this time bed ridden, being eighty two and gouty, sooner is a mystery.[64]

It would only be in the afternoon that the council would finally call Boyd, an ADC to Jefferies, to come before them and to prepare a letter which would describe to Admiral Byng the situation within the fort of St Philip.[65] He was to be rowed out of the harbour from St Stephens's cove, on the southern side of the harbour. His leaving attracted the attention of some of those besieging the fort and they fired on him with muskets and then cannons, none of which hit Boyd's boat. However, the time lost in waiting for the council of war meant that Boyd was going to find it very hard to catch up with Byng's squadron.[66] The six-oared boat pulled away from the shore toward Byng and his squadron.

It was just before sunset that Boyd set off towards the ships standing just off Port Mahon with a letter from Blakeney, which, after all the deliberation, omitted most of the salient details of the true situation the defenders found themselves in. This detail was left to Boyd to convey once he had got on board the Admiral's flagship.[67]

Whilst the British sought to open communications between their squadron and the fort, the French under La Galissonnière were aware that the British were in the offing. This was in part due to the *Gracieuse*, which had been off Palma and had been driven off, a factor which had allowed Augustus Hervey in the *Phoenix* to join Byng.[68] On 19 May, at the same time that Hervey was off Port Mahon, the *Gracieuse* joined up with La Galissonnière at 6am, informing his Admiral that the British were off the island.[69] What La Galissonnière decided was that he had, in accordance with his instructions from Louis XV, to interject between the British squadron and Fort St Philip. He weighed and got underway before setting a north-west course for Port Mahon.[70] His ships were, as others have pointed out, just out of the dockyard, and they had not spent the previous fighting season patrolling in the chops of the channel or crossing and re-crossing the Atlantic.[71] They should have been in good condition, notwithstanding the problems with manning which plagued both sides, and, if the intelligence was correct, their shortage of ordnance.[72] In fact as late as December 1755 the arsenal at Toulon was short of 714 cannons of all calibres for Galissonnière's squadrons. One month later there was shortage of ninety 24- and 12-pdrs for the squadron, which forced the substitution of a third- and a fourth-rate for two second-rate ships.[73] This is an interesting counterpoint to those historians who have sought to show that Byng's squadron was under-gunned in comparison with its French counterpart. If the establishment is looked at, i.e. those guns which should have been aboard, then this is true: however, as is often the case, the reality is much more complex as the forgoing has shown. What is not in dispute is that some of the French ships were more heavily gunned ship for ship than the British, but they still had problems finding sufficient ordnance of the right type to fit them out to full establishment.[74] There has also been much debate, both then and now, as to the relative sailing qualities of both British and French ships of the line.[75] In particular this focuses on the seventy four gun ships, such as the *Invincible*, captured in 1747 from the French. She was indeed a fast and weatherly vessel. However, she and her counterparts in the French Navy had lighter hulls and were, in general, less rugged than their British counterparts, at least in the opinion of the Navy Board officers: at least as far as the British were concerned, it was they, by and large, who held sway in ship design.[76] It cannot be doubted that some of Byng's ships were in a poor state, nonetheless La Galissonnière had had problems, and as well as trouble fitting out, he had received more restrictive instructions from the French Court, which circumscribed his actions, than Byng had received from the Admiralty.[77]

As sunset drew on the French squadron came into view of the British, at first from the mastheads of those vessels inshore, and it was *Phoenix* that made the signal to the Admiral by hoisting a flag and firing three guns, 'Enemy in sight to the south-east.'[78] The signal was repeated by the *Experiment*, which was acting as repeater between Hervey and Byng onboard the *Ramillies*. There was little doubt what Byng had to do: he recalled the ships he had detached inshore to join up with the squadron, as they would be vulnerable if they were left where they were.[79]

Whilst all of this was going on Boyd was still being rowed out to meet the *Phoenix*, expecting from thence to be transferred to Byng's flagship. However, as luck, or misfortune would have it, he was setting off just as the French were seen hull down on the horizon and, once the signal from the *Phoenix* had been repeated and received and all the frigates recalled, there was no way that his boat could catch up with them before dusk. As darkness fell he lost sight of them. Thus Byng lost his only chance to have a verbatim account of what was happening ashore, as against the opinions of men who had not been in the fort for some time whose opinion was rendered at the Council of War at Gibraltar.

Much has been made of how Byng might have acted had Boyd come aboard instead of his having to return to Fort St Philip. However, Byng knew what he had to do and once he knew that the British were still in control of the fort he might have seen a chance to relieve it. He ordered all his ships to close up and hoisted the signal for the line of battle to be formed.[80] The sighting of the French squadron in the offing gave him the chance to defeat the French at sea, thus leaving the French ashore in a parlous state.[81] As the sun waned in the sky the two squadrons were edging closer, with the French approaching from the south east having the wind with them, which was also out of the south east. This gave the French the weather gage. By about 7pm the wind freshened as the two squadrons slowly edged closer. With the French having the weather gage, it would be down to them to decide whether to engage before dark or not. However, at the same time that the wind rose both the British and French tacked almost simultaneously.[82]

At this point they were just about six miles apart, but it was past dusk and neither Byng nor La Galissonnière wanted a night action. This was not something most sea officers of the eighteenth century would have contemplated with equanimity, with all the difficulty of signalling during daylight multiplied by a factor of at least ten. It would be a case of holding the squadron together overnight whilst at the same time trying to gain the wind.[83] On sighting the French Byng had hoisted the signal for the line to be formed. As darkness enveloped the fleet this was lowered. Overnight Byng would try and keep his squadron together by hoisting blue lights in the top-masts so that all the ships in the squadron could keep station on each other, or failing that could at the very least keep close together, before the morrow and the hope of action. During the hours of darkness Byng's squadron stood on and off the island of Minorca and hoped that the French had stayed to fight and that there would not be a long and fretful day of searching out their opponent.[84]

As the sun came up on the Mediterranean lookouts on all of Byng's ships scanned the faintly-lit sea for their compatriots and their enemy. In this first early light, although Byng's squadron was in sight the French were not. However, the sea was not empty; there were two small craft in sight. These were tartans, a lateen-rigged type of vessel found in the Mediterranean, and they were flying blue flags, but more importantly they were carrying French troops.[85] These troops had been sent from shore by Richelieu at the express request of the French commander at sea La Galissonnière, whose ships, with exquisite irony given Byng's problems with manning, were also short of men.[86]

In fact there were seven such tartans sent off from shore to reinforce the French squadron, and unfortunately for these two it was the British squadron which they ran into. The previous night La Galissonnière had taken one hundred and fifty men from the frigates to ensure his ships of the line were fully manned.

As any good Admiral would do Byng ordered that the strange sail be investigated and, if at all possible, captured. For this purpose he sent three of his squadron, the *Defiance*, the *Captain* and the *Princess Louisa*, to intercept them. Byng was sailing to the south-east and the two unidentified vessels were being left astern and, while Byng wished to gain what intelligence he could, he also did not want to do so at the expense of keeping his squadron together, and with this in mind Byng tacked. The time was about 6.15am.[87]

It was not long after the British squadron had settled on its new heading that a signal was made by one of the detached ships, the *Princess Louisa*, as she had seen ten ships to the north-west: the French squadron had been found. The *Trident* also made a signal that she saw a fleet, this time to the south-east, which seemed to show the French coming from the opposite direction to that which the *Princess Louisa* had signalled.[88]

Byng recalled the three ships which he detached and there seems to be a little confusion as to what time these signals were made. Yet, whether it was at 6.30 or 7am is in some ways irrelevant: neither squadron was close enough to come to action anytime soon as they were about twelve miles apart, and there was the matter of who would gain the all-important weather gage.[89] One of the tartans had been taken by the *Defiance* and once she had seen the signal for the recall of the detached ships she sank the little vessel. Only two of the three detached ships responded straight away; one remained intent on the chase, the *Princess Louisa*. Byng could not form the line of battle or think of coming up with the French until such time as all of his ships were back with the rest of the squadron.

It was only at 9am that the *Princess Louisa* at last saw the recall signal and came about to rejoin Byng.[90] It would be another hour before the three ships had closed sufficiently on the *Ramillies* and Byng gave the order to alter course towards the French, who were indeed to the south-east of his squadron with the wind at that time coming from the south-west blowing what was then called a small gale.[91] Once his squadron was in close order Byng hoisted the signal to form the line of battle and that the distance between ships in the squadron should be two cables, i.e. 400 yards.

An hour after this Byng signalled once again, this time that the distance between ships was to be reduced to half a cable, 100 yards, and at the same time he ordered all ships to crowd on all sail to get to windward of the French squadron.[92] Byng also ordered the 48-gun vessel the *Deptford*, the weakest of his ships and one which under no circumstances could be seen as ship of the line, out of the line. This evened up the numbers with the French squadron at twelve apiece.

Whilst both squadrons clawed for every bit of advantage that the wind could give them, each ship in the British and French squadron went through a similar process of preparing for the upcoming battle. Onboard the British ships it would be a well-worn routine. The decks were quite literally cleared, this was especially the case for the lower decks. All obstructions were to be removed, many of the bulkheads and cabin partitions were either struck down, or in some cases where they where hinged swung up to the deck head. If time permitted furniture and other such items would be sent down to the hold. In the hanging magazines powder for the great guns was measured out into paper cartridges: shot too would be placed close to the guns.

These, perhaps the most important instruments aboard, would be tended by up to thirteen men, each with their assigned task. So many men were required for each gun that only one broadside could be fully manned at any one time: if both broadsides were simultaneously needed in any engagement then guns crew numbers for each gun had to be halved, with a consequent slowing in the rate of fire.[93] The guns would have also to be run in, as whilst on voyage most would be lashed up to stop them moving as the ships worked in any kind of seaway.

The port lids would be opened. Some might have a lion's head painted on the interiors which, when raised, showed its face to the enemy, but many, if not most, were painted red, giving a strange checker board effect to the ship's side. Inboard, the rammers and sponges to swab out the barrel between firings and to extinguish any residue were checked. Buckets of water were placed between the guns for the same purpose, and, at the same time the decks would be sluiced with salt water as a precaution against fire. Down on the orlop deck the surgeon and his mate, if he had an assistant, prepared to receive casualties, setting out instruments and placing forms and tables to make makeshift operating tables.

Whilst all of this was going on between decks, the boatswain would be supervising the reinforcing of the running rigging and the yards would be slung in chain slings to prevent them being shot away during the action: if that were to happen it could either stop the ships from making way, or at the least foul the upper deck and hinder the guns' crews. Sheets and braces for the topgallants and royals would be doubled up, again as an insurance against damage from enemy fire.

The carpenter and his crew were also preparing in case of damage, having made a variety of conically-shaped plugs to drive home in shot holes and readied lead to seal holes which might be made between wind and water. Once in action, the carpenter's crew would be stationed below the wings of the ship. Had they been aboard the marines would have taken up their positions on the quarter decks and in the tops, but in Byng's squadron their place was taken by the men of Bertie's infantry. All of this was a well-organized confusion of men going hither and thither on the sound of drums beating to quarters, often to the rhythm of some well known tune.

The French ships hove into view from Byng's squadron sailing on a north-westerly course with their port tacks aboard, whilst the British were on the starboard tack sailing on a converging course with both squadrons trying to hug the wind.[94] Dudley Pope's description of the two squadrons at this time is the most apposite when he describes the course steered, 'as if travelling down each arm of an invisible V inscribed on the surface of the sea'.[95] As the British and French drew closer the first battle was to see who could gain the weather gage, with both seeking to sail as close to the wind as their ships could go. Square-rigged line-of-battle ships could not sail directly into the wind and no closer than perhaps six compass points. (Each point in this case is equal to eleven and a quarter degrees, meaning that they would be forced to sail off the wind by sixty-seven and a half.) It was down to the masters and quartermasters at the helms of the British ships to keep to the wind, and to their French counterparts to do the same. The irony of this is that for all their supposedly inferior qualities, the British ships and their crews were able to stay closer to the wind and gain the advantage of the weather gage. This was so important precisely because ships could not point into the wind, with the result that if you were to windward of your opponent you could sail down to engage or refuse action, whereas to leeward it was all but impossible to claw to windward and attack an unwilling enemy.

As Byng watched the French squadron they were on his port bow and it would be a close run thing as to which of them got to the intersection of the converging courses and thus gained the advantage. Both sides stood on, hoping either to weather their opponents or perhaps believing that as the sun got high in the sky the direction of the wind would alter and thus aid them.

Earlier, Byng had made the signal for his ships to form 'the line' and it is important to understand what 'the line' means in the context of a naval battle and why it was to assume such importance during the upcoming action. To quote Falconer's Marine Dictionary, it is: 'The order in which a fleet of ships of war are disposed to engage an enemy. This disposition, which is best calculated for the operation of naval war'.[96] With most guns carried along the broadside it made sense to fight in line astern. The line of battle was also a way of controlling a fleet in action. From the late-seventeenth century onward there were attempts to formulate and codify action at sea, and this was mainly down to the limited means of signalling and the need for the admiral to remain in control once an action had started.

The need for small ships to stand to leeward of the line to repeat signals was vital to fighting in line ahead because, although signals were usually hoisted at the main mast-head of the flag ship, as battle included the clawing and hauling up of sails and the firing of guns, flags were hoisted from all three masts. Yet still ships in line astern could not read the signals from flagships in the midst of an action because of the large amount of canvas and all of the smoke which would be generated obscuring the view. The small ships to leeward could see the signals and relay them virtually unimpeded to the ships in the line. This goes a long way to explain why Byng made such a fuss before leaving Portsmouth requesting frigates, this and the need to have scouts for the fleet to gain intelligence. The codification of action at sea became the 'Sailing And Fighting Instructions' which, via the Admiralty, were given legal sanction, and the punishment for breaking them could include the death penalty.[97]

Both Byng and La Galissonnière stood on, seeking to gain the advantage the weather gage would give them. It was at half-past twelve that the wind changed; it veered and this allowed the British squadron to put their bows more to starboard. As they were already on the starboard tack (i.e. the wind was coming over the starboard side of the ships) this meant that the British squadron was easing across the bows of the French and would gain the weather gage, just where Byng, and the fighting instructions, wanted it to be.

This movement was confirmed when the French ships eased off from the wind, as they could no longer keep as close to the wind now that it veered round.[98] Thus far what was happening off the island of Minorca seemed more like a sailing match than a sea battle, but for all the reason already mentioned this sailing match was carried out with deadly intent.[99] In fact the wind shifted to such an extent that the French would have to bear away by more than eleven degrees and this meant that the squadron could not hold its present course and would have to reform to leeward of the oncoming British. Byng was where he wanted, and needed, to be: all he had to do now was execute the manoeuvres which would bring both squadrons into action. At approximately 12.45 Byng made a signal for the squadron to alter course to port which would bring them back parallel to the French on their new course.[100] Both squadrons were now advancing on each other in parallel lines on opposite courses. Byng, according to contemporary evidence, was on the quarter deck, along with the other senior officers aboard the *Ramillies*, and in his hand was a copy of the sailing and fighting instructions, which he perused at the pertinent section.[101] It was also reported that the Article he was looking at was number XVII and this dictated that when two fleets were opposite each other but sailing on different courses the British should tack to come on to the same course as the enemy.[102]

Once they were sailing on the same, but parallel, course the British could tack again and, being to windward, force the French to fight. There is also reported an affecting scene where Byng's secretary George Lawrence, 'Took the Liberty of observing to the Admiral that agreeable to the Article the fleet should then tack'.[103]

Why would a man who has been described as by turn haughty and proud, and if some historians are to be believed both incompetent and defeatist, take the advice of his secretary?[104] Might it be just the outward sign of a man thrust into supreme position of authority showing that doubt which accosts many at such a time? He must have known the sailing and fighting instruction well, if not by heart. He had already exercised authority when he commanded of the squadron off Scotland and when he was sent into the Mediterranean at the end of the last war. In both cases no battle ensued, but still he would have had to have had more than a passing acquaintance with this document. Many historians seem to read this, alongside his self-deprecating use of language in his official letters, as a sign of things to come, leading inexorably to one thing: disaster when the test came.[105]

However, Byng had not at this point failed; he may have been swayed at the Council of War at Gibraltar, but he had not given up. He had sailed and was attempting to open communication with Blakeney when the French first appeared. Whilst this was not unexpected, Byng did the right thing, neither he nor La Galissonnière risked a night action and come the dawn he sought out his opponent and with the help of the change of the wind was in the best position to affect an action.

What is of interest and perhaps some significance is that Byng was loath to appoint any of his captains as a Commodore, should he need to do so. Under his command were thirteen ships which could normally stand in the line. Usually these would have three flag officers in command when going into action: the Van in the lead, the Middle (normally the station of the commander of the fleet or squadron), and the Rear. Each of these would have had at least one flag officer commanding them, and in a larger fleet more than one such flag officer to each squadron. In Byng's squadron there were only two flag officers, himself and Rear Admiral Temple West. Why did Byng not appoint one of the senior Captains to act as commodore in the upcoming action? His stated reason was that he did not know any of them well enough.[106]

What Byng chose to do was have just the two flag officers and their positions within the line of battle which was, as it turned out, to carry major consequence, although at the time it does not seem from the evidence that Byng felt any disadvantage would flow from this decision.[107]

This on the face of it does not seem to be an unnatural thing to have done: it is all too easy to read everything as if it were a self-fulfilling prophecy, and it was not as if Byng could control who his opponent would be or how they would act if faced by a British squadron. La Galissonnière was one of France's most distinguished commanders and an excellent handler of fleets, but he was constrained by his instructions from Louis XV.[108] The supposedly conventional Byng had decided on an unconventional method of approaching his opponent which he hoped would mean that, as they came into action, he would not be exposed to the broadside fire of the French without being able to reply, only of their bow chasers. He would do this by allowing his squadron to pass the last of the French ships, both still sailing parallel but opposite courses and, unlike Article XVII of the sailing and fighting instructions, he would then have his ships tack. As the two squadrons stood at this moment it would mean that the British would come onto the same tack as the French, the port tack, but would not, as they came about, be opposite their intended opponent, but would have passed them. As they tacked they would then have to make what was known as a 'lasking' approach, that is, an oblique angle to their French target.[109] The wind would be coming over the quarter of the vessel, not quite dead across the stern. This would, in theory at least, allow some of the broadside guns of the British to bear as they came into action.

What Byng was doing was, of course, not known to the French commander. La Galissonnière, after ordering his squadron to bear away, had had them reform their line with their main course (sail) clewed up and just the topgallants were kept to maintain as little way on his ships as possible, consummate with keeping them under control. It is likely that he was expecting Byng to carry out the manoeuvres which have already been touched on under Article XVII: there is even some speculation that he may actually have had a copy of the British sailing and fighting instructions, although there is no hard and fast evidence to prove this one way or the other.[110] However, judging from the movement of Byng's squadron, it appeared to the French command as if the British were looking to attack one part of their squadron and attempt to defeat it in detail. Given that by this time Byng's leading ship had passed the rear of the French squadron this looked like it would be the case. La Galissonnière would have to take some action to preclude the British doing just that.[111] If the British were allowed to stand on as they were and if they did attack the French rear, the French van would be unable to come to the aid of those ships quickly, due to the time it would take to tack or wear and come up with the British. What La Galissonnière planned to do to counter this was to back his sails, thus bringing all of his ships to a standstill, which should mean that the British would overshoot and thus thwart the British plan.[112] By the time the two were in this position it was 1.30pm and things were about to come to a head, as Byng decided that his squadron was in the right position for him to order them to tack in succession and come down on their French opposite number on a lasking course.[113] This movement would be started by the rear ships in his line, followed one after the other by the succeeding eleven ships. This would entail all of the ships coming about on the port tack and then approaching the French on the diagonal in such a way as to give them some hope of engaging the enemy whilst they closed the range.

With that in mind, Byng ordered the signal for the ships to tack in succession to be made.[114] As his ships started to prepare to tack it became clear that the French had backed their sails and by doing so would force the British to pass the French and thus be out of place to carry out their attack. To counter this he cancelled the signal for the ships to tack in succession from the rear of the line, and instead ordered them to tack together. This would bring his squadron into action just as he hoped it would.[115]

It was not to be: the *Defiance*, which was now leading the British line, should have tacked and sailed down onto her opposite number in the French line, the *Orphee*, and pounded her into submission, although it is doubtful that Byng himself thought in such colourful terms. This did not happen; she came round to port but did not lask down on her opponent and instead took up a course parallel, but a mile from, the French line. While this was technically within the range of the guns aboard, for any serious damage to be done the ships would have to be at pistol or half pistol shot range, about 20 yards apart, not 1,760 yards as they appeared to be.

As the ships of his squadron came out of their stays and on to the new course they all followed in the wake of the *Defiance*. One after the other the *Portland*, the *Lancaster* and the *Buckingham* all stood on this new course. Fully a third of the ships Byng had in his line were not following what Byng thought he had ordered them to do.

What could he do to correct this mistake by his subordinates? According to the trial reports there was another of those telling exchanges between Byng and Captain Gardiner and Lord Bertie, with Byng expostulating on what Captain Andrews of the *Defiance*, might or might not understand of the sailing and fighting instructions.[116] What perhaps is interesting, given Byng's previous acknowledgement, is that he was expecting his subordinates to carry through a complex manoeuvre and to some extent second guess the commanding officer's intentions. It is all too easy to look to later success and see what officers could do on their own initiative: this was not the Navy of 1756 and individual initiative can only be exercised within a fleet where all parties have total confidence in each other, and, most importantly, where they know what the intentions of the commander are in the first place. None of these preconditions held true on 20 May 1756 under John Byng. He was a man of his time and accepted that sailing and fighting were part of the framework of a well-regulated service. He was not a Nelson, but neither was the Navy in which he served that which had the habit of victory; that was to come after 1759. Byng's Navy was much more uncertain than that of Nelson's day. It had just come through a series of revolutions, including that of 1688, the settlement of 1701 and a change of monarch in 1713, and had suffered some reverses in the last two wars, all of which influenced those, like Byng, who learnt from the experience of their mentors, not through books or staff colleges, that discipline and staying within the rules was vital. The lesson he learned from the court martial of Mathews and Lestock in the last war merely reinforced the point; stability was to be gained by following the rules, not overthrowing them.

However, Byng was now faced with the problem of communicating his wishes via the limited means that he had at his disposal. The decision he came to was to order the leading ship to turn one point to starboard. This, he thought, would make clear his plan that they should engage their opposite number. To that end he hoisted a blue and white striped flag and fired one gun to signal the turn.[117] The captain of the leading ship of the line saw his duty every bit as much as Byng did in following the instructions his commander gave. Thus it was that Captain Andrews of the *Defiance* turned one point (11¼ degrees) to starboard in accordance with the signal flying aboard the flagship. This would not close the distance between the two squadrons so that they could come into action. Byng did not have recourse to a vocabulary signal system; he could not spell words. The signals he had could only say certain set things, such as the enemy is this or that way, or the fleet is to turn this way or that way. The only way to communicate the fine points would have been either to have discussed his plan with his captains beforehand, or to have sent the ship's cutter with an officer with verbal instructions. The one was not done prior to the engagement and the other was almost impossible during the action because of the distance between the flagship *Ramillies* and the *Defiance*.

One of the ships which had followed the *Defiance* around was the *Buckingham*, which had on board Rear Admiral Temple West, Byng's second in command. It would appear from his action that he too, albeit that she was the hind-most of the quartet, either took no action or did not know what Byng intended by the initial manoeuvre and the subsequent signal. Either way, Rear Admiral West followed the other ships and sailed one point to starboard.

Whatever the cause, the British squadron was not going to come into action unless Byng could get the head of his line to come in on a diagonal, which the first signal had failed to do. Given the limited choice available, Byng could do little but have the signal just made repeated, which he did, and in obedience to it the *Defiance* and her followers altered course a further point to starboard.[118]

There were to be some unintended consequences from the two evolutions carried out by the leading British ships. The two lines of ships, British and French, had been converging like two sides of an arrow head; even after the

French bore away before the wind the two were not perfectly parallel, and the two one point turns made by the four leading British ships put the head of the squadron much closer to the French than the rest, which meant that it would come into action sooner than the middle and rear. Byng was to try one more thing to get his squadron where he wanted them, alongside the French. There were no more signals or Articles save one which might force the ships into action: a plain red flag, usually hoisted at the main mast-head – the signal for general action which would fly as long as the Admiral wished the engagement to last.[119]

Byng ordered the signal to be made to bring on the general action. *Defiance* and her consorts put their helms over, put before the wind, and at last sailed down perpendicular to the French.

There was but one problem with this: the head of the British line was now just a mile from the French whereas the middle and rear were between two and three miles from the enemy. The lead British ships would be unsupported by some of the heaviest ships, including Byng's flagship, for quite some time. It was a complete reversal of what La Galissonnière had feared would happen to his rear. Now the British van might be punished without the rest being able to come to support them.

As all of the ships in the British line turned in response to the signal, this should have been what brought all to a bloody but glorious climax. But the manoeuvres that had brought Byng's squadron close to the French meant that even the rear of the line was not in good order. The irony is that some of the ships closest to Byng's flagship *Ramillies* steered differing courses to bring them into action. The *Intrepid* turned to run straight down on her opponent the *Revenge*, by coincidence almost following a lasking course down onto the waiting French. *Intrepid* was followed by two ships, the *Princess Louisa* and the *Trident*.[120] These two also took a diagonal approach, which caused problems for the next ship in the line to these vessels. This vessel was Byng's own ship the *Ramillies*, which turned, as the admiral intended, straight down on to her opponent. The next in line was the *Culloden*. She too took a slanting course. This meant that the vessels immediately ahead and astern of Byng were on a slanting course whilst he had turned at right angles to the French line. Some historians see Byng's frustration with what was occurring as an obsession with the line of battle and the fate of those, such as Mathews and Lestock, who broke with it.[121] Yet it is more likely that he was concerned that all ships got into action in as short a space of time and in as good an order as possible so that the battle did not descend into an uncontrollable melee. It is true that, as evidence at his trial showed, he did indeed mention what had befallen Mathews at Toulon, and the significance taken is that Byng was refusing to break the line lest the same fate awaited him.[122] Whilst he mentions Mathews, his referral to the case is because this action was the best example of what could happen if a British fleet came into action piecemeal against a coherent and well handled French fleet. Byng was facing just that, a well handled French squadron under La Galissonnière, on 20 May 1756. His reaction appears to be the natural one for someone in command: what he wanted was for the action not to miscarry, rather than any slavish adherence to the sanctity of the line of battle.

Be that as it may, what Byng now faced was a situation in which his van was all but in action, and he and the bulk of the squadron were two to three miles off. How could he get them to close more rapidly and in a coherent way? Byng wished for the sail aboard the *Ramillies* to be shortened, Captain Gardiner argued that they should crowd on more sail and thus reach the French sooner and receive, he hoped, less damage and by the same token set an example which the other ships on the lasking course would follow. Byng was not convinced by Gardiner's argument. He did not want it to appear as if he were taking part in a single-ship action by leaving the line and bearing down on the French flagship ahead of the rest of the rear of the squadron.[123] Pope and Tunstall see this as either stubborn adherence to an outmoded doctrine or as a loss of nerve on the part of Byng.[124] This too would seem to miss the point. Byng needed to retrieve a situation so that he could beat the French and thus relieve Blakeney in Fort St Philip.

Byng instructed Gardiner to shorten sail so that the others could catch up with the *Ramillies* and at the same time Gardiner and the Army officer readied their men for action. All the guns aboard the flagship were to be double-shotted, the 12 and 24 pdrs with a mix of grape and round shot, the 32pdrs with two solid shot per gun.[125] At last action was imminent and it was already past 2pm.

At 2.30pm the French opened a long range cannonade of the leading British ships. The *Defiance* came under fire from the French *Orphee*, but although Captain Andrews brought his ship about to run parallel to the French ship he was still standing about 300 yards from her. Given that all the French had to do was cripple some of Byng's ships to stop him from breaking the French siege it is unsurprising that La Galissonnière accepted action at this range. With his ships to leeward their batteries would be firing at an upward angle, rather than at the level or on the down roll, which at this range would carry shot into the masts and rigging of their opponents where it would do the most damage to the motive power of the British.[126] If the French could cripple the masts and yards of the British squadron it would be restricted in what it could do to interfere in the French plans and may even have to retreat for repairs.

What happened aboard the *Defiance* was that she took heavy damage from the French *Orphee*, as the shot damaged her masts and yards and she also took some damage to the hull . Within a short time of her coming into action she had lost thirteen killed and forty five wounded. One of those killed was Captain Andrews.[127] The cumulative effect of the French fire was that the *Defiance* was becoming more and more difficult to handle and she was losing way, she had four gun ports smashed, and all of her boats were destroyed. It is difficult to convey the sense of a sea battle between-decks aboard a ship of the line as there are few firsthand accounts. The senses would be assaulted, with sight obscured by smoke, the smell of the smoke and the reek of burnt powder, the sounds of the discharge and the recoil of eight or ten heavy guns, the orders given being shouted above the din, and the tearing crash as French shot hit the ship, plus the sounds of the wounded and the dying, mingling into a devil's chorus.

The next ship in line to come under fire was the *Portland*. She came into action shortly after the *Defiance*, matched with the *Hippopotame*, and also received heavy fire from the French ship. She too had a torrid time as the *Hippopotame* moved ahead of the *Portland* and her place in the line was taken by the *Redoutable*, which was the flagship of La Galissonnière's second in command Admiral de Glandevez. She bore away out of the French line a short distance and her place was taken by a third French ship, the *Sage*, who also pummelled *Portland*. The enemy caused damage to the *Portland's* upper-works and to the masts and yards, and killed six of her crew and injured twenty more.[128] Next to come down onto the French was the *Lancaster*, who was to come up on the *Redoutable*. The *Lancaster* opened a smart fire on the French ship, which returned it with interest, doing great execution on the British ship. The *Lancaster* was seconded by the *Buckingham*, with the combined fire of the British ships causing the French ship to forge ahead, and in the process take the place of the *Hippopotame*, and shortly thereafter come into action with the *Portland* as described above.[129] The *Buckingham*, which had seconded the *Lancaster* so ably, was Rear Admiral West's flagship, and before she fired upon the *Redoutable* had herself come under fire from at least three other ships in the French line. The vessel which was the *Lancaster's* opposite number was the *Sage*, with whom she started to exchange a brisk fire, and despite the often cited disparity in the number and weight of fire it was to be the *Sage* which bore away. The wind at this point in the action, around about 3.30pm, was light and ships under topsails were ghosting along, with the smoke from the discharge of both great guns and small arms not being whipped away on a strong breeze but hanging in the air like thunder clouds.[130] The lack of visibility caused by this fog of battle and the consequent loss of control was just what the line of battle, with its repeater frigates on the disengaged side, was supposed to preclude. It was difficult for either Rear Admiral West or Byng to have a clear picture of how the action was unfolding or, if either did, for them to communicate that one to another or just as importantly to their subordinates in the squadron.

Having punished the *Sage*, and she having left the line, the *Lancaster* and the *Buckingham* sailed on to give support to the *Defiance* and the *Portland*, which by this point were in a parlous state. According to Dudley Pope, it was the sanctity of the line which stopped the British from following up their forcing the French ships out of the line.[131] However, Tunstall makes the case that these French ships were operating on a preconceived plan, in which once they had inflicted sufficient damage they were to withdraw.[132] The most up to date account makes no mention of any such plan: it does however make it clear that the French were suffering as much as the British were.[133]

The next ship from the British line to come up was the *Captain*. Her opponent was the *Guerrier*, but she had come under fire from others in the French line and she seems to have fired just four broadsides at the *Guerrier*.[134] The *Captain* herself was badly damaged, her bowsprit was shot away, her foremast was hit by shot ten feet above the deck and the main and mizzen were also heavily damaged by enemy fire.[135] As well as the running and standing rigging, the sails were also shot through, which all meant that the ship became much more difficult to handle. She had also been badly hulled by enemy shot. Five of the twelve ships were now in action but not in the way that Byng had hoped. They were coming into action singly and were suffering the consequences.

The next in line to come up to the French was the *Intrepid*. She had not had the best of luck thus far and her misfortune was, although her crew did not expect it, to continue. The ship she was to attack was the *Fier*, but as she sailed down on her she also drew the attention of the French flagship, the *Foudroyant*. The latter was a powerful eighty gun ship, the former was a fifty gun ship. Both these ships mauled the *Intrepid*. Her mainmast was hit, but not brought down, her bowsprit was shot through and her jib-boom was damaged. Then, as so often in war, one incident occurred which was to flip the whole action. A shot went through the fore-topmast and brought both it and its attendant yards down, which, along with the damage to the bowsprit, caused the ship's head to come up into the wind.[136]

What this meant was that whilst eleven British ships had ghosted into action on a light breeze, the twelfth was now athwart the line, that is, at right angles to the British line of approach. The result was that there would be a hiatus astern of the *Intrepid* as vessels astern would have either to pass her to leeward, which was the easiest course, or weather her, or wait until she cleared the line once she had regained control, if she could. Failing any of these she would have to be towed by one of the frigates out of the line. What this also did was to open a gap in the British line: the ships ahead could quite simply continue on their course but those astern had to manoeuvre to pass her. By default the cohesion of the line had been lost by this point.

The next in line to the *Intrepid* was the *Revenge*. What happened next has been described variously as either a farce or as a gallant gesture by Captain Cornwall of the *Revenge*. As the *Intrepid* came round into the wind, and whilst the crew were seeking to clear the decks, the *Revenge* sent a boat carrying a message. There are two versions of what was contained in the message. One states that Cornwall asked whether his ship the *Revenge* should pass ahead of the crippled *Intrepid* so that she might support the vessel ahead of her.[137] The other version, which is more in the tradition of the nobility of war, has the question asked whether the *Revenge*, 'for the Kings service', should stand to leeward to protect *Intrepid* from the enemy's fire.[138] Whatever the case, Captain Cornwall hove-to astern of the *Intrepid*, waiting for the response of Captain Young.

The story as laid out by Pope, and as supported by the evidence given at the court martial, was that Captain Cornwall aboard the *Revenge* saw Byng some way astern when he looked out from his Great Cabin, and, having hove-to shortly afterward, the *Princess Louisa* loomed out of the artificial fog created by the cannon fire and passed so close astern that her jib-boom came over the *Revenge's* taffrail (i.e. stern rail) as she passed.[139]

Some little time after that she saw the *Trident* pass by and only saw her at the level of her topsails, so dense was the smoke from the action. If Captain Cornwall's action were to interpose his ship between the *Intrepid* and her principal tormentor the *Foudroyant*, she did not take any serious damage from the enemy (she was struck by just three shot) and was one of those British ships which had no casualties aboard due to enemy action.[140]

Some of his contemporaries felt that Cornwall was at best being laggardly in coming into action, at worst just plain stupid. Whatever motivated him, be it bravery or stupidity, the net effect was more disruption in the British line. Further confusion was caused when the *Princess Louisa* came under the *Revenge's* stern. The *Princess Louisa* should have been the next to come into action in an orderly fashion, but this was disrupted by the *Trident*, which appeared on the *Princess Louisa's* starboard side, forcing her to turn to port and hence across the stern of the *Revenge*.[141] This all meant that the *Princess Louisa* had problems firing on a target in the opposing line, yet she took quite a lot of damage herself. Captain Noel was hit by a shot which carried away one leg and eventually the wound would prove fatal.

The *Trident*, as with the *Revenge*, provides a problem for the historian studying the subject. Her captain, Durrell, makes little mention of why he took the course which ended in her closing on the *Princess Louisa*. However it was her action which was to affect Byng directly, as it was his flagship the *Ramillies* which was next astern. Durrell claimed that he, like the Captain of the *Revenge*, was coming to the aid of the *Intrepid* and the *Princess Louisa* by sailing between them and the enemy's line. It was from this position that the

Trident opened fire on the French, yet he also backed his topsails. This had the effect of bringing the *Trident* to a stop.[142]

What had happened thus far was that Byng's ships had arrived at the French line and had inflicted damage on their opponents, but they had not arrived in a coherent way in which any individual success could be exploited.

This had little to do with any slavish adherence to the line of battle and more to the simple fact that the nature of the ships' arrival did not allow a concentration of force on any part of the French line. The effect of this was akin to a slow moving traffic accident in which the cumulative results were greater than the individual damage. The bunching and agglomeration of ships was at the end of a slowly moving line and almost two thirds of Byng's ships were caught up in it.[143]

Aboard the *Ramillies* the troops and seafarers were ready for action and had the most difficult part to endure, the wait for the shooting to start. Shot from the French started to cross the *Ramillies* and some went through topsails and cut some of the upper rigging aboard the flagship.[144] At around 12.50pm somewhere on the upper deck a gunner fired without orders from the lieutenant in command of that battery. At this point the *Ramillies* was approximately half a mile from the French line, and at this range, as with the French, the cannonade would be to a great extent ineffective.[145]

Why Byng, this supposed martinet, did not order a ceasefire is an open question. There is some speculation that Byng thought that the discharge from the guns and the attendant smoke would mask the flagship from the French line as she made her final approach.[146] Why Byng thought at this point that he needed to hide his flagship from the French is odd; at no time up until this point or thereafter did Byng show any fear of the upcoming engagement, either generally or as it might affect his flagship. He walked about the quarterdeck as one might expect a flag officer to do, giving orders in a cool and collected manner.[147]

Why, apart from coming into action undamaged, would there be the need for a smoke screen? It could be that Byng felt that, albeit the shot was at long range, it was better for him and the flagship to be taking the enemy under fire, and that to hold fire now would have a bad psychological effect on the crew. There is little evidence in Byng's own hand to explain the reason why, and therefore his motives must be adduced from his actions – or in this case the lack of them – in not ordering the guns silenced. Be that as it may, what happened next would be the culmination of all of his previous actions.

It would fall to Lord Bertie, whose regiment was still aboard Byng's flagship, to report sighting a vessel crossing the starboard bow of the *Ramillies*. From her position in the line it could only be one of Byng's squadron and it would take some smart work to stop her being fired on by the *Ramillies*. Orders were sent, carried by Bertie, to Captain Gardiner to stop them firing into her. Meanwhile, Colonel Smith, another officer being carried aboard the flagship for Minorca, had also spotted the colours of yet another vessel, this time off the *Ramillies'* quarter and ordered the stern guns not to fire on that vessel.[148]

In this sudden flurry of activity Byng also made a decision which is still debated, in historical circles, to this day. He gave Captain Gardiner an order to back his fore-topsail, the effect of which would be to bring the *Ramillies* to a slow halt. This was a controlled version of what in effect had happened to the *Intrepid* a little earlier.

Byng's planned attack had fallen by the wayside. As he ordered his flagship to bring-to, he found that he had the *Trident* 200 yards off his starboard bow and the *Princess Louisa* close off his port bow. His next order was even more controversial than his last as he wished to avoid collisions between his own squadron, and in particular the rear ships of his line: that at least is how he explained it in evidence.[149] He ordered the signal to be made that all ships in the squadron should brace-to, and come to a stop.

This was laudable in theory but lamentable in practice. He had clear evidence earlier in the engagement that the Captains did not always read the signal in the spirit in which it was meant, for example in the actions of Captain Andrews. In this case Byng wanted to bring the rear of the line to, but allow the remaining ships to carry on and straighten the line. His only means to do so was to fly a general signal.[150] What happened was that all vessels brought to and thus the whole attack stalled.

This does not seem to be an act of cowardice, more a man seeking to make order out of a chaotic situation, some of which was of his own making, some of which was not. Whatever the rationale in the heat of battle, in the cold light of day it did not do what Byng wanted and in fact exacerbated the situation. Yet it was a case of being damned if you did and damned if you didn't. The great fault was that Byng did not inform his Captains as to how he would attack the enemy. Even if he had not the personality or preconditions of a Nelson, he might have informed them in general terms of what he intended. If there was fault it was the aloofness, or perhaps shyness which manifested itself in bombast, which precluded this from happening and precipitated the tragedy which followed.

Within a few short minutes the ships had drifted cleared of one another, and at the same time the French had spied an opportunity to divide the British line by forcing through between the *Captain* and the *Revenge* with seven of the French line who were relatively unscathed. This plan came to nought as Byng ordered the signal to 'brace-to' hauled down and the rear of the British line closed on the damaged ships.[151] At around the same time Byng ordered the *Deptford* to return to the line to add weight to the renewed attack. The last two ships in the British line, the *Culloden* and the *Kingston*, followed *Ramillies* out from the confusion but did not fire a single shot at the French.

In a short time La Galissonnière saw Byng's ships coming-up and he stayed on his course to the north-west, cannonading the head of the British line as he did so. Byng is purported to have made a remark to Captain Gardiner about how the French ships out-sailed the British under foresails and topsails, which is odd given how well the British had weathered the French line before the action was joined.[152] He also expressed the desire to have had more ships so that, as he perceived the French bearing away, he could have continued the action with a general chase.[153] The French bore away to leeward and for all practical purposes the Battle of Minorca was over. All that was needed was the butcher's bill on both sides. In this, as in much else, they were evenly matched, the French losses amounting to 213 killed the British 207.[154] As Dull, in his history of the French Navy in the Seven Years War, points out, whilst the French casualties were spread out amongst the French squadron it was the leading ships of the British line which had a disproportionate number of the losses.[155]

What the French had done, but perhaps were unaware of, was stopped the reinforcement of the garrison on Minorca in the short term, although some of their ships were disabled in their masts and rigging and some to be sure were even more short of crewmen as a result of the action. Byng still had a force which on the face of it could have interrupted the French proceedings at sea and thereby caused great harm to the French attempts on land to besiege Fort St Philip.

First Byng had to gather information on the state of his ships, ascertain what if any repairs needed to be undertaken and whether they could be done at sea, or whether it required any of the squadron to return to Gibraltar and undertake the work in the comparative shelter of the yard there.

Chapter Five

Council of Despair?

The action was over with neither side having a great advantage over the other. La Galissonnière had stopped the British for the time being, but Byng was still off Minorca and, for all he knew, Byng would seek to renew the action as soon as it was feasible. Both sides had continued on a north-north-west course, the French about two miles to leeward of Byng's ships, which Byng then tacked, in succession, at about five o'clock. With Rear Admiral West's ships in the van, this placed Byng in the rear and closer to the French.[1]

For Byng's part, he wanted to ascertain how things stood on his ships, but as night fell he would try and keep his ships together. They would all, once the signal for general action was hauled down, stand off the island under easy sail.[2] He was also unsure what effect his ships had had on their opposite numbers.[3] Yet from all appearances the French had not received much punishment, which might put Byng at a disadvantage if he sought to re-engage straight away. In any event, with the distance between the two increasing and sunset fast approaching it was unlikely that the French would stand to and accept action even if Byng tried to force the issue.

Byng wrote a letter to his second-in-command, quoted by both his previous biographers, in which he is effusive in both his praise and concern for his second in command, Temple West: 'I hope you are well and have not received any hurt yourself tho' I see that your ship has greatly suffered', the language then rising to the more hyperbolic, 'Your behaviour was like an angel today'.[4] Perhaps this is part of the clue to the character of the man: passionate but well aware, like any who read Chesterfield's advance to his son, that such displays had to be kept within bounds in polite society. He restrained the display and was therefore acting like a gentleman should.[5] This is what he in fact was, but he had to act and sound as such in word, deed and speech. Whether that made him look haughty and disgusting, as Horace Walpole said, is another matter.[6]

After this exchange Byng waited for the coming of the dawn, when he could plan what he would do next. He was, in theory at least, in a position where he could still stop French reinforcements from reaching the besiegers outside Fort St Philip. At sunrise Byng's squadron was about 25 miles north-west of Cape Mola, and hull down on the horizon the French squadron could still be seen. Byng detached his frigates to look for two of his number which had parted company with the rest during the night, the *Intrepid* and the *Chesterfield*. Of the two it was the *Intrepid* which had been worst hit in her masts and rigging, and therefore it was of greater concern that she had not strayed too far from the rest lest she be caught by the French and overwhelmed before assistance might come.[7] They in fact would not be sighted again until 22 May, two days after the battle, during which time the rest of the squadron repaired the damage it had received in its topmasts and yards. In fact the weather would also take a hand in the proceedings: it turned thick with a heavy swell which would make it difficult for ships with damage to their topmasts and yards to do anything other than keep under easy sail to reduce the strain.[8] In such conditions Byng's avowed intention to renew the action would come to nought.

Byng had other issues on his mind. He was less than happy with the conduct of several of the captains, especially those toward the rear of the line. How he was to deal with them would be a leitmotif of the next few days.

What happened over the next two days after the battle on 20 May was that the ships in Byng's squadron continued to repair the damage they had received. Further, there was the question of who was to replace Captains Andrews and Noel, of the *Defiance* and *Princess Louisa* respectively, who had been killed in the action. This was Byng's prerogative as the commander of the squadron. He chose to appoint Augustus Hervey to the *Defiance* and Lloyd to command the *Princess Louisa*.[9] Hervey is much quoted because of the journal he kept, which was edited in the 1950s and published. He was certainly less than happy with the ship he took command of, calling it, 'a perfect wrack' and 'the worst-manned ship in the service now'.[10] And, even allowing for his natural tendency for the dramatic, the *Defiance* was in a parlous state. She had a complement by establishment of 400. When they left Gibraltar there were fifty-three men in the hospital and they had had a further fifty-nine killed and injured on 20 May. These were offset by approximately 20 men who had been transferred out of the frigates.[11] Despite this it was a major promotion for Hervey, coming out of a twenty-gun sixth-rate ship in to a fourth-rate 60-gun ship, with an attendant increase in pay, allowances and status.[12] Hervey has attracted criticism from some who see him as one of Byng's cronies. Hervey was certainly one of Byng's favourites, but this does not in and of itself negate what he said about the situation immediately after the battle of Minorca; even allowing for some of his more eccentric behaviour in the light of subsequent events.

Byng's next communication with Rear Admiral West was on 23 May, when the French squadron was sighted once more. In it he set out his thoughts on whether they were in any condition to engage the French. He felt that they were not. Rear Admiral West's response was to attend Byng aboard his flagship, and, in the oft-quoted second line: 'should be glad to give my opinion at a council of war'.[13] There is no record of what was said between the two officers when they met aboard the *Ramillies*, only that Rear Admiral West wanted to be able to express his opinion in a formal setting.[14] Thus was set in motion one of the most controversial acts in naval history. A Council of War was to be held aboard the flagship on 24 May. The signal was made that all Captains should attend the flagship. This in itself was to cause trouble, as Rear Admiral West is reported as not wishing to sit with three of the Captains , Parry, Ward, and Cornwall, all of whom he thought had failed to act in the appropriate manner during the action in not supporting the van. There followed, according to Rear Admiral West's account at the court martial, an exchange with Byng in which Byng recognized that they may have failed but said that he had reprimanded them, or would do so, and that they should sit at the Council. West acquiesced to this in terms that he was not in a position to judge, as his ship was at the head of the line and thus obscured from those at the rear.[15]

Much has been made of this, to the effect that by the time that evidence was given Rear Admiral West was less keen to point out the failings of these Captains, although others, such as Hervey in his journal, alleged that Rear Admiral West had already wanted the three court martialled.[16] The point that this illustrates is that there was tension within the squadron. It can be suggested that if there had already been or if there was later a whole-hearted victory, these tensions would have been swallowed up in the general acclamation. In the event that did not happen. Byng also asked the three most senior Army officers present to attend. With the thirteen sea officers and Byng this would make a convocation of seventeen officers who met in the great cabin of the flagship. As yet no one knew what Byng would bring forward for them to discuss.

Once again the question arises as to why Byng had thought it necessary to hold such a meeting. Pope is of the opinion that a more determined commander would not have relied on such a council and it materially helped in his downfall.[17] Tunstall was even more forceful: 'they (the officers present) were about to endorse one of the most disastrous expressions of opinion ever made in the annals of our Navy'.[18] This is strong meat and he goes on to link this gathering directly to Byng's execution. There is no private letter or journal which hints at why Byng felt that he had to summon a Council.

These bodies, much abused but not unusual, were often seen both at the time and subsequently as the last resort of either scoundrels or of the weak.

Byng might have been many things but even his worst enemy did not accuse him of being devious or a scoundrel. This implies that he was not bad, but, perhaps even worse, may have been lacking in courage: not of the physical kind, although George II subsequently thought so, but in moral courage. To do what was right and to act as a sea officer he should have acted aggressively, albeit with a fine calculation of what damage he could do to the enemy without immolating himself and his command to no effect. Byng was fussy, which might come across as dithering, and he also wrote in an orotund style which was self-deprecating. While neither of these traits are the archetypes of what a sea officer was supposed to be – horny-handed sons of toil – they were perhaps closer to those of a country gentleman, which, from his building projects at Wrotham and his acquisition of land at South Mimms, would be appear to be what he wanted. Whether this had a bearing over his decision to call the Council is difficult to ascertain. The need for external reassurance concerning decisions made, or about to be made, is a complex and controversial subject to this day.

What Byng did on 24 May was to lay out for discussion by the Council the information to hand, to whit:

1. His instruction from the Board of Admiralty dated 30 March
2. Orders with regards to Lord Robert Bertie's Regiment of Fusiliers
3. The opinion of the artillery and engineer officers on the predictability of landing troops at St Philip's
4. The opinion of the Council of War held at Gibraltar on 4 May
5. The state of the sick and wounded as of 24 May, which was as follows: sick, 389 on board and 71 left at Gibraltar; wounded 168, killed 43. Total of killed and wounded 671.[19]

Also laid before them was the current state of the ships in the squadron. The *Defiance* would have a new foretopmast swayed up by nightfall and the *Captain* had also fished her foremast ('fishing' in this case means attaching a length of oak, concave on one side and convex on the other, to the mast by lashings to strengthen it) and was fit to sail.[20] The *Portland's* masts were sound but her knees in the head of the ship ('knees' were curved pieces of timber used to attach beams to side timbers) were loose; in this case, from the description it could be the knee of the head, which ran under the figure head of the ship.[21] In any account, it could not be repaired at sea and needed the attention of the dockyard artificers at Gibraltar. The *Intrepid* was running under jury topmasts and would have to be towed to Gibraltar. Rear Admiral West's flagship the *Buckingham*, the *Revenge* and the *Princess Louisa* were all fit for action.

Like so many important discussions there is only one first hand account, by Hervey, and as has been said before he was one of Byng's favoured officers. Nonetheless, this of itself does not discredit his account, which in broad terms was that several of the officers present thought that Byng's instructions from the Admiralty were 'absurd' and agreed that the squadron was not in a fit state to face another action with the French. In Hervey's account, Rear Admiral West was strongly against renewing any action with the French under the current circumstances, although Byng in a telling phrase is supposed to have said that, 'if there was any officer that thought we ought, he would attack tomorrow'.[22]

It is significant how passive Byng appears to be at this point. If what Hervey reports is the truth, he may have already been convinced, as many of his detractors have stated, that an action was not possible. They ally this with what he said just after the action: that he would have given chase to the French had he had greater numbers. In this they follow the lead of Sir Julian Corbett with his view of a 'man half-beaten'.[23] Others admit that this is odd but seek to explain it away by the general situation of the squadron at the time. It can be interpreted as operating in the same manner as the later court martial, in which the junior officers gave their conclusions first so that, in theory at least, they were not unduly influenced by the senior officers present. Hervey's own actions would tend to tell against this theory, as he supposedly spoke out for staying off Minorca and awaiting any reinforcements which might be sent out. Although more were on the way, none of those present was aware of this at the time of the Council. More importantly when it came to voting on the resolutions of the Council Hervey did not vote against any of them.[24] There is little reported on what the Army officers present thought or said excepting only their record in the vote at the end of the proceedings.

This still leaves the question open as to why Byng resorted to such a council in the first place. He had been in the service long enough to know that in the end the commander of the squadron was the one who would take the lion's share of praise or blame. Yet a Council of War might provide an excellent audit trail as to why a particular action was or was not carried out.

But in the end it was the action or lack of it that would be judged and as Byng was the one who commanded, it would be he who was judged by what he did or did not do, irrespective of any advice proffered.

The Council was held and in the end, after all of the debate – or lack of it – there would have to be a formal resolution on which all of those present would be asked to vote. It was down to Byng to bring forward the questions which had to be answered, and these too were to be even more controversial than calling the council in the first place. Perceived by even those favourably disposed to Byng as biased, they are perhaps an object lesson in asking what might be called 'closed questions'.[25] In this case there would be five questions put before the officers gathered aboard *Ramillies*, and once the vote had been take all of those who were in favour had to sign the resolution.

There were five questions on which the members of the Council of War were asked to vote. They were as follows:

1. Whether an attack upon the French Fleet gives any prospect of relieving Minorca?

Unanimously resolved that it would not.

2. Whether, if there was no French fleet cruising off Minorca, the English could raise the siege?

Unanimously the opinion that the fleet could not.

3. Whether, Gibraltar would not be in danger by any accident that might befall this Fleet?

Unanimously agreed that it would be in danger.

4. Whether, an attack with our Fleet in the present state of it upon that of the French, will not endanger the safety of Gibraltar and expose the trade of the Mediterranean to great hazard?

Unanimously agreed that it would.

5. Whether it is not the most for His Majesty's Services, that the Fleet should immediately proceed for Gibraltar?

We are unanimously of the opinion that the Fleet should immediately proceed for Gibraltar.[26]

It is often said that a week is a long time in politics. The five days which followed the Battle of Minorca on 20 May seem also laden with significance. The inaction in the first days or so after the battle is understandable in terms of the damage to the ships and the need to refit and repair.

The five propositions which were recorded can, and have been, read and reread in light of what happened subsequently, and in that they are no different to any text which can be reinterpreted after the event. Do they show that Byng was trying to argue from the position where he had already made up his mind and was merely looking for legal cover to try and escape the consequences?[27] Byng's behaviour and reaction after his relief by Admiral Hawke would seem to point the opposite way: he did not see that he had committed any great sin of omission or commission. He felt that it would all be sorted out. Courts martial were an occupational hazard. He had already raised the spectre of Admiral Mathews during the action. It does not appear as if it paralysed him either then or after the action. He was mindful of what had happened, but that is different to being held captive to either the fate of a fellow flag officer or to the Sailing and Fighting Instructions.

It was entirely within his power to call for advice from the officers under his command and those in the Army who it was his charge to take to Minorca. This did not mean that he lacked physical courage: his demeanour during and subsequent to the action was to give the lie to this. However, did he lack moral courage, one of the charges made to the court of public opinion and also in private by the King?[28] This is something that subsequent historians have seen in his actions after the battle of 20 May.[29] Furthermore, some of them in have taken his whole career as leading inexorably to this point.[30] If this were true it would indeed be a Greek tragedy; Byng marked out by birth or fate to carry out the actions he did. More probable, if less dramatic, is Byng the sea officer exercising his judgment of the situation as he saw it at the time.

That the judgement was flawed is clear: whether he exercised his judgement to the best of his abilities is not. This does not mean that Byng lacked either tactical insight – his sailing match with the French showed that – or that he lacked the will to serve and knew what should be done. What he lacked, alongside a great many other flag officers before and since, was the strategic vision as to what the consequences would be if he did not stay off his main objective – in this case Minorca. Gibraltar was important, but Minorca was vital: lose that and Britain lost a base of operations off the French coast. Lose Minorca and the law of unintended consequence came into play. France had attacked to divert attention from the Americas; to take Minorca was one thing, the political turmoil which followed was quite another. Byng was either stunningly naïve in terms of the politics of the situation, or, more likely, was doing the utmost he could to carry out his orders and could not fully grasp the full ramifications of his actions.

What compounded this was the fact that Byng only wrote his despatch to the Admiralty on 25 May, after the Council of War, and, if he is to be believed, with the help of Captain Hervey. He enclosed with it the deliberations of the Council of War and sent it home through the Straits aboard a frigate.[31]

This despatch, which under most circumstances would not be hugely contentious, was also to become a political tool. British ministers would use it against Byng in a cynical attempt to avoid any responsibility for what had happened. And, as luck would have it, they were aided in this by the fact that La Galissonnière had written to the French Minister of Marine on 21 May and sent it into Toulon.[32] He made no claims of victory, but bad news can be half-way round the world before the truth has got its boots on and in this case it proved to be true. The French dispatch was printed and passed on to the ministry at home before Byng's had arrived, thus giving them time for political manoeuvring, much of which will be dealt with later on.

Suffice to say that an edited version of Byng's despatch was printed when it did arrive. The despatch itself is a classic example of Byng's prolix style. The excisions are telling: the text in bold is that which was cut by the ministry from the version printed in the London Gazette. It is dated the *Ramillies* off Minorca 25 May, 1756:

Sir,

I have the pleasure to desire you will acquaint their lordships, that having sailed from Gibraltar the 8th, I got off Mahon the 19th having been joined by his Majesty's Ship *Phoenix* off Majorca two days before, **by whom I had confirmed the intelligence I received at Gibraltar of the strength of the French Fleet, and of their being off Mahon. His Majesty's Colours were still flying at Castle of St Philip's, and I could perceive several bomb batteries playing upon it, from different parts. French Colours we saw flying on the west part of St Philip. I dispatched the *Phoenix*, the *Chesterfield*, and the *Dolphin* ahead, to reconnoitre the harbour's mouth and Captain Hervey to endeavour to land a letter for General Blakeney to let him know the fleet was here to his assistance, tho' everyone was of the opinion we could be of no use to him: as by all accounts, no place was secured for covering a landing could we have spared any people. The *Phoenix* was also to make the private signal between Captain Hervey and Captain Scrope, as this latter would undoubtedly come off, if it were practicable, having kept the *Dolphin's* barge with him; but the Enemy's Fleet appearing to the South East, and the wind at the same time coming strong off the land, obliged me to call those ships in, before they could get quite so near the entrance of the Harbour, as to make sure what batteries or guns might be placed to prevent our having any communication with the Castle,** falling little wind, it was five before I could form any line, or distinguish any of the enemy's motions: and not at all to judge of their forces more than by their numbers, which were seventeen and thirteen appeared large: they at first stood towards us in a regular line , and tacked about seven, which I judged was to endeavour to gain the wind of us in the night; so that being late, I tacked in order to keep the weather gage of them, as well as to make sure of the land wind in the morning; being very hazy, and not above five leagues off Cape Mola. We tacked off towards the enemy at eleven: and at day light had no sight of them. But two tartans with the French private signal, being close in with the rear of our fleet, I sent the *Princess Louisa* to chase one, and made the signal for the Rear Admiral, who was nearest the other, to send ships to chase her: the *Princess Louisa*, *Defiance* and *Captain* became at great distance: The *Defiance* took hers, which had two captains, two lieutenants and one hundred and two private soldiers, who were sent out the day before with six hundred men, on board tartans, to reinforce the French Fleet, on our then appearing off the place. The *Phoenix*, on Captain Hervey's offer, prepared to serve as a fire ship, but without damaging her as a frigate, till the signal was made to prime: when she was then to scuttle her decks, everything else being prepared, as the time and place allowed of.[33]

It can already be seen that the tenor of what was left out was Byng's explanation of why certain actions might not be undertaken. The despatch itself was nearly 2,000 words long and the excisions were quite extensive and were not , as was shown above and will be discussed later, just made for the sake of brevity.

Whilst the British and French despatches wended their way, something else had occurred which materially changed the situation in the Mediterranean. This was the arrival of Rear Admiral Broderick. He had been ordered to sail on 8 May with five ships of the line to reinforce Byng. With Broderick were the *Prince George* 80, the *Hampton Court* 70, the *Ipswich* 70, the *Nassau* 70, and the *Isis* 50 guns.

They sailed on 20 May, the same day that Byng engaged La Galissonnière off Minorca, and arrived at Gibraltar on 15 June.[34] This would give Byng the extra ships he said he was in need of, and one, the *Prince George*, was the same rate as his flagship. One 80-gun ship and three 70-gun ships of the line would be a major strengthening of the fire power of the British line.

Three days prior to Broderick's sailing, on 17 May, King George II formally declared War on France and at about the same time ordered three regiments to be sent to Gibraltar for its defence.[35]

The first of Byng's squadron to encounter Broderick was Hervey, who had been sent ahead by Byng in the *Defiance* to ensure that all was ready at Gibraltar, and especially at the Hospital, in order to receive the squadron and its wounded. Byng, with the remainder of his squadron, did not arrive off Gibraltar until 20 June. Having landed his sick and wounded at the hospital, Byng was now in a much better position: even if the two most heavily damaged ships, the *Portland* and the *Intrepid*, were excluded, he had eleven of his original ships in fair or good condition plus Broderick's five, making sixteen ships of the line to renew any assault upon the French.

Now at last Byng could go toe-to-toe with La Galissonnière with the advantage being with him. What happened was the complete opposite: whilst Byng had every intention of returning to the fray, his plans were derailed by one of his Captains demanding that he, the Captain, be court martialled. The officer in question was Captain Cornwall of the *Revenge*.[36] When Captain Cornwall arrived at Gibraltar he heard certain remarks, made by fellow officers, concerning his conduct in the late battle and to clear his name demanded that he be court martialled. At first Byng refused his request, most likely on the grounds that any such Court would require the squadron to say at Gibraltar until the matter was resolved, due to both the number of officers required to sit as part of the Court and also the fact that the main witnesses would also be fellow officers from the squadron. [37]

Cornwall persisted in his request and eventually Byng relented. Rear Admiral West was to be the President of the Court and three Captains, Hervey, Lloyd and Amherst, all of who had command the frigates would also sit on the Court: they had been to windward during the battle and thus had a better view than most of what occurred with the *Revenge*.

The court was to convene aboard Rear Admiral West's flagship the *Buckingham*. However the proceedings soon dissolved in farce when Hervey, Lloyd and Amherst refused to sit as they felt sure that they would be called to give evidence as to what Cornwall and the *Revenge* had or had not done.[38]

This caused the Court to be adjourned for two days. However, prior to the Court rising, Rear Admiral West spoke to all assembled there to the effect that it was he who was blamed for the remarks concerning Captain Cornwall's conduct, an allegation he denied in the strongest terms. He went on to say that the van had beaten the French van and it had not been properly supported by the rest of the fleet, however he did not know the cause of this nor was he accusing anyone, even allowing for the fact that he refused to sit at a Council of War with some of them. He also stated that courts martial brought disgrace on a fleet.[39]

What followed according to Hervey was a series of exchanges between himself and Rear Admiral West as to who he would not sit with and more to the point that he, Hervey, knew Rear Admiral West's opinions concerning the conduct of Cornwall, and that his ship might have passed the *Intrepid* just as Rear Admiral West's flagship *Buckingham* had passed by the *Defiance*. Hervey also felt very strongly that Rear Admiral West was being critical of Byng for the first time in public, and said so to his face. This occasioned a series of increasingly bitter exchanges between Captain Hervey and Rear Admiral West.[40]

Reports of this, when relayed to Byng, meant relations between him and his second in command were soured to such an extent that General Fowke asked Hervey to act as peacemaker between them; a request, not unnaturally given his part in the affair, Hervey declined.

The Court resumed on 28 June and no one came forward to give any evidence against Cornwall. There, as far as Cornwall was concerned, the matter could rest: honour, in a strange way, was satisfied. Some three days later Byng and Rear Admiral West seemed, to the outside world, to have reconciled their differences and were seen coming ashore together.[41]

What this shows is just how much tension there was just below the surface, and that any slight or imagined insult or chance remark might bring it to a head. What Byng needed to do was sail as quickly as possible from Gibraltar with Broderick's ships and make his way either off Minorca, to find out what had happened, or to sit off Toulon, which if Minorca had been lost would be the best place to watch the movements of the French fleet – if it was there. If it was not, Byng's presence in the vicinity would cause problems for the French and draw the French fleet to him.

However, events at home were to cut short any putative plans Byng may have had to renew his campaign in the Mediterranean. News would arrive on 1 July overland at Gibraltar which gave the first inkling that what had transpired thus far was not sitting well with the ministry at home. With a degree of irony it was to be Rear Admiral West who received the first news of how the action of 20 May was received at home and from his reaction anyone could see that it was not positive. His frosty demeanour toward Byng returned and all the resentments which had so recently surfaced and seemed to have gone away broke out once more, and this time they could not be put back in the box. On 2 July the *Antelope* arrived in the Bay of Gibraltar. Aboard was Admiral Hawke and with him was Rear Admiral Charles Saunders. Hawke carried orders to supersede Byng. Yet it was not just Byng that was being replaced: Rear Admiral West, as well as Fowke, the Governor of Gibraltar, and General Stuart were all dismissed.[42] And there was worse to follow, as all three were not just dismissed, they were to be sent home under arrest.[43] What had happened at home to cause such draconian measures to be taken that flag- and general-officers should not just be superseded but sent home under arrest?

Chapter Six

The Politics of Execution

When did the ministry at home first get news of Byng's action off Minorca? Timing is everything, and in this case Hawke had been sent with Saunders to replace Byng before Byng's official despatch arrived in London. Hawke sailed on 16 June and the official despatch did not arrive until 23 June.[1] The sequence went further back still even than this – the news of the French attack on the Island of Minorca had been received in London on 6 May.[2] It was at this point that reinforcements were ordered to be sent to the Mediterranean by the Cabinet Council under the Duke of Newcastle.

It was at this point that the unease about the decisions made by the ministry started to come to the surface. The Treasurer of the Navy, George Dodington, recorded in his memoirs how Newcastle and Henry Fox both felt that not enough had been done to protect the island, but at the same time both denied that they were personally responsible.[3]

Newcastle pointed the finger of blame at Anson, which was technically correct as he was the principal naval adviser, although it was Newcastle and Fox along with the King who set the national priorities.[4] Fox on the other hand sought to portray himself as having always wanted more ships to be sent out with Byng.[5] Newcastle censured Anson for how the navy had been deployed, and the whole affair left Newcastle and his ministry open to attack from his political opponent, Pitt, who believed that Newcastle had totally misread the situation and had failed to act in the best interest of the country. The affair was not helped by the fact that Henry Fox also harboured the view that Byng would not relieve Minorca, and as such he was loathe to overtly defend the Duke of Newcastle.[6]

Matters were made worse when a despatch Byng had sent after his first arrival at Gibraltar reached the ministry; this was on 31 May. This despatch, which recorded the outcome of the Council of War held with General Fowke and supplied information on the situation as Byng found it at the time, was not one to lift the spirits of Newcastle and could only give succour to his enemies both within and outside the ministry.[7]

The final blow came on 2 June when the Spanish ambassador handed over a copy of La Galissonnière's despatch to the French Court. According to John Cardwell it was Byng's tone in the Gibraltar despatch combined with what La Galissonnière had said in his report which sealed Byng's fate.[8] La Galissonnière reported that it was Byng who had broken off the action and that Byng was content not to try and bring reinforcements into Fort St Philip. All of this alienated Newcastle from Byng and on 2 June, without having received Byng's formal despatch on the events of 20 May off Minorca, Newcastle ordered First Lord Bedford to relieve Byng of his command.[9]

This move, however, would not in and of itself protect Newcastle and his ministers from the charge that in fact it was they and not Byng who had been at fault in not sending sufficient forces into the Mediterranean.

What Newcastle and his ministers did was convince themselves that the personal ramifications of the loss of Minorca would be severe and, conscious of their own culpability in the loss, they lighted on Byng's supposed lack of initiative and, as they saw it, loss of nerve as the main reasons why Minorca would fall.[10] Thus in their minds they exculpated themselves completely from any responsibility for the reverse.

Henry Fox was of the opinion that, given the tenor of the despatch from Gibraltar, shortly thereafter another would follow saying that Byng had retreated and that it would be accompanied by a resolution of a Council of War.

When at long last Byng's despatch arrived in London – on 23 June, nearly a month after it was written off Minorca – it seemed to confirm the ministry's worst fears and at the same moment gave them, potentially, the evidence to shift all of the blame onto Byng instead of standing jointly accused of the miscarriage which had occurred. They made the decision, on 25 June, that Byng should be tried at court martial under Article XII.[11] The irony of the situation is that it was one of Byng's supposed strongest supporters who had given the ministry warning of what was coming and the kind of criticism they would face. Augustus Hervey had sent a letter home with Byng's despatch addressed to Henry Fox in which he described the Council of War and also the great concern of all the officers over the state of the fleet. Hervey wrote: 'everyone here calls out loudly on the manner this fleet was sent out and how late ... The Council of War had likened to have strong reasons for their resolutions'.[12]

This was not the kind of view which would sit easily with the Duke of Newcastle and his riposte gave an indication of just how defensive the ministers were: 'The sea officers should be learnt [not] to talk in this manner and not to think to fling blame upon civil ministers'.[13] Newcastle and his minister knew that what was happening in the Mediterranean was also holding the public's attention. There were high hopes of what Byng might do and grizzly expectations that the French Army's Commander Richelieu would end up with his head on a spike atop Temple Bar in the City. Even when the First reports from the French came in there was an air of disbelief that it might just be French mendacity, and the British press printed rumours which had first circulated in Spain reporting that it was Byng who had driven off the French and landed troops on the Island.[14]

In most parts of the United Kingdom the predominant feeling was that Byng had won and with the time it took for the official despatches to arrive in London there was nothing to contradict the various reports which were, at this time, emanating mostly from the continent. This only increased the tension and the anticipation of their arrival with news of a great victory. Cardwell quotes from a Reading innkeeper how the news was transmitted throughout the country: 'on a letter from Barcelona great rejoicing were made in several places, on account of Admiral Byng having drubb'd the French'.[15] There is more to this quote which will be brought out later, but it shows how speedy and widespread the news of events were: something the ministry would initially use to its advantage concerning what had transpired in the Mediterranean. Until the official version of events was placed before the public, the overwhelming sense was one of disbelief and the beginnings of discontent, which at this stage could either impact on the ministry or on Byng.

The ministry managed the expectations at this point with some finesse. They printed, prior to their having any formal notification, an account of Byng's retreat to Gibraltar designed specifically to point the finger of blame at Byng.[16] This was important as part of the process to sway the opinion of the political class, as well as the population at large, towards the conclusion that it was wholly Byng's fault and not that of the ministry. The next step was the release of a bowdlerized version of Byng's despatch of 25 May, part of which has already been quoted. On 26 June it was released through the government-controlled paper the *London Gazette*. It not only had the excision previously quoted, but anything which looked as if it might reflect badly upon the ministry was cut, as was any reference to the unanimous decision of the Council of War.[17] One word was also cut from the last line which in the view of John Cardwell was the most spiteful: this was the verb 'cover', which was excized from the last sentence 'am making the best of my way to[cover] Gibraltar'.[18] This made it seem that he was not carrying out a staged plan to cover the last base wholly under British control, but simply fleeing in the face of the French.

What has only recently been uncovered was who edited the piece: the evidence is that it was Henry Fox. He wrote to another member of the Board of Admiralty concerning the publication and was dismissive of Byng's claims that he was out-matched by the French squadron: 'He says He beat them; but they were stronger than Him: and some other Absurdities, which We leave out'.[19] The impression that Byng had run away from the French was added to by the fact that the casualty figures were included in the *Gazette* and it has been suggested that this was to show how his flagship the *Ramillies* had not had anyone killed or injured.[20] To add insult to injury, the number of guns of the two fleets, something subsequent historians have fixated on, was also printed, once again in an attempt to show Byng in a bad light.[21]

This was unpleasant in the extreme, but it has to be said not unusual in terms of how politicians attacked each other. However, the depth and ferocity of the coming storm which was to break over Byng was almost without precedence.

The next step in this particular part of the government's plan may well have been the beginning of the use of propaganda, with the article placed in the London Press, which in turn would be picked up by the then flourishing regional press. The first of these attacks was published on the same day that the 'official' version of Byng's despatches was printed. This makes it almost certain that someone within the ministry, or at least close to it, passed on a copy of Byng's original despatch.[22] In this case it is thought that it was Lord Royston, who happened to be Anson's brother-in-law and who later helped the ministry in other ways and had contacts within the London Press.[23]

With the start of this campaign the government sought to ride the tiger of public opinion by publishing material which would divert attention away from themselves. There was much interest in knowing what had happened off Minorca; witness the Reading innkeeper previously quoted, and in his case the last line of the quote shows how quickly triumph and joy turns to dismay and anger: 'the Gazette was called for. The oldest gentleman in company was desired to read it. But alas! The alteration that appeared in every face was not to be described'.[24] The attacks on Byng were not just within the London press; the regional press from Edinburgh to Dublin also took up these attacks, as well as something like twenty local papers within England. As well as the straight press there was a flood of scurrilous verse, as well as a host of satirical prints. Some, including Cardwell, argue that Byng's style underlined his unfitness for high command, citing the use of his language and mingling this with the oft-quoted assertion of his pride.[25] Whilst it is true that he was a proud man, and his style of writing was both prolix and self-effacing, this is not necessarily a reason for his not holding high command. It was however ripe for parody from the acid pens of the hacks of Grubb street.

They lighted in particular on the opening of Byng's despatch in which he stated he had: 'pleasure to desire you will acquaint their lordships'.[26] The polemics were vicious:

Curs'd be the wretch, that glories in his shame,
Eternal infamy still brand his name
His hasted name, who basely dar'd repeat
The tale with *pleasure* of his own defeat.[27]

This is one of the kinder verses printed in response to the release of the edited version of the Byng despatch. It was published at about the same time as copies of the French despatch were being printed, first in London and subsequently in the provincial press. All of this was feeding on the expectation that Byng would have triumphed, and the subsequent disillusionment when the true information started to come out was an explosive mixture, which, once ignited, would be all but impossible to control. Another barb pointed up the difference between the French and the British versions of events:

If you believe what a Frenchman say
B—G came, was beat and ran away
Believe what B—G himself has said
He fought, he conquer'd then he fled
To fly, when beat, is no new thing;
Thousands have don't, as well as B—G
But no man did before B—G say,
He conquer'd then run away.[28]

It got worse than lampooning in the press and pamphlets, with the feeling that there was more to this than just a miscarried action. Now in the press there were accusations that the whole battle had in effect been stage-managed and that Byng had received money to not press home his action, and in fact to ensure that it failed. This of course was in no uncertain terms accusing Byng of treason. While there is no evidence that this was government-sponsored, it further soured public opinion against Byng, and most of this was already in print before Byng returned home and he cannot really have had any idea as to just how virulent the attacks upon him were.[29]

Having gone from anticipation to expectation and then complete and utter bewilderment, the flow of material never ceased. He was variously accused of selling his property, and that his family were in league with him and warned him that if he returned he would face condign punishment.[30]

The battle, if battle it was in the minds of those who published accounts of it, was fought out in print with every bit as much vigour as the proponents of both Admirals Mathews and Lestock had done during the previous war. Not just text accounts but maps, supposedly giving an accurate representation of the two fleets, were printed, and correspondents like those of the *Gentleman's Magazine* fought and re-fought the battle giving their expert opinion on what Byng might have done – all of it a house of cards conflated from the edited version of what Byng had actually said.[31]

Having set in train this campaign the ministry had also confirmed what it should do and how it should proceed. Having made the decision to dismiss all of the general- and flag-officers, Henry Fox wrote, in a private letter to Fowke, to explain why he was being dismissed. The nub of it was; 'His Majesty could by no means brook you calling a council of war on orders directed to you singly'.[32] He continued in the same vein, saying that the King had had difficulties with this and that the danger of attempting a landing was a strange reason for not doing so: Major Mace was also found to be at fault for the advice he had proffered.[33] Shortly after the release of the official version of Byng's despatch, Anson, along with the Duke of Bedford, was at the Admiralty to draw up orders for the officer who was to replace Byng in the Mediterranean, Sir Edward Hawke.[34] At the same time that the decision to recall Byng in disgrace was taken at the Admiralty, those in attendance at the Board – namely Anson, John Bateman and Richard Edgcumbe – decided to recall all six of the lieutenants aboard Byng's flagship the *Ramillies*. As is usual with Admiralty minutes they do not give the reason why a particular action was taken; they simply record decisions made.[35] Why all of the lieutenants from the *Ramillies* were to be recalled can only be guessed at, although with a court martial on Byng being enacted they would almost certainly be needed as witnesses to his action and demeanour.

As well as Admiral Hawke the Governor of Minorca, Lord Trawley, who despite being prodded by the Duke of Newcastle had not stirred from Blackheath before Byng had sailed, was to go out and was reportedly confident that Minorca could be saved.[36] However, he was less than impressed when he arrived at Portsmouth to board the *Antelope* for his voyage to the Mediterranean, finding ships not under orders to sail and going in and out of Portsmouth to clean which seemed to infuriate the Lord.[37] The *Antelope* with all of the sea and general officers sailed for Gibraltar on 16 June and two days after the ship sailed, and one month after Britain had declared war, France formally declared war on Britain.

With the onset of a war in Europe Newcastle had to worry about more than just the French, as he had received intelligence via the Spanish Ambassador that Austria and France were now to be in alliance.[38] This would be a complete reversal of the situation for the last fifty or more years, in which the Houses of Bourbon and Habsburg vied to be the power-brokers on the continent of Europe. How this came about is long and complex; suffice to say that this, if it were true, would leave Britain without a major ally on the continent of Europe.

This would add to the angst of the ministry over how they had managed affairs thus far. Another factor in the equation was Newcastle's difficulties in keeping his ministry together and having the right people speaking for him, and by implication the Crown, in the House of Commons. As a peer the Duke could not speak in the House of Commons and the one person who was most effective in that role was, at the very moment Newcastle needed a united front, seeking promotion to the House of Lords from the Commons. This was William Murray the Attorney General, who wished to be appointed Lord Chief Justice and have a peerage to go with the dignity of that office.[39] If he were raised to the peerage and went to the Lords this would leave Henry Fox as the only speaker of any note for the ministry in the House of Commons. This was something the Duke of Newcastle could not allow. It was not that Fox was not effective: quite the contrary, he was a rival who could not be allowed free rein.[40] All of this was swelling around at the same time that the decision over Byng was being made. What the ministry needed was to keep attention off themselves and on Byng and the unfortunate Army officers who had been recalled.

The situation was neatly summed up by William Pitt: 'We are as helpless and childish as ever, and worse still, if any amongst the Ministry are to disposed to be men, I hear they would be madmen'.[41] He goes on to say; 'probably many an innocent and gallant man's honour and fortune is to be offered up as scapegoat for the sins of the administration'.[42] Pitt, it has to be stressed, was a political rival of the Duke of Newcastle and therefore his comments should not be read without a hint of self interest in them

If the political classes were in uproar, what of the sea officers? How did they react to the proceedings in the Mediterranean? Admiral Boscawen wrote on 11 June:

> Our disgrace in the Mediterranean has so filled my spirits that I could not sleep all night. What shall we come to? Sir Edward Hawke was chased yesterday by some of my squadron and sent me the whole news, as did Lord Trawley, and the French and English Gazettes containing the accounts ... I should have gone to Minorca to have retrieved it if possible, but the back game is hard work. If courage will do it, that won't be wanting.[43]

It should be remembered Boscawen was not just a sea officer: he was, although junior on the list, one of Byng's professional rivals. He went on to say much more in a further letter: 'they have left Gibraltar with an Intention not to fight or relieve Mahon, which Mr Byng must know he could do if he could beat the French'.[44] He pointedly showed that Byng above all others should know the Mediterranean through experience from when a boy. His conclusion was scathing: 'What a scandal to the Navy that there should be premeditated cowards that have been so long bred to arms. I should think for the future no man should command that had not given proofs of his courage'.[45] This was another line of attack on Byng as a coward and it is interesting to note, even allowing for the partisan nature of the witness, that some in the Navy, as well as the ministry, thought this way.

Others shared the view expressed by Boscawen, for example Captain Samuel Faulknor who wrote: 'No doubt but Mr Byng's behaviour on the late occasions off Mahon must anger and surprise you and every thinking man in the Kingdom. Sad indeed: he's brought more disgrace on the British flag than ever his father Lord Torrington did honour to it'.[46]

Just as Boscawen had, he drew an unfavourable comparison between father and son and, like the Admiral, implied that the habit of fathers taking sons into the service was undermining its morale and fighting spirit. Another letter, quoted by Rodger, implies that there was more criticism within Byng's squadron than Hervey would allow for: 'All the fleet are opened-mouthed against Byng, his own division more than ours, as well as all of the land officers that were on board to be landed at Minorca'.[47] Perhaps this somewhat overstates the case, given the unanimity of the Council of War. Certainly there was a general level of disquiet at what was supposed to have happened, considering that many of the early letters were written before any of the officers who had participated had returned or any correspondence from them was in wide circulation.

Rodger also brings up the subject of honour which, as he rightly says, is dangerous for historians to interpret at this time.[48] He cites a number of examples of the need for justification of actions taken or not taken by sea officers and why they felt it was necessary to do so. Rodger lights upon Arthur Gardiner, Byng's Flag Captain, who, he asserts, was aware of Anson's opinion that Byng had brought disgrace on the nation and dishonour upon its officers. So much did this burn in Gardiner's soul that in February 1758, when in command of the *Monmouth* 64 he came upon the *Foudroyant* 80, he engaged in a running action. The *Foudroyant* had, of course, been one the principal protagonists in the battle off Minorca. During the course of the action Gardiner was killed, although the French ship was, despite the disparity in firepower of the two, taken.[49] As Gardiner was killed it is difficult to be certain of his motives and it is unlikely that he would wish to immolate himself. There is no evidence that Gardiner had not been an aggressive commander prior to 20 May 1756. However Rodger should not be dismissed lightly, as both ships and men gained reputations, some good others bad, but perhaps what was unique here was the febrile atmosphere which surrounded everything around Byng after his return.

Away from the growing ferment at home, when Hawke arrived he handed over the letters entrusted to him by the Admiralty to Byng. By all accounts he was shocked by their contents. He had not thought he would be recalled or that he had done anything other than his duty. One letter was from the Secretary of the Admiralty, Cleveland, which expressed in trenchant terms why Byng was to be sent home: 'His Majesty having received an account that the squadron under your command, and that of La Galissonnière came to action off the harbour of Mahon the twentieth of last month; and that the French, though inferior to you in force, kept before the harbour, and obliged you to retreat'.[50] The sting was in the tail: 'His Majesty is so much dissatisfied with your conduct, that he has ordered their Lordships recall yourself and Mr West'.[51] To add insult to injury, the Admiralty had enclosed a section of the French Admiral's report to the French court, and his own despatch is not mentioned, so it would have been obvious to Byng that his recall was based on French reports of his actions. There was a second letter from the Admiralty which required Byng to strike his flag, stating as well that Mr West and all of the officers of both the *Ramillies* and *Buckingham* respectively were to be sent home at the same time.[52]

According to one source Byng was in such a fury that he threw his coat over the side of the *Ramillies*, and whilst it is a nice story that when Hawke and Byng met they were in the great cabin, it is highly unlikely.[53] What is true is that his response was measured in its tone: 'I have only to express my surprise at being so ignominiously dismissed from my employment, in sight of the fleet I commanded, in sight of the garrison and in sight of Spain'.[54] He continued in the same prolix way that he was: 'most injuriously and wrongfully attacked now on the grounds of a false gasconade of an open enemy to our King and country'.[55]

The tenor of this letter picks up on the points of both personal and professional honour already alluded to. It is striking that Byng felt as much hurt about where the events took place: not just in front of his squadron, but in front of the British garrison on Gibraltar. Equally as important was the fact it was also carried out off Spain, always seen as a potential enemy, in front of whom no such signs of weakness or discord ought to be displayed.

He went on to say that he was sure that he and West would both clear their names and that in fact, far from censuring him, when the full facts came out he would gain the approval of both his King and the country at large.[56] If he had any inkling of what awaited him at home, it would be unlikely that a man such as he would have thought anything other than that a great injustice had been done. But, given the opportunity, it would be a fairly straightforward matter to set things right. This either betrays stunning naivety or, as has already been discussed, it was the act of a gentleman-officer who forgot that he was dealing with high politics – which would seem odd for the son of one of the most politically dextrous sea officers.[57]

However first he had to take passage home and this was to be aboard the *Antelope*, the ship which had brought Hawke and Saunders out. Aboard the fifty-gun ship were not just Byng and West, but both their Flag Captains as well as all of the lieutenants of both flagships.[58] Also aboard was the former Governor of Gibraltar, General Fowke and his wife, and according to Augustus Hervey there were near on forty people aboard when she finally weighed and made sail out of Gibraltar Bay on 8 July.[59]

Whilst Byng and his companions in ignorance made passage home, the printing press and acid-ink scribblers were still hard at work, including those which touched on the tactics employed and which formed a piece with the armchair sailors , already alluded to:

> With thirteen ships to twelve cries B—g;
> It were a shame to meet 'em
> And then with twelve to twelve a thing
> Impossible to beat 'em
>
> When more's too many, less too few,
> And even still not right
> Arithmetick must plainly shew
> 'Twere wrong in B—g to fight[60]

There was now a concerted effort to show that the lack of casualties aboard Byng's flagship was down to the cowardice of the admiral and nothing else. While Byng came in for withering sarcasm, West was on the whole praised and held up as a counterpoint for Byng's supposed failings:

> Mr W–st who loves to fight, behav'd like a Man.
> Tho' he sai'd in the Rear, yet he fought in the Van:
> If I fought, you'll believe the Engagement was hot.
> But I wisely kept out of reach of their shot.[61]

What this piece points to is the continued attacks on every single aspect of what Byng did, both before, during and after the battle. There was even a piece published which mocked all of the manoeuvrings before the action and twisted to imply that the tactics used showed that he was trying to avoid action rather than seek battle. The attacks on Byng also focused on his supposed lack of courage as compared with those who were killed or injured aboard the ships of West's squadron.

Formal three-quarter-length portrait of John Byng painted just after the end of the War of the Austrian Succession. As with all such portraits it depicts a Sea Officer of some status and wealth. (*National Maritime Museum*)

A very unflattering portrait of John Byng taken from a contemporary history book, Hervey's *History of the late War*.

George Byng, Viscount Torrington, First Lord of the Admiralty between 1727 and his death in 1733 and the Hon John Byng's father. The young John first went to sea with him in 1718 and saw his only fleet action, at Cape Passaro, until his ill-fated action off Minorca in 1756.

A contemporary map of the island of Minorca with details of both the harbour and fortifications at the mouth of the Harbour. French siege batteries commanded both sides of the harbour mouth.

Edward Boscawen. His action off the Newfoundland Banks in 1755 precipitated the naval action of what was to become the Seven Years War. His squadron returned from Newfoundland with the loss of 2,000 men who had died of typhus; this shortage of men was to adversely affect Byng's squadron.

Boscawen as a Lord of the Admiralty and Admiral of the Blue. He was a rival of Byng's and criticised Byng's action off Minorca, while his wife Fanny was acerbic in her views of Byng's sense of dress and mode of speech. It was to fall to Boscawen to decide where Byng was to be executed aboard the *Monarch*.

Admiral Lord Anson, First Lord of the Admiralty under the Newcastle ministry. He was the man who insisted that the Western Squadron was vital to Britain in the spring of 1756 and in consequence left few ships for Byng's Mediterranean squadron.

Admiral Sir Charles Saunders was one of a number of officers who were critical of Byng's actions off Minorca and how it reflected badly on the Navy. Saunders found fame taking Generals Wolfe's force up to Quebec in 1759.

William Pitt, a vociferous critic of the Newcastle ministry, was to be appointed Secretary of State for the Southern Department in the coalition ministry under Devonshire; he was politically too weak to overturn the result of Byng's court martial.

Captain Keppel was a member of Byng's court martial and also one of those who wished to be released from their oath. He himself was to undergo a similar experience to Byng after his miscarried action off Ushant in 1779; Keppel survived and subsequently became the Head of the Board of Admiralty.

Admiral Lord Hawke was sent out to relieve Byng in the Mediterranean. His greatest feat was the action in Quiberon Bay in November 1759, part of the *Annus Mirabilis*.

General Lord Blakeney, the octogenarian Lieutenant Governor of Fort St Philip on Minorca. He held out for over fifty-two days against the French and was lionised on his return to England. His insistence on having a Council of War everyday after noon delayed the sending of boats to Byng's ships waiting in the offing.

The execution of Byng on the quarterdeck of the *Monarch*. Originally, Boscawen had ordered that Byng be shot on the forecastle like a common seaman. After protest, the place of execution was moved to the quarterdeck, the natural domain of an officer. Only six of the nine marines fired, one missed; the remaining three were to finish him off if he were not killed outright. (*National Maritime Museum*)

Another avenue of attack was on the Council of War which he had called. Such Councils were often seen as contentious things, as Cardwell has pointed out.[62] Often called when joint operations between the Army and Navy was concerned, they had, to say the least, an unfortunate record. Stretching back to previous wars they had been seen in general as at best a necessary evil and at worst a legal way of avoiding action. Not content on venting their spleen on Byng alone, upon his arrival he was to be visited at Portsmouth by his brother Colonel Edward Byng, who was not a well man and in fact he died shortly after seeing Byng. This tragedy for Byng, and his family, was turned against him, with the accusation that his brother collapsed and died from grief and shame at Byng's actions. A barb which, one can imagine, a private man from a large family would feel all the more.

Before Byng himself and his forty odd companions arrived back at Spithead, and while Grub Street continued unabated in its attack on him, there were moves to add to his woes and humiliation by having him arrested. This was a most unusual event – many other officers had been relieved under suspicion of having failed to carry out their orders; few of such rank were placed under arrest. This was what might be saved for someone suspected of treason. The decision to arrest Byng was made on 25 June but the orders were written 29 June, when Fox wrote to the Admiralty signalling the Kings instructions that: 'Admiral Byng be put immediately under arrest, and sent forthwith to England, in order that he may be brought to trial'.[63] The orders also stipulated that Hawke was to look into Byng's conduct both off Minorca and subsequently, and why he had left the island exposed. In July, worried in case the orders to Hawke had not arrived in time, further orders were sent to the Commander-in-Chief Portsmouth and also the Commander-in-Chief Plymouth, as well as the flag officers of the Downs, making it plain that in whatever vessel Byng was to arrive he was to be arrested.[64]

The biting irony of this Admiralty order was that one of the Commanders-in-Chief to whom it was sent was Henry Osborn at Portsmouth. Osborn was Byng's brother-in-law, being as he was the brother of Sarah Byng's husband John Osborn.

When the *Antelope* finally arrived at Spithead on 26 July it would be down to Admiral Osborn to go aboard and acquaint Byng with the fact that he was now to be placed under arrest and placed in the charge of the admiralty marshal, William Borough. Byng may not have been told formally of his imminent arrest prior to his meeting with Osborn on that day. However, to say, as others have, that he had not even thought this would happen is stretching credulity to breaking point. He had, after all, sat on courts martial precisely to adjudge on the kinds of thing for which he was recalled.[65] When he did respond specifically to his arrest he named Mathews and Lestock as precedents for his release on shore.

Having spoken with Byng aboard the *Antelope*, Osborn wrote to confirm to their Lordships that he had carried out their instructions: 'To acquaint their lordships of the arrival of the Antelope, and of my having caused Admiral Byng to be arrested on board the said ship'.[66] Aboard the *Antelope* Byng was to be kept under armed guard lest he tried to escape, and the captain of the *Antelope* was ordered by the Admiralty to supply as many guards as Burrows thought necessary.[67]

Rear Admiral West, whose pride – both personal and professional – had been insulted alongside Byng's, was not placed under any restrictions and was soon penning an angry and aggrieved letter immediately prior to his disembarkation from the *Antelope*. He wrote that: 'the mortification of his public disgrace cannot be sensibly felt by an officer whose utmost endeavour all his life long has been to serve his King and Country'.[68] However, Rear Admiral West need not have worried, as George II fully approved of his actions on 20 May and received him with much favour at a Levee.[69] The importance of this was that such public marks of favour were reported in the press, and despite the abrupt nature of his recall and the perceived humiliation he quite rightly felt, he was soon to be re-employed.

What Byng would have faced, had he been allowed ashore and not detained aboard ship, was not just the bile of Grub Street but also of the mob. This was precisely because the regional press was so extensive and because, as with the Reading Innkeeper and his patrons, the broad population were comparatively well-informed on events and were hungry for news; something the ministry had played on up until this point. One piece of news of which they would have been aware was the ministry's decision to hold Byng under arrest. News of this had been passed on to the London Press the day after the letter from Secretary Fox instructing the Admiralty of the fact had been sent.[70]

One of those closest to Byng, his brother Edward, had travelled down from London, once he had received news from Admiral Osborn that his brother had arrived, and he would have seen the mob call out against his brother in virulent terms. Edward does not appear to have enjoyed the best of health and at least some sources have it that the news and the stress hastened his end, which has already been alluded to.[71] What is certain is that he could, once he had been rowed out to the *Antelope*, give his brother an idea of how his action had been portrayed, and also relay family news – specifically the death of their mother, Lady Margaret Torrington. Edward was to stay aboard the *Antelope* overnight. He was tired and ill and the next day found him in a worse condition – so much so that that the ship's surgeon was called to attend him. All of this was to no avail and Edward died that afternoon from fatal convulsions brought about by a weak constitution.[72] On the following day Byng started what was to become a long series of letters to and from the Admiralty, concerning everything from his arrest, to his place of confinement, to the number of witnesses he wished to call at his court martial. In this case his letter to their Lordships was about his confinement aboard the *Antelope* and that he needed to be released from confinement in order to be able to prepare his defence, as had other officers who had in the past been in similar circumstances.[73] The response he got from the Admiralty the next day was short and to the point that: 'orders would be given next week for your being brought to Town'.[74]

Any illusion he had harboured about the seriousness of his circumstance must have evaporated once he had received that letter from the Admiralty Board. He also wrote on the same day to his sister-in-law, Lady Charlotte Torrington, for permission for Edward to be buried at Southill.[75]

Whilst Byng chaffed at his confinement aboard the *Antelope* and the mob threw abuse on his head from afar, members of the ministry had other worries – for example where Byng was to be held. Being under arrest aboard ship was one thing, where he was to end up was another. In strict terms Byng was not a political prisoner; he was under the Admiralty's jurisdiction. If he was accused of piracy or the like he could, in theory, have been sent to the Marshalsea. However his offences were more akin to those of Walter Raleigh or other gentleman prisoners who were held in genteel incarceration in the Tower of London. An exchange between Lord Anson and Henry Fox took place, with Fox opening the proceedings with a letter dated 30 July. In the letter he outlined why Byng ought to be kept under close arrest. This was to be in stark contrast to Fowke and Rear Admiral West, both of whom were free to go about their business. However, in Byng's case he was: 'to be brought by land, under strong guard, and lodged in the Tower. If your Lordship will consider what would be said and believed if he should escape, I am certain you will think it ought to be made possible'.[76] He then expressed the one fear; that perhaps 'if he should die before trial, it would be bad'.[77] Fox ended with the hope that Byng should stay in good health, and for whom he had a hearty wish that he should remain in that rude health.

Anson drafted a reply which agreed in broad terms with Fox, adding that because of his former position in the fleet he might, if he was minded to escape, effectively do so if he were kept aboard ships.[78] He also wrote out the details of how it might be affected that while Byng was to lodge in the Tower he was still in the charge of the admiralty marshal.[79] It was a day later that the Duke of Newcastle sent a letter to the Board of Admiralty reflecting the concerns expressed by Fox, and already aired with Anson, the professional head of the Navy. His words echoed Fox and Anson: 'to prevent the possibility of escape, and can best be done by sending for him immediately by land under a strong guard and committing him to the Tower'.[80]

When the Board of Admiralty met it was decided that Byng would be moved out of the *Antelope* to the *Royal Anne*, a 100-gun first-rate ship of the line with, as the order puts it: 'a proper and efficient guard of Marines'.[81] This was temporary while full arrangements could be made for Byng to be sent by land to the Tower. The commanding officer of the 3rd Regiment of Dragoons received instructions from the Secretary of War to send a detachment of fifty troopers to Portsmouth, which were in addition to the marine guard that the Admiralty were to provide. They were to escort him from Portsmouth as far as Kingston, where they were to be relieved by a detachment from the Horse Guards. As well as instructions to the troops, these orders also required the civil magistrates to co-operate with the Dragoons as they escorted the prisoner.[82]

Byng was to be landed on 5 August and Admiral Osborn was then to hand him over to the escort, and thence he was to be taken up to the Tower. There was however a hiccup and new orders were sent to Osborn to delay the transfer as it was not at all certain that lodgings in the Tower could be found. There is an air of farce about all of this, as Byng was already in a coach on the way up to London with fifty dragoons as escort, whilst an Admiralty messenger was riding post-haste in the opposite direction on the same road. They did in fact cross and it was only when the messenger arrived in Portsmouth and was told by Osborn that he set off in pursuit. The messenger intercepted Byng and handed over the orders to the admiralty marshal, as a consequence of which Byng was returned to Portsmouth and thence he went back aboard the *Royal Anne*. Once he was back aboard the ship he sent an angry letter over his treatment to the Admiralty.[83]

The Admiralty had changed its mind: Byng was not to go to the Tower, he was instead to be held by the Admiralty at the Seaman's Hospital at Greenwich to the south of London. His first move from Portsmouth had been on the Thursday; he was to be landed on the Monday and start afresh. On Monday 9 August Byng came ashore again from the *Royal Anne* and once again with the admiralty marshal and fifty dragoons set off for London and thence across to Greenwich.

Byng had also turned his attention to how he was to defend himself against the charges – he would need to gather evidence and being under close arrest would hamper him to a very great extent in doing so. He would need officers from his squadron, not only those from his flagship but from others who had either been in the van or saw the action from frigates and other ships. The letter requesting the officers was sent to the Admiralty two days before he came ashore for the second time. At about the same time the Admiralty started to garner evidence to carry out a successful prosecution, creating a digest of papers; a boon to researchers, but one to be wary of on account of what they omitted.

Others too started to muster the documents which were necessary, and many of these were gathered by the politicians. Both the Duke of Newcastle and also Lord Chancellor Hardwicke, the father-in-law of Anson, have extensive material in them. This includes copies of nearly all the intelligence received by the ministry, and copies of official correspondence, as well as private letters between members of the ministry. The great care with which all of this is enumerated and bound in volumes, both in the Admiralty record and in the Hardwicke papers, show the level of preparation and concern which pervaded the powers that be.[84]

While all of this was going on Byng trundled his way toward the capital and thence onwards to Greenwich, the Horse Guards having taken over at Kingston, and it was there that according to surviving sources he learnt that he was to be incarcerated at the Seaman's Hospital.[85] He was to be kept in Queen Ann block, and when he arrived the deputy governor Isaac Townsend was to be his gaoler. Byng was placed in the south range of buildings, in a bare room with little or no furniture, with guards on the stairs and outside his door. All of this was a great insult to someone who was an Admiral of the Blue as well as a Member of Parliament.

If he was kept in such a way for any length of time it would be all but impossible for him to carry out any kind of co-ordinated gathering of evidence for his defence.

While Byng was taken into incarceration at the Royal Hospital at Greenwich, the public mood was still essentially against him but there were just a few who were starting speak out on his behalf. However, the predominant feeling amongst the populace, as much as can be gauged, was one of outrage.[86] The extent of this popular protest was underestimated and modern research has shown that it was not just in the metropolis and principal city of the Three Kingdoms, but across the country where demonstrations against Byng broke out, which were often well organized and financed.[87]

Byng had one home at Berkeley Square and was building a new one at Wrotham Park, and also rented one not far from the site of his new house. Wrotham was designed by Isaac Ware, who was known to Byng via his sister Sarah and her son Sir Danvers Osborn. Ware was well known for his translation of a book on Palladian architecture, and he had also carried out speculative building works in the West End of London and was undertaking commissions, of which Wrotham is one of the few still surviving at the time of writing. Wrotham Park, in Barnet in Hertfordshire, was not far from other property which Byng had leased in 1751 in South Mimms.[88] However, it was the then as-yet-unfinished house at Wrotham which bore the brunt of the mob's anger at Byng's supposed failings, to such an extent that they nearly burnt it down.[89] This attack took place just prior to Byng being landed at the end of July. However, other demonstrations took place in August and in these Byng was either hanged or burned, sometimes both, in effigy.

The demonstrations were kingdom-wide following the wide circulation of the bowdlerized version of Byng's despatch, as well as the other material put in the public domain by the ministry.[90] The list of places drawn up by Cardwell is quite impressive. Outside of London there were ceremonies to burn or hang Byng's effigy in; Birmingham, Newcastle, Gateshead, Sunderland, Leeds, Tynemouth, Dudley, Bewdley, South Shields, North Shields, Darlington, Higham Ferrars, York, Richmond, Cleveland, Market Harborough, Exeter, Devizes, Falmouth, Worcester, Hertford, Salisbury, Southampton, Gravesend, Bristol, Isle of Wight and Dublin.[91] This list excluded those demonstrations in the Capital. However, it does point up just how widespread anti-Byng feeling was, and not just in large metropolitan centres, but in county towns, as well as sea ports. Pope's assertion that the main focus of discontent was in London barring a few provincial towns is wide of the mark.[92] According to Cardwell at Market Harborough marchers accompanied the effigy with a monumental scroll and in Southampton the dummy had a note on its chest confessing to treason.[93]

It was in London though that some of the largest protests, in terms of numbers, took place. At Tower Hill Byng's effigy was paraded in full uniform and carried in a sedan chair. It went round the streets with much flag waving and was followed by a mock trial and confession and then the dummy was pelted by the crowed with whatever was to hand and set afire. When the head fell off it was kicked down the hill.[94] All of this shows just how deep the resentment and anger against Byng was, but the mob was known as the most dangerous, fickle entity in eighteenth-century politics. Once unleashed it followed content, not logic, and was difficult to control, something the ministry of whatever strip would find out in due course.

As well as the physical abuse to which Byng, or more properly his effigy, was subjected to, he was still vilified in print and verse, picking apart not just his actions – or lack of them – off Minorca, but also his taste and habits, and even his masculinity. This was not directly about his sexual orientation, but more his taste in clothes, his collecting of fine china – the subject of a number of biting satires as to why, in the author's view, he had not engaged more closely during the battle. His manner of dress and his mode of speech were all taken to be effete, a kind of moral and social degeneracy which was undermining the aristocracy and gentry and more especially the sons of the nobility, who in previous generations had martial success, such as Byng's own father George Viscount Torrington. The effeminacy was seen as alien, corroding the moral fibre of the country.

Whether it was his collection of fine china or his dress and deportment, all were fair game. There was no attack on his sexual predilections: the fact that at the age of fifty two he was unmarried – albeit that he had a mistress who had died in December of the preceding year – was not used overtly against him. The charge of effeminacy and being likened to the Romans or Greeks also carried a much darker undertone. He does not appear from all the surviving evidence to have formed any other lasting relationships with women, and to be sure if he had the hacks of Grub Street would have exposed it. Despite the modern, at the time of writing, imputation that those who do not form such relationships are either inadequate, in one way or another, or closet gays, no such implications can be drawn about Byng. He seems to have lived a self-contained life, with little room for many close friendships of either sex, something a psychiatrist or psychotherapist could make much of if it weren't for the fact that the patient is long dead and unable to attend therapy. Historians can only adduce that he was happy with his mistress Mrs Hickson, and her death would have been a blow. The fact that the relationship grew when it did, during one of the few times Byng was unemployed on half-pay between wars, points more closely as to why perhaps nothing of the sort had happened sooner, and hence the lack of its being used as a point against him.

While Byng suffered the slings and arrows, General Blakeney and his garrison had held out for most of July and had made it quite hard for the French to overcome them. However, with no hope of relief eventually he had to capitulate – which was just as well for the French, who were also having such difficulties that Richelieu had decided to take the fort by storm. The assault having been successful in taking the outer works, Blakeney was left with little option. Richelieu resolved that the best solution, as well as following the normal conduct of a siege, was that if the outer works were lost the commander could sue for terms. As the citadel of St Philip was still in British hands, Richelieu allowed the garrison to leave with drums beating and arms at the slope with the full dignities of war. This would be something else which, when the news got back to Britain, would be sharply contrasted with Byng's supposed behaviour before Minorca.[95] In fact, many of the times at which Byng was hanged or burnt in effigy in August there was a deliberate juxtaposition of Blakeney the hero with Byng the coward.

The political world was on the turn: what had, until now, been a torrent of abuse aimed almost exclusively at Admiral Byng was now attacking Newcastle's ministry. Rumours and speculation abounded as to what the ministry had or had not done.[96] A fake advertisement gave the tenor of the nature of the attack: 'Now selling by Auction; By Order of Thomas Holles of Newcastle, Great Britain & the Dominion belonging thereunto. Gibraltar and the Port Mahon were disposed of the first Day, and the latter is already delivered'.[97] Holles of course was the family name of the Duke of Newcastle. This could in some circumstances be seen as seditious and that is how the ministry took this particular squib. However, it was not just personal attacks, there was a broader feeling welling up that the ministry had not handled the war well so far.[98]

This was not a ground-swell or the mob, but was a move by the county gentry. In Dorset the MPs and Justices of the Peace sent a loyal address to the King asking for an inquiry into the state of affairs. The loyal address was an ancient means to petition the monarch of grievances. Dorset was not the only place to put forward this device. In Bedfordshire, Byng's home county, the judges asked for an enquiry, as well as Bury St Edmunds and Hereford.[99]

These appeals were followed by others in fairly quick succession across the country. However as yet perhaps the most important had not yet spoken up: London. By the end of the second week in August, on the twelfth, the City of London also followed suit.[100] The petition was to be presented in person by a delegation of City Aldermen to the King on 20 August. It was not just an overt political action, as the hacks of Grubb Street continued their assault.

In light of this, abuse of Newcastle continued apace; he was accused of pacifism and of squandering the best natural harbour in the Mediterranean. In this there were classical allusions, for example Hannibal, who had first used the harbour at Port Mahon as a base of operations against his enemies.[101] His personal habits, and more particularly his ability to spend beyond his means, were picked over by Grub Street. The annual income from his estates was estimated at around £27,000 per annum[102] This was something which had attracted adverse comments long before the outbreak of the Seven Years War. He was regularly accused of embezzling state funds, with attacks stretching back as far as the 1740s. However, they were given greater strength and urgency with the perceived mishandling of the war thus far. The writers of verse did not let him go and gave him a similar treatment to the one meted out to Byng:

> To pay thy Duns off and replenish thy chest
> To wallow in lux'ry, and feather thy nest
> If thy Country is ruin'd thou thinkst it no matter
> So B—g Minorca and slighted the rest.[103]

One print which was against the ministry showed devils gnawing on the bones of Newcastle, Fox and Byng, as the Duke's love of fine food and drink – particularly in the French style – was well known. As Cardwell has shown quite clearly, from just before and during these events there was a strong anti-French sentiment in the country at large. This was so pervasive that the more radical view of this took any sign of French influence as a French plot to undermine British morals and corrupt society prior to its overthrow.[104]

Nor was it just Newcastle and Fox who came in for attention: also vilified in print and verse was Lord Chancellor Hardwicke, yet given how close he was to them both politically and personally this was not at all surprising. In Hardwicke's case he was seen as predatory and somewhat like a vulture, and as a consequence he was often depicted in prints and verse literally feathering his own nest at the expense of the national well-being. His attentions to the careers of his two sons, one in the Army, the other the British minister at The Hague, were also put under scrutiny and found wanting. His previous legal career was also looked into with a great deal of disfavour.[105]

These were the overt political attacks; however, Hardwicke was seen by some as the éminence grise of the Whig administration, with Newcastle, who was thought of as panicky and febrile, as his puppet. The attacks were also much more personal on Hardwicke, whose daughter, as has already been mentioned, was married to Admiral Lord Anson, the professional head of the Navy. It was alleged by his detractors that he had sacrificed his daughter to Anson, an older man, who according to the same source was unable to consummate his marriage, for the sake of politics.[106] He was also accused after the court martial had sat of making sure that Byng would not be pardoned, in this case to save his son-in-law Anson.

Although Grubb Street had, by and large, switched its attacks, Byng was by no stretch of the imagination out of favour as a target. In fact what tended to happen from August of 1756 onwards was that Byng, Newcastle and Fox, were lumped together, as either bungling incompetents, or with Byng as venal, Newcastle as Machiavellian, and Fox as cunning. This was more a case of a plague on all of your houses rather than playing one off against the other. Later on the pendulum would swing further away from Byng towards Newcastle and the other ministers.

With all of this going on Byng, even allowing for his incarceration at Greenwich Hospital, also had his defenders other than Hervey, and once he had returned a number of pamphlets were published which were quite obviously written by either Byng or by someone close to him. These were aimed at highlighting the incompetence of the ministry with regards to the number and quality of ships, their manning and the state of the Dockyards at Gibraltar.

To this end Byng's despatch to the Admiralty was printed in full for the first time, as was his letter from Gibraltar which outlined his concerns over the decrepitude he found at the yard there. There was also a campaign to show where the anti-Byng feeling was coming from, with some pointing the finger at one of the clerks in the Victualling office.[107]

This was not a small or under-funded fight back by Byng and his friends: once again Cardwell asserts that something like 10,000 copies of one piece alone were printed and distributed around the London coffee houses and public houses.[108] This was highly successful, and turned the tide in terms of the polemical war which was being fought in Byng's favour. Once the full despatch was out in the open the ministry found itself wide open to attack by friend and foe alike. It was not long before the ministry's hand was being seen behind all, or nearly all, of the anti-Byng material which was then in circulation. Though this was of course not entirely true, it was close enough for it to be very uncomfortable for the ministry and their allies.

Members of the ministry were aware of how damaging the censoring of Byng's despatch was to them, and the London Press had also lighted on this fact as therein showing their guilt. Horace Walpole, who was at first against Byng and his supposed action off Minorca, having read his full despatch changed his mind and instead of finding him 'haughty and disgusting' became a defender of his cause.[109]

Another avenue of attack which now opened up was that all of the press coverage, the pamphleteering and the versifying was going to be wholly prejudicial to the course of justice at Byng's court martial. Furthermore, the assault was not stopping and it was Anson, who had already traduced Byng, who was to be the focus once more of the satire.

Anson was picked out because of the failure of the naval strategy. He was also pilloried for his age, being nearly sixty, and often the two were linked. The overblown – as it was seen by some – fears of invasion were seen as the failings of an old and timorous man. The fact that the intelligence was misread and the station of ships was, according to the critics of the ministry, mishandled was also put down to the senility of Anson.

Byng all the while was seeking to come to terms with the fact that he was not just to be court martialled, but that he would remain under arrest for the foreseeable future. Given that there were something like 3,500 in-pensioners at Greenwich Hospital as well as Byng, there are some grounds for having sympathy for Isaac Townsend as he sought to confine his famous prisoner. However, he does appear to have been excessively zealous in imposing conditions on Byng whilst he was at Greenwich. Given that he was a middle-aged, portly man and that he was being held to answer charges under Article of War number XII, they were excessively severe. Yet Townsend was asking by mid-August for more guards, writing on 14 August that he felt that there was a need for eight more privates to keep the prisoner safe.[110] Some sources also mention that as well as the troops the boatswain, who was in charge of the wards, along with twelve of the in-pensioners also kept guard.[111] In case Byng was to try and ascend the chimneys, bars were to be fitted across them as well as bars on the windows to stop his escape. There is little remaining evidence at the time of writing of this diligence to detain Byng: the south range, now the home of the Business School of the

University of Greenwich, has many fireplaces, most if not all bricked up in Edwardian times, and there are no signs of bars on the windows.[112]

There were also the wholly false allegations put abroad in the press that Byng had tried to escape, dressed in women's clothing and more particularly those of his sister Sarah Osborne, who had visited him at Greenwich. There is no evidence that he even thought of escape, although some of his supporters, such as Hervey, did harbour such thoughts after the court martial verdict.

While all of this was going on Byng also had to look to his upcoming court martial, and he needed to gather evidence to clear his name. He had already sent the Admiralty a letter with the names of possible witnesses, and he wrote again on 6 September, about a month after his arrival, from Greenwich to ask for more officers for his defence. The Admiralty had already recalled all of the officers from Byng's flagship the *Ramillies*, as well as Rear Admiral West's *Buckingham* and their response pointed out that there were twenty officers already at home who might be called. His first request, on 4 August, was for thirty-seven officers, of whom twenty three were still serving under Hawke, and all had been recalled. Now he was asking for thirty-one more witnesses. At this point the Admiralty declined to act, accusing Byng of meanly wishing to spin out proceedings rather than coming to trial.[113] However, what is most important about this exchange is that the drafts still exist and show how Anson responded to Byng. A phrase which has divided opinion then and since was: 'Their Lordships are desirous of giving you the earliest opportunity of acquitting yourself if possible from so heavy a charge'.[114] Pope sees it as a sly way of insinuating the reverse of innocent-until-proven-guilty. Byng also felt that there was a presumption on the part of the Board of Admiralty that he was guilty and he wrote to express his feelings on the matter: 'I shall not comment upon that prejudging expression of yours, an opportunity of acquitting myself, if possible, – it seems sufficient to explain itself'.[115] He then vented his spleen over his treatment after his arrival back in Britain, especially how his being moved back and forth was not showing, as he put it, any indulgence to him as the Admiralty letter had implied; rather the contrary. He also complained, with some justice, of the fact that he was not allowed visitors to stay after dark, not even his own servants. He saw all of these things, and expressed as much in his letter, as studied insults to a man of rank who as yet had not been convicted of any breach of either civil or military law.[116] He ended with a series of complaints about Isaac Townsend and the petty indignities which he, Townsend, seemed to delight in.

It does appear that Townsend did take his duties as gaoler to the extreme. While Byng was most certainly a high profile prisoner, the bars and extra guards do on the face of it seem more to injure Byng's pride than to stop the portly Admiral from escaping. As to the Admiralty, or more accurately Anson's responses, it is always difficult to gage. However, he knew what was resting on the trail; he, if not directly, was part of the ministry which had attempted to shift the blame onto Byng. If the court martial acquitted Byng, he along with his colleagues would be in an even more precarious position than they already were. Notwithstanding that knowledge, and the fact that it appears as if Anson's true feelings about Byng's behaviour spilled out in the passage quoted, he was right that there were only so many officers who could be recalled. Added to which, the fact that Byng could not name all of them would seem to imply that he was simply trawling for as much support as he could.

At the same time, the discomfort on the part of Anson and his ministerial colleagues was getting to the point where they were looking to take legal action against some of those publishing anti-ministry material. The Admiralty in one case at least looked for advice as to whether they could sue one of the London papers and the author of the article. The Solicitor General gave the opinion that so much else of a libellous nature was already in the public domain, it would be difficult to choose that one to make a stand upon and have any chance of success, and so the matter was allowed to drop.

While the ministry could to some extent shrug off the attacks in the press over their handling of the situation in the Mediterranean, what could not be ignored were the tensions between ministers. This was particularly the case between the Duke of Newcastle and Henry Fox. Things were made worse by the fact that William Murray was still wanting his elevation to the peerage and with it appointment as Lord Chancellor. If that were to happen, Newcastle would be left with Fox as his spokesman, not something he could consider with any degree of equanimity.

Things between Fox and Newcastle were to come to a head over political appointments and more to the point who was, or was thought to be, responsible for the debacle off Minorca. Fox wanted his nephew to be appointed to the staff of the Prince of Wales and he was relying on the Duke to intercede with the King on his and his nephew's behalf. He also wanted to avoid responsibility for what had happened in the Mediterranean. At first all seemed well, when the Duke appeared to have persuaded the King that Fox's nephew should have the place. However, at the start of October this decision was reversed and Newcastle wrote to Fox to tell him so.[117] While all of this was going on Fox had also said that he would resign in favour of William Pitt as Secretary of State for the Southern Department. This was a calculated move which, it was hoped, would appease Pitt. In the Byzantine manoeuvring of eighteenth-century British politics, Pitt was Paymaster but now had gone into opposition against Newcastle. Fox hoped to manoeuvre himself into a better position. He also had strong allies as he was very closely linked to George II's son the Duke of Cumberland.[118] Fox took things very badly when he received the news that his nephew was not to gain the place at the Prince of Wales' Court. He felt that he had been: '"used like a dog" and did not consent to Mr Pitt should have my place.'[119] Of course he had no say in who had which places, as that would be down to Newcastle; however, he could precipitate a crisis by resigning. In that case it would also force Newcastle to resign as he would not have any effective support in the House of Commons.

If Fox went, Newcastle would seek to gain support from one of, if not the, most effective speakers in the House of Commons, William Pitt. And Henry Fox did indeed resign his office on 13 October. He explained his decision in a letter: 'no power of making a friend or intimidating an adversary: and yet to attempt to lead a House of Commons with less help even in debate on our side than was known'.[120] He went on in the same letter: 'It is absolutely impossible to get on with him. I therefore must get out of court ... I find my credit in the House of Commons diminishing for want of support'.[121] This shows how far things had changed since the start of the year, or even since Fox had written in a bellicose way about shifting the blame from the ministry onto Byng. Now he was out of office and Newcastle was forced to rely for his political survival, in the short term, on persuading Pitt to join his ministry.

This, at least at the present, Pitt could not and would not do. Partly this was down to his antipathy towards the Duke, but also especially due to the alliance which both Newcastle and the King were proposing – that is, concerning alliance with Russia, and security for Germany, and Hanover in particular. It was on 15 October that George II authorized Newcastle to speak to Pitt, and it should be remembered that, as with Military appointments, the King was no mere cipher in the process. If the King did not want, or could not be persuaded, to have a minister, they would not be appointed.

Given how critical Pitt had been of Newcastle, what would it take for him to be brought into the King's service, and would the political price be too high? Pitt would not serve under the Duke of Newcastle. Despite his protestation of affection for the Duke in person and their disagreement over a number of issues, such as the treaties with Russia and the German states, it was in fact association with the Duke's links with the miscarriage in the Mediterranean which Pitt sought to avoid.[122] Pitt was offered the post of Secretary of the Southern Department: the King would not countenance his being given the North Secretaryship, as this would involve Pitt in German affairs, which the King would not allow. However, Pitt did not want to be part of a reshuffle, he wanted a break with the past, and having been offered the Secretaryship on 19 October he wanted Newcastle to resign and there to be enquiries into both what had happened in America to Braddock, as well as the events which had led to the surrender of Minorca.[123] He also deemed that all foreign troops in British pay should be dismissed. Pitt also wanted a Militia bill put before the House. He made it quite clear that these terms were non-negotiable. However George II would not acceded to Pitt's demands and there appeared to be a stalemate. Newcastle had in reality only two options: either appoint Fox as leader in the Commons and accede to his request, or appoint Pitt and take on board his. In the end, Newcastle could not accept either man and on 26 October tendered his resignation to the King.

Five days prior to this Pitt had gone to see the Countess of Yarmouth, the mistress of George II, and had put forward a proposal by which the Duke of Devonshire would head a new ministry, with Pitt as one of the principal Secretaries of State. Devonshire was seen as someone who could bring together the disparate divisions of the Whigs.[124] The day after Newcastle's resignation, 27 October, the King gave Henry Fox authority to form a coalition between Fox and Pitt. Yet this was precisely what Pitt did not want. He did not want to be in any ministry in which Fox had a leading part, but things were to be held up overlong, as on the thirtieth of the month Pitt informed the Duke of Devonshire that he was withdrawing some of his demands. This included any inquiry into the war. There was now enough room to build a coalition of former Newcastle supporters, as well as those within Pitt's circle, under the nominal leadership of Devonshire.[125]

It would take until the early weeks of November before a new ministry was almost all in place. Devonshire was to be First Lord of the Treasury; Earl Temple was to be First Lord of the Admiralty; and Pitt Secretary of State for the Southern Department. This last position was only finalized in early December of 1756, when George refused to accept Pitt at the Northern Department again. Pitt now became the principal speaker for the government in the House of Commons. Like so much of politics this was not a case of out with the old and in with the new; many of those who were in office under Devonshire had also served under Newcastle.[126]

In terms of the effect on Byng, the new ministry was in theory more favourably disposed towards him. This should not be overstated though, as it was a coalition of opposites. Pitt had carried out some very successful political manoeuvring, yet he had little party support or even backing more generally within parliament, and this would circumscribe his areas of action. An MP, Lord Crayford, summed up the situation in November of that year: 'I think the present political system of administration seems too narrow and confined to last long. It is constituted principally of one single family against the united force of the principal nobility'.[127] Even Pitt was uncertain about the future of his ministry, this despite the fact that the Duke of Devonshire, being First lord of the Treasury, was the titular head of the administration. The Ship of State, to use the old phrase, was a wreck, and he wrote: 'I am, in all senses, unfit for the work I am going to set my feeble hand to ... Be the event what it may, as soon as I can crawl I will embark, and perhaps on board wreck: and trust I shall have your honest and kind wishes for a fair wind and favourable sea'[128] This letter, written to his friend Charles Lyttelton, smacks a little of self-effacement but it also summed up the situation he faced when he received the seals of office. The King was also less than favourably disposed towards Pitt and his ministry and this did not bode well for Byng and his trial.

Chapter Seven

An Opportunity of Acquitting[1]

While all of the high politics was going on the process of preparing for the court martial went ahead. In October of 1756 the Board of Admiralty, still under the old commission with the Duke of Bedford and Anson at its head, wrote to Byng to advise him that the *Colchester* had returned from the Mediterranean with some of the witnesses for his trial. While Byng was pleased that this group of witnesses had returned, he had not as yet received an answer to his letter requesting further witnesses, and wrote a letter in an aggrieved manner. The tone of his letter perhaps betrays the stress which he was under rather than his general outlook on life: 'My case is sufficiently hard if indulged with every legal advantage for I have too much reason to believe that my prosecution is carried on by persons too powerful for me to contend against'.[2] In this respect Byng was most assuredly right about the forces which had been gathered against him. He also refuted the suggestion that he was in any way wishing to postpone his trial, and from his point of view there was every reason why he should want the trial to go ahead as quickly as the right course of justice would allow.

The Board was not moved by Byng's eloquence and expressed themselves surprised by some of the passages within his letter; their response was written on 25 October.[3] When the officers who had been brought home arrived, Byng was anxious that he should speak to them before anyone else, but it was the Judge Advocate who did so. He wrote to Captain Lloyd in this vein: 'I beg that you will favour me with an opportunity of asking you some questions on that subject previous to your being examined in court...a favour that you run no risk in granting because I have a legal right to demand it'.[4] Byng would return to this subject on 27 November writing about the constraint under which he laboured to put his defence in place: 'Illegally to discover my defence, and expose me to the malicious and virulent attacks of my enemy', but he would not receive a reply to this letter from the new Board which was now headed by Earl Temple.[5]

A week earlier, 19 November, the new Board had met for the first time. It was at this meeting that they looked at Byng's request for more witnesses.[6]

The new commission of the Admiralty (the Office of Lord High Admiral) under the Devonshire-Pitt ministry was as follows: the First Lord of the Admiralty was Earl Temple: other members of the Board were; John Pitt, George Hay, Admiral Boscawen, Admiral West and Gilbert Hunter. Only Admiral Boscawen remained from the old Board. Rear Admiral West was Byng's second in command in the Mediterranean.[7]

They had before them a request for relief from the requirement that no one was to be allowed in his rooms at Greenwich after dark. The Board interrogated the admiralty marshal as to whether there were any objections in granting Byng's request. Mr Brough, the admiralty marshal, had no objections. The Board seemed to be in favour until they were shown the order made by Henry Fox in August which forbade anybody staying and, most likely for political reasons, did not reverse that order.[8]

The reason why Temple and the Board did not overturn this decision was most likely the fragility of the new coalition headed by the Duke of Devonshire. Their stated reason was recorded in the Admiralty minutes of 24 November: 'they did not know on what grounds so express an order was founded, they did not think it proper to take on themselves to make any alteration'.[9] The last part is the most revealing – the fact that it was Fox who wrote the last order shows how carefully the new ministry had to tread in the case of John Byng.

Whatever their reason it would place Byng at a disadvantage when seeking to interview potential witnesses, such as those who had just returned from the Mediterranean. All told there were twenty one sea and warrant officers who could give testimony as to Byng's action before, during and after the action off Minorca. Also brought home were the Army officers who could give testimony as to what occurred during the Councils of War at Gibraltar and off Minorca. Byng rightly stated that: 'the most essential time for preparing my defence can only be commenced from the arrival of my witnesses'.[10]

Amongst those who had come home from the Mediterranean was Augustus Hervey, who, once he had travelled to London, was seen by Earl Temple the First Lord and assured that Byng would have a fair trial. It was shortly after this meeting with Captain Hervey that Temple met with the new Board and decided against Byng being allowed visitors after dark.[11] This shows the fine line which Pitt and his ministers, and it should be said family, as Temple was his brother-in-law, had to walk.

Byng was a very useful scapegoat and while Pitt might have wished to pile all of the blame for what had gone wrong onto Newcastle, for the population at large it was Byng who was to blame. And to make matters worse for Byng, arriving back at the same time as his witnesses was General Blakeney, who was showered with honours for his conduct, despite the fact that for most of the siege he had been bed-ridden with gout and command had devolved upon his subordinates. He was created a Knight of the Bath and a Baron.[12] Only those Army officers who were still under investigation were snubbed by their not being allowed to attend Court until after any inquiry into their conduct was concluded.[13]

On his return Blakeney had an interview with the Secretary of War, Barrington – still in place as part of the Faustian pact Pitt had made – at which he declared that it would have been possible for Byng to both communicate with Fort St Philip and land if he had chosen to do so.[14] Barrington passed this to Newcastle who then wrote to Hardwicke on the subject, since it seemed that all their actions had been justified by what the hero of the hour had reported.[15] Blakeney totally failed to mention the long delay incurred when he did not allow a messenger to row out from the fort to Byng's force. This was down to his need to have everything considered by a Council of War before anything could be done.

Newcastle made certain that all interested parties were aware of what Blakeney had had to say on the matter of the relief of Fort St Philip. Sir John Ligonier, who was conducting an investigation into the officers in the Mediterranean, was also alerted and Blakeney repeated his story to him as part of the investigation. Hardwicke was further of the opinion that the Admiralty too ought to be informed of what the general had said, and furthermore he should be called at Byng's trial as a witness.[16]

The officers who had been sent out with Byng and recalled with him in disgrace were acquitted of any wrong doings by Sir John and his fellow officers; as the letter to the Secretary of War put it: 'each of them is clear from any suspicion of disobedience of orders or neglect of duty'.[17]

Strange as it might seem Newcastle was not happy with this outcome and expressed his frustration in the strongest terms to Hardwicke. Thinking perhaps that this might be the way that Byng's trial would go, he wrote: 'all possible care be taken about Byng's trial, for there the whole question ought to turn'. He went on to say that two members of the Board, Boscawen and Cleveland, were against Byng, and could make those more in his favour see reason and avoid a barb at them being: 'ashamed of protecting or conniving at Byng's acquittal, if the facts comes out, as we have the strongest reason to think it'.[18]

All of this high, and low, politics was not a good augury for Byng's court martial, for whatever the outcome there would be those who would find it difficult if he were acquitted and likewise if he were found guilty. He was in the worst sense caught in between two rival factions both of whom were trying to avoid the public and political opprobrium of the reverses in the Mediterranean.

When and where the court martial was to take place was something that was down to the Board of Admiralty under the direction of the Devonshire ministry. The Houses of Parliament started their new session on 2 December 1756, with the King's speech which laid before Parliament many of the things which Pitt had argued for in his manoeuvrings for office. This focused on what was happening in the Thirteen Colonies; and as well as these there was to be a Militia bill, something which Pitt and his followers felt passionately about as it meant, in theory, that foreigners (i.e. Hanoverian and Hessian troops) would not have to be stationed in Britain for home defence. This was part of the long running debate about the influence of the King's German ministers and his preoccupation, as many saw it, with his patrimony in Hanover.[19]

There was something else which had to be done at the start of the Parliamentary session, which was to inform the House that one of its members was under arrest. This task fell to a fellow MP and flag officer, Boscawen, who since his appointment to the Board had been appointed Vice Admiral. Boscawen was no friend to Byng, as has already been mentioned: 'The King and the said Board (of which Boscawen was one) having been dissatisfied with the conduct of Admiral Byng in the late action with the French fleet in the Mediterranean, and for the appearance of his not having acted agreeable to his instructions for the relief of Minorca. He is now in custody in order to be tried by court martial'.[20]

Neither was Boscawen's promotion to Vice Admiral of the White the only promotion which was conferred at the beginning of December: Rear Admiral West was also promoted to Vice Admiral of the Blue. Thus it was that the man who had raged against the public disgrace of his recall was in less than six months promoted and a member of the Board of Admiralty; such are the twists and turns of fate. It was on 14 December that the Board wrote to Admiral Smith to inform him that he was to be President of the court martial which was to try Admiral Byng.[21] Smith was at that time in command of the squadron off the Downs (the sea area off the Kentish coast between the North and South Forelands, which includes Sandwich, Deal and Ramsgate). He was at the same time sent material which would help with the case as well as the instruction that the trial was to start two days after Christmas on 27 December.[22]

Byng was to be escorted from Greenwich and then taken aboard one of his Majesty's ships, where he was to be held during the course of his trial. The trial itself was to be convened at Portsmouth and hence Byng would return to where he started once again under guard, something which involved a further exchange of correspondence between the Board of Admiralty and the Secretary of War to arrange an appropriate escort.[23]

Byng wanted to stay ashore rather than be confined aboard ship, which would be just as oppressive as his incarceration in Greenwich. On this point the Board relented and Byng was to be lodged in the Royal Dockyard at Portsmouth.

The trial itself was not to be held ashore but was to be convened aboard one of the ships then laying in ordinary (reserve) in the harbour. The ship chosen by Smith was the *St George*, which was ordered to be fitted with all despatch as per the Admiralty order.[24] Byng himself was taken, by coach, from Greenwich on 21 December with the admiralty marshal and fifty troopers as escort. The journey would take two days and when he arrived he was given lodgings in one of the officers of the yard's houses, in this case the Boatswain of the Yard, Edward Hutchins. Most of these houses were built in a row and were quite substantial, as they were the residences of the Navy Board officers who supervised all of the works of each yard and as such reflected their status.[25]

Many of the witnesses, as well as Byng's friends and some of his relations, also travelled down to Portsmouth just before or after Christmas Day. Included amongst them was one Benjamin Gage, who, as Pope says, was acting as Byng's agent at Wrotham Park, at Gages Farm, and at South Mimms, which was the house Byng had rented back in 1751 – presumably that is why he was appointed as agent rather than any friendship between his wife and Byng's mistress, as Pope speculated.[26]

Also arriving at Portsmouth were Admirals Broderick, Holbourne and Norris, all of whom where to be part of the court martial. As a senior flag officer was on trial there was to be no possibility for anyone to make the accusation that the Board did not carry sufficient weight in terms of its seniority. The question of what – if any – bias it had was a wholly different matter.

The full membership of the court was as follows: Admiral Thomas Smith (President of the Court), Rear Admiral Francis Holbourne, Rear Admiral Harry Norris, Rear Admiral Thomas Broderick, and eight post captains; William Boys, John Simcoe, John Bentley, Peter Dennis, Francis Geary, John Moore, James Douglas and Augustus Keppel.

Admiral Smith had been Commander-in-Chief of the Downs and it is not too much to say that Smith was not the most distinguished officer of his generation. He was also related to Pitt by marriage in what one author has called the cousinhood – Smith was the natural son of Sir Thomas Lyttelton who in turn married into the family of Sir Richard Temple.[27] Other members of this extended family included George Grenville, who was the Treasurer of the Navy, Richard Grenville, Earl Temple First Lord of the Admiralty, and, of course, William Pitt, Secretary of State for the South Department. Of the rest, Norris was the son of Admiral John Norris, one of the leading officers of the Georgian Navy who had first gone to sea in 1680 and was still in service at the age of eighty nine in 1749. His son had a lot to live up to.[28] One of his sons, Captain John Norris, had already disgraced himself and his family at and after the action off Toulon and in 1744 he was to have been court martialled: however he fled to Spain and remained there.

Francis Holbourne was to hold command in both this war and in the American Revolutionary War, as would Francis Geary, who in the later war was a flag officer. The one officer whose career in some ways was to mirror Byng's was Augustus Keppel. In the American War he was to command the Channel Fleet and have the misfortune of engaging in an action against the French which would miscarry and end in court martial. In Keppel's case he would not suffer the same fate as Byng. Another thing that marked out Keppel from his fellow members of the court was that he was one of the officers who had circumnavigated the world with Anson, many of whom reached prominence within the Navy.[29]

The Court itself was governed by the regulations of the Articles of War of 1749, those which had been brought in after the upheaval of the Mathew and Lestock affair. They were to be carried out in accordance with the 'Articles and Orders in the Act of Parliament in the 22nd Year of the Reign of King George'.[30] These Articles and instructions amongst other things laid out what the Judge Advocate's duties were: 'the Judge-Advocate is to take Minutes of their Proceedings, and to advise them of the proper Forms, when there shall be Occasion, and to deliver his Opinion in any doubts or Difficulties in their Methods'.[31]

Once all the evidence had been heard the accused was removed from the court, as were those who had just come as observers, and the court would debate the evidence. One procedure which was designed to make sure that the junior members were not too overawed by their fellow members was the process of asking the junior members for their opinion and vote first. This voting was on the guilt or innocence of the accused. As a court could have not less than five members and not more than thirteen, this should produce a majority verdict. The other thing which the court then had to do was decide on the punishment for the offence, if the defendant was found guilty, within the regulations.[32] In Byng's case the court would have no latitude over what punishment would be awarded if he were found guilty: under Article XII of the Act of 1749 there was only one punishment for a guilty verdict, and that was death.

The actual process of the court martial was similar but not congruent with what happened in the civil court. The orders from the Lords of Admiralty were read, which gave authority for the court to sit. The officers of the court were sworn in and the defendant brought in to the court and all of the witnesses were examined under oath.

Courts martial were not without their critics, even in the eighteenth century. These criticisms were on the lines that the defendants were denied their basic rights. In the 1740s there were those who thought that members of the court should not just be drawn from officers, and also there was some debate, although not within the Admiralty, as to whether there should be a jury sitting with the court to help with their deliberations.[33] Markus Eder in his work on crime and punishment in the Navy during the Seven Years War has called naval courts martial elitist. He bases this on the fact that there were only three hundred post captains who could sit as members of courts martial, alongside a number of Admirals. Eder estimates that less than one percent of the Navy could function as judges in comparison with the civil courts in which between twenty and thirty percent of the adult male population could be empanelled as a juror.[34] He also dismisses the defence that they were constituted that way because of the need for discipline aboard ship.[35]

He misses the point, however scrupulous he was, that the Navy was almost wholly different from civil society in one major aspect, and that was that all members of the ships company had to be trained to kill, or take instruction which meant they might be killed. Whether a more democratic form of court would have done, such as he posits happened in the interregnum period, is perhaps only in the realms of speculation. In the mid–eighteenth century the court which would sit was entirely comprised of officers, and in the case of John Byng it is to be suspected that is how he would have wished it – to be tried by his peers.

One of the other criticisms levelled at the system in place at the time of Byng's trial was that the Judge Advocate was unqualified in the civil law and was in some ways little better than a clerk. This may or may not have been true, but in Byng's case it was the composition of the court that was a problem; in particular the fact that Smith was part of the Pitt-Grenville political family and hence biased more toward Byng, given the strength of some of Pitt's attacks on Newcastle in the Commons.

From the evidence it does not appear that Smith was partial in his judgement of Byng, he could not be too overt but notwithstanding what happened after the trial, which will be discussed later, the decisions made, based on the evidence given and the cross examination undertaken, were all unanimous.[36] However, there was suspicion on both sides of the argument: Admiral Boscawen, according to Horace Walpole, felt that those who would have him condemned were in the majority: 'well say what you will, we have the majority'.[37]

Although this was not a comment that can lightly be dismissed given that Boscawen was now on the Board of Admiralty, he may however have been referring to professional sentiment rather than political bias, in as much, as has already been touched on, that there were those within the Navy who felt Byng had brought disgrace upon the service and therefore was deserving the most condign punishment.

The Court itself was to be held aboard the *St George* in the great cabin. Moored in Portsmouth harbour, all of the witnesses, as well as those who constituted the Court, would be rowed out before the day's business started and rowed ashore when it was finished. They would not be held in the solemn silence of modern courts – there would be friends, family and witnesses all crammed aboard the *St George* and all in the great cabin. Although more restrictive, the Courts were in some ways like their civil counterparts.

The first day that the Court was due to sit was Monday, 27 December, as the President of the Court Vice Admiral Smith's flag was flown aboard the *St George* and at the appointed time a Union flag would also be hoisted as a sign that the Court was sitting; the Union flag would be hoisted at the peak of the mizzen.[38] Finally, a single gun was fired and, on hearing this, all post captains were supposed to come aboard the *St George* to witness the court martial. The Court would sit until dusk every day.

All of the captains had with them their commissions, which is how the nine who have previously been listed were chosen: in effect it was the most senior captains present who would make up the Board.[39] As all of the captains responded to the signal and came aboard they gathered in the great cabin. It would take some little time to go through their commission dates and it was nearly midday before the process was complete. In fact it took such a time that Admiral Smith adjourned the Court until Tuesday, 28 December when the first witness would be heard.[40]

Pope makes a salient point when he notes that the day-to-day working of the *St George* carried on regardless of what might be going on in the great cabin. She was first and foremost a ship of war and the Court sitting was just a transient event in her thirty-four years of active life.[41] The one coincidence was that the *St George* had been fitted out as Admiral Hawke's flagship in 1755 at the start of the quasi-war.[42] Those who look for studied insults might find one here, however it seems more likely that she was the largest second-rate in home waters, and, given the number of people who were in attendance, such a large vessel would have been needed – if only for the sheer space aboard.

Byng, now in his lodgings, was to be escorted by a special detachment of marines. These were supernumerary to the normal ship's company and would be in attendance throughout the trial and would then either execute the sentence of the Court or, if Byng was acquitted, march off into historical obscurity.[43] On 28 December they formed up outside the Boatswain of the Yard's house and escorted Byng and Admiralty Marshal Brough to a cutter, which then rowed them out to the *St George* moored in the stream.[44] Pope felt that this was a ludicrous spectacle; Byng with a marine escort with fixed bayonets marched to and from the harbour's edge. In some ways it was a fine line which the new ministry was walking and it is difficult to see what else could have been done.[45] With public, and political, opinion so inflamed it was a case of damned if you did and damned if you didn't.

Whatever the circumstances it was obvious that this was a show trial, albeit one where the jury was not rigged, as was usually the case, and a show trial in the sense that the ministry of whatever composition had to be seen to be doing something.

Once the Court was assembled Byng was brought in and was seated to the left of the Court in front of the table at which the officers sat, with Smith in the centre, the other three flag officers flanking him and the nine captains arrayed around the rest of the table. Byng was allowed a scribe as he appeared to have contracted a cold whilst incarcerated at Greenwich which was, he said, affecting his sight.[46]

With all present the Judge Advocate read out several documents including the Admiralty warrant which called the court martial into being as well as the charge against Byng: 'That the said John Byng, having the command of His Majesty's Fleet in the Mediterranean... on the 20th of May last, did withdraw, or keep back, and did not do his utmost to take, seize and destroy the ships of the French King... and for that the said John Byng did not do his utmost to relieve St Philips Castle'.[47]

The oath was taken by the Court, as it was by every officer who sat on a court martial. Pope made much of the fact that part of this oath meant they could not disclose the votes of the members of the Court except if required by Act of Parliament – in his view they were all going to have trouble with this after the verdict.[48] However, if Boscawen was right that the majority were against Byng, then they would quite happily stay in the shadow of legal anonymity.[49]

An opening statement was read, by the Judge Advocate because of the state of Byng's eyes, where Byng in essence set out in his own prolix style that he was happy that the trial had now started and that he could prove all that had happened to him was cruel and unjust. He also asked that one of his witnesses be dismissed, since his station on the *Ramillies* was on the middle deck, and therefore he was not in a position to see the motions of the fleet or anything else which might be material to the case.[50]

It was the usual quotidian start to legal proceedings – there were to be no oratorical flourishes: this was not the way with military tribunals. Smith then called an adjournment whilst the Court discussed certain points, one of which was central: under their warrant the Court was to look into events on and around 20 May 1756. What Smith and the rest of the members of the

Court decided upon was that this was too narrow and they would expand their frame of reference to include all events from the time of Byng's sailing from Spithead.

This according to Captain Hervey caused a great stir when Smith reconvened the Court after approximately two hours. In fact Hervey, as might be expected, was outspoken in his journal about this, although it must be remembered that the journal itself was, as has been touched on, not written until a number of years after the event. It therefore reflects Hervey's views as filtered by the knowledge of the outcome. However even allowing for this it is one of the only firsthand accounts, with the exception of the trial transcripts, which give a view, however partial, of events at the court martial. This legal manoeuvring took up most of the day and the Court was adjourned and ordered to reconvene the next day, at which point Byng was once again rowed ashore guarded by the marines.

The following day, 29 December, the same routine as the previous day was followed, with signals and flags and outside the Boatswain's house the file of marines arriving to carry out the twice-daily ritual of escorting the Admiral to and from the *St George*. Around the ship, boats and cutters came and went carrying members of the Board, all before eight in the morning.

Once aboard the soon-to-be-familiar Court routine was gone through and soon the Court was ready to examine its first witness. The first witness called was Vice Admiral Temple West, now a member of the Board of Admiralty and from all the marks of favour shown to him since his return totally exonerated from any blame for the miscarriage off Minorca.[51]

The opening questions concerned the squadron at St Helens, whether there was any delay in the passage from St Helens to Gibraltar?[52] To which West replied that there was not any which appeared to him. Was the stay at Gibraltar of six days justified? A question which West had to be asked in two different versions: he stated with all his responses he would not proffer opinions on matters of fact. All of this was just the preliminaries to what happened off Minorca. The next series of questions was about just what happened once the squadron had arrived off Minorca. West made it clear to the Court that Hervey had been sent inshore to open communications with Fort St Philip and what Hervey had done to try to gain the attention of the fort.[53]

The Court's next series of questions, unsurprisingly, was on the motions of the French squadron and when and where he had first seen it and what action was taken by Byng to counter them. To all of these, West gave slow and methodical answers building up an intricate picture of the manoeuvrings which took place as a prelude to the action opening. It would be the President of the Court, Smith, who asked the question which was central to the charges under Article XII: 'How did the Admiral's ships and the rest of our fleet proceed from the time of our van beginning to engage, till the engagement was over?'[54]

West circled the question rather than, in his own terms, answering to the facts. He did not know the movement of the British squadron until after the French fire had ceased; however, as the French rear advanced he remembered the orientation of the two fleets, that the English were well astern and that at times some of them appeared to have their maintopsails aback and at others they seemed to fill and sail towards him.[55]

Next was the question of what might have stopped Byng from coming up with the van, and again it was Smith who asked about the state of the wind: was it contrary? Could Byng's division have got up and engaged as closely as West's? The answer West gave was yes, as it appeared to him – he was in all his answers careful not to directly criticize Byng – and that he saw no impediment. Yet he made it clear that that should not be taken to mean there was none, just that he was not in a position to see because of how the fleets were engaged.[56]

Smith probed the matter further, asking if he expressed an opinion about the behaviour or proceedings of any of the officers or ships, or, and this again went to the heart of the matter, the behaviour or proceedings of the Admiral. This was a very clever and all encompassing question, the maritime equivalent of 'when did you stop beating your spouse?' His response according to Pope was to bluster before answering that it was not a matter of fact, which of course he said he would answer. He then went on to say that he could not but be dissatisfied with the appearance of it, the squadron's motions, but qualified it by saying: 'I saw the Fleet in that situation but cannot tell the reason'.[57] As Pope pointed out he had been so dissatisfied with at least three of the captains, Ward, Parry and Cornwall, that he did not want them at the Council of War, although he subsequently relented.[58] The shambolic court martial held at Gibraltar was also entirely down to West, all of which he most likely would have wished to keep out of the view of the court. All in all West had, despite his action during the battle off Minorca, done things which he did not want too closely examined, and more particularly since his return and promotions, both in flag rank and his position on the Board of Admiralty. His last answer pointed generally in the direction of Byng: who else would have been giving orders to the rest of the squadron to back or fill their sails?

West's evidence took up the whole of the twenty-ninth and the Court sat until dusk, at which point it was adjourned until the following day. The same routine was followed with Byng rowed ashore under guard back to his lodgings, where he was free to talk with his cousins and friends who were there to support him. There is no independently-surviving evidence as to what Byng's state of mind or thoughts were at the end of the first full day of evidence. However, his second in command, with whom it should be recalled he had fallen out at Gibraltar, had tried to give just the facts, although he was less than fulsome in his defence of his Commander-in-Chief. West was to return on the thirtieth to give further evidence.[59]

The next day West returned to be examined more on what happened when the squadron had arrived at Gibraltar. What intelligence had Byng given him after he was informed of the French invasion off Minorca? West was again careful to say that Byng had consulted him, but not in a way that was determent to Byng carrying out his instructions. He was asked whether Byng had consulted him, West, or any others for their opinions after the battle but prior to the Council of War. West answered that when he went aboard the flagship he found that Byng was very unhappy with the conduct of some of his captains and West thought he should not allow them to continue in their commands. He also took the opportunity to mention that Byng had sent him great expressions of gratitude for his part in the action.[60]

Now it was Byng's turn to examine the witness and he asked West about the Council of War, realising that this was the crux of his defence if he could prove that all that was done was the custom and practice of the service in particular circumstances. He started by asking whether that business transacted between the sea officers and the general officers was not usually done in writing and he also asked whether he thought that what transpired were private conversations or part of the service. West's response was that he thought that: 'the manner in which the transaction passed had very little of the air of business about it'.[61]

Byng followed this question with one concerning the need for provisions to be taken aboard as the enemy had command of Minorca and no supplies could be expected from there. Byng was once again seeking to show that what he did was prudent in light of the evidence which he had received since arriving at Gibraltar; West could hardly refute that it was an important step to secure supplies for the fleet.

Byng asked West fifty questions on what had happened to the squadron, and in particular he pressed West concerning the manning issue, which was another of the cards Byng would play during the trial. Byng pressed West on whether it was right and proper, given the proximity of the French fleet, which was known to be in the offing, not to have just sent one ship inshore to try and open up communications with Fort St Philip. He also pressed West on whether or not it would have been advisable to try and send troops ashore which would have materially weakened the manning of the fleet.[62] The most potent of Byng's questions on this was when he asked West whether if: 'it been practicable to land the fusiliers who were acting as marines, would the ships than have been fit for action?'[63] The answer Byng received was an emphatic: 'No I think not'.[64]

Both Tunstall and Pope make much of West's evidence, as he was Byng's second in command, and, as Tunstall points out, he was a member of the Board of Admiralty, something which is mirrored above.[65] West did back Byng on the difficulties, although he also qualified this by saying that he was following the lead of the general officers who had given their opinion that it was not possible.

Something else on which West concurred was the state of some of the ships in the squadron: the *Captain* was leaky and her crew sickly and not fit for foreign service; the *Portland* was very foul, in other words had weed and so forth on her bottom, and did not have enough crew for the guns she carried; the *Defiance* was ill-manned; the *Princess Louisa's* crew were unfit for service; and the *Revenge* was also under-manned.[66]

All of this was contrary to what the ministry had been saying; that is that Byng had been give the appropriate number of ships at the right time and that by and large they were in a good state for the service to be undertaken. Now both the Commander-in-Chief of the squadron and his second in command disagreed. In fact if the evidence was correct then fifty percent of the major warships with Byng were defective in one form or another.[67]

According to Pope this evidence was so damning that the President of the Court ordered the Court cleared so that they could discuss this turn of events. The clear implication is that this was not what they wanted to hear. When the Court reconvened Smith asked West about the state of his squadron which had done so well against the French. West replied that his ship was well found and overmatched his opponent, and having driven her off he was able to come to the aid of the other ships in his squadron.[68] With this attempt by the Court to probe West on this subject his evidence came to an end.

The next witness was to be far more difficult for Byng to counter – he was the hero of the siege of Fort St Philip, General Blakeney. This gouty, dyspeptic eighty year old was going to be a far more dangerous witness for Byng to deal with. He had already won the battle for public sympathy after the garrison had held on for more than fifty days and the full honours of war had been granted to him and his troops. He had been ennobled and lionized by the state and public alike.

As with West the President of the Court opened the examination of the General.[69] Smith started with questions as to how easily communications with the fort might have been. The general said that the sally port, where troops might enter or leave, had been blocked to stop any desertion, however it could be opened up quickly.

Blakeney's answer was on the face of it perfectly straight forward and plausible. However it was not the answer which tweaked Byng's attention, it was the fact that Blakeney was reading from a piece of paper. Byng challenged the general on this point and the President of the court Admiral Smith also asked him when he had written the paper – if it was written at the time of the events or subsequently, when he was examined by the Judge Advocate, prior to the trial. Blakeney made the admission that he could not rely upon his own memory and that the paper was the work of several others. To suggest who these others might have been, given there is no surviving evidence to test where it came from, would be in the realm of speculation and dependent upon your particular point of view.[70] As far as the Court was concerned, the answer was to point out that the general must: 'put it in his pocket and not refer to it'.[71]

Having got over this setback, the General's answers to the questions put by the Court were lucid and to the point. When asked whether troops might have been landed elsewhere, he replied that he thought there were several other places for troops to come ashore. In response to the question as to what effect the landing of the reinforcements would have had upon the garrison, he felt they would have helped as it was short of junior officers. He was more circumspect when asked whether Bertie's regiment would have made a material difference to the outcome of the siege, replying that there were too many incidents in war so the question could not be answered.[72]

When it came to be Byng's turn to examine Blakeney his prolixity in speech, as well as writing, would be a handicap. Asked as to whether troops would be discommoded by enemy fire when landing, the general stood upon his dignity to state that there were always those possibilities within war. Byng would have done better if he had asked his second question first. This was about the siting of batteries and something which caused the general, dare one say it without his crib note, something of a problem: a problem in as much as he contradicted himself as to whether the batteries were or were not a danger to troops landing, and also whether they did or did not fire on Boyd when he tried eventually to row out to the fleet. All the surviving evidence is that they were taking the fort and potential landing places under fire and that they fired upon Boyd also.[73] Boyd had had some experience of landing troops, as he had been with Vernon at the start of the previous war, and this may have coloured his evidence. That expedition was not a success story in terms of joint operations, as Richard Harding has shown in his work on the subject.[74] With the question as to landing settled, Byng asked one final question of the general and that was what time Boyd had been sent, to which the answer was between 3 and 4pm, although the squadron had been seen from the fort at 10am.[75] To this question Blakeney could only say that the boat with Boyd aboard had been sent as soon as possible, forgetting that Boyd had had to wait for the Council of War, which is how the General ran the garrison.[76]

31 December saw Robert Boyd being called to give evidence. It will be remembered that it was he who had tried to reach Hervey's ships when they

were in the offing. He had also come under fire from both muskets and the batteries set up by the French opposite Fort St Philip; something that Blakeney was, to put it mildly, confused over during his evidence on the previous day. Boyd would have been in a position to corroborate what steps Byng had taken to open communications with the garrison, and likewise how long it took to respond.

For once, as Tunstall points out, Byng made the most of the opportunity presented by Boyd being on the stand. First of all he asked Boyd what time the English Fleet had appeared. Boyd response was that it was about noon (it was actually 10am). Byng then asked what time did he make the proposal to Colonel Jefferies that he might go off. Boyd's answer was slightly evasive; he said as soon as he believed it to be the English fleet. Byng pressed him as to the time, as this was all too important to him; Boyd responded that he could not be certain of the hour.[77]

Byng returned to the point asking whether Boyd thought it was it was an hour or two after he saw the Fleet that he made the proposal to Jefferies. Boyd repeated his previous answer that he made the proposal as soon as he thought that it was the English fleet. Byng pushed this further asking whether it was one or two hours or perhaps five?[78]

For all of the good work done in undermining Blakeney's testimony about the garrison and how quickly or otherwise things might have happened or where boats may have landed with troops to reinforce the garrison, this was a subject which he should have left alone; it was better to undermine the credibility of the witness than to get speculation on this particular point.

The questions asked by Byng concerning the numbers of boats which might or might not have been landed allowed Boyd to speculate. He was asked by Byng how many boats might have been landed on 19 May, to which Boyd responded: 'as many as might have been sent'.[79] Byng kept going, trying to get Boyd to admit that it was impossible to land any boats, but this was something Boyd would not do, however hard Byng pressed him. After three or four attempts Byng gave up on that point. As it was nearly dusk Byng requested of the Court that the next day General Blakeney be recalled as he had a further question to ask of him.

The next day that the Court sat was 1 January 1757, and the question which Byng wished to put to Blakeney was as follows: 'If the whole of the detachment which was ordered from Gibraltar had been landed at Minorca, could you have saved the Island?'[80]

His answer is instructive, as he said that since he did not understand the question: 'It is impossible to tell', which would seem evasive on his part.[81] Blakeney, both to this Court and prior to this to the Secretary of War Barrington, had said that if he had had the troops he could have saved the island. Blakeney chose to answer by stating half the truth, that he might have saved the island if he had enough troops to drive the French off.

Byng asked again, in a modified form, this time whether Blakeney had declared that if he received the seven hundred men from Gibraltar he could have saved the island. Blakeney tried to slide out of a direct answer by saying he might have held out until Admiral Hawke arrived. Hawke did not arrive off Minorca until 18 July and Blakeney surrendered on 28 June, after 52 days under siege.[82] Byng would not let the matter rest there, and he again asked Blakeney whether he had made such a declaration. Eventually the general had to admit that he had.

The point of this as far as Byng was concerned was not to show that the troops ought not have been landed, but to show that Blakeney was not in touch with the true situation on the island, and that seven hundred men added to the garrison would have made little or no material difference to the outcome when set against the fifteen thousand French troops already besieging Fort St Philip. Having answered Byng's question, in a manner of speaking, Blakeney was excused by the Court and given leave by them to return to London.[83]

Having taken evidence from the general officers and from Rear Admiral West, it was now the turn of the sea officers aboard the ships which were present at the battle off Minorca. Of these Lieutenant John Bower, who had been the first Lieutenant of West's flag ship, was questioned. Most of this evidence concerned whether he perceived any delay in taking on water or stores at Gibraltar, to which he confirmed that from his perspective there had been none. Prior to that question he had been asked about sailing from Spithead to the Straights, and he had confirmed that there were no delays except those caused by contrary weather.[84]

In succession he was followed by the second, third and fourth Lieutenants, all of whom had been recalled at the same time as Byng and West. In this case their evidence was very narrow, given their stations during the battle aboard West's ship. In most cases it revolved around the state of the weather on the day of the battle and little else. With the conclusion of their evidence ended an eventful but mixed day for Byng, and the Court concluded.

The 2 January, it being a Sunday, the Court did not sit, therefore it would reconvene on Monday, 3 January when Captain Everitt of the *Buckingham* would be examined by the court and then cross examined by Byng. Captain Everitt could happily agree to most of the negative questions: i.e., that sailing from home or Gibraltar was not delayed and that the fleet would have been weakened by the loss of Bertie's regiment if it had been landed.[85] What he was sure of was that the rear of the line could have made more sail and come up with the enemy.

Given their positions aboard West's flagship the *Buckingham*, many officers, including Everitt, were not in a good position once the action was joined to give a clear account of the motion of Byng's division. It would be the frigates which, in theory at least, should have had the best view of the action. They were on the disengaged side of the British squadrons and their whole purpose was the repeating of signals.[86] From this vantage point they could track both the motions of the fleet and, as importantly, the signals which were made by Byng in the *Ramillies*.

The first of those who commanded these vessels to give evidence was Captain Gilchrist of the *Experiment*. Pope makes much of how antagonistic Hervey was towards Gilchrist; his evidence was most certainly not a ringing endorsement of his commander's actions. According to him, the van bore down on the enemy as they should have done.[87] Byng and the rear: 'Did not bear down before the wind upon the enemy, nor any of his division'.[88] This was not what Byng wanted to hear or have entered into evidence to the Court. Pope points out the contradictions in Gilchrist's evidence, which came to light when he was asked about the distance at which the rear opened fire. At that point he mentioned that three of the rear ships which came into action, the *Trident*, the *Revenge*, and the *Princess Louisa*, all made so much smoke that he could not judge how far off the French they were. It should be noted that the *Experiment* was stationed so as to repeat West's signals from his flag ship the *Buckingham*.

He was asked by a succession of members of the Board as to whether or not he had seen Byng's flagship the *Ramillies* engage, and whether he saw her firing. Another taxed him on what he meant when he said as part of his evidence that *Ramillies* was: 'firing and not engaging'.[89] Gilchrist had to admit that his view was occluded by his position on the disengaged side of the British squadron and he could not see the enemy relative to Byng's ships. Pope again labours the point that Gilchrist appeared not to understand the tactic employed by Byng during the action.[90] However it is quite clear, even allowing for the occasional wilful stupidity of some of the Captains, that most of the fleet did not understand what Byng was trying to achieve with his lasking course.[91]

Next to take the stand was Captain Hervey, and if the preceding witnesses had been unduly negative it might be supposed that Hervey, given his feelings of loyalty toward Byng, would have veered in the opposite direction. The opening questions from the Court to Hervey asked him to give a description of the battle from his position as the repeater frigate for the *Ramillies*. This he proceeded to do, but his testimony took so long that dusk fell before the Court could ask him any questions on the evidence he had given.[92]

According to Pope, quoting from Hervey's journal, Hervey went to Byng's lodgings that evening and had dinner with him, and records how pleased Byng was with his evidence. This was not anything out of the ordinary for the time. However, it says much that it was thought acceptable that a witness of either side could carry on in this manner. It would be anachronistic to measure eighteenth-century court martial standards by those of the twenty first, not the least that at the time of writing such tribunals are under attack for how partial they are today.[93]

When the court reconvened the next day Hervey was cross examined. The court probed Captain Hervey as to the details of the action which he had laid out so precisely the previous day and there were a number of sharp exchanges between Hervey and members of the Court. He was questioned on whether Byng might have set his topgallants, to which he responded that being out of the line he could not judge; he did however admit that the weather was suitable for that evolution. Just as importantly he felt that the French had withdrawn on a signal made by the flagship *Foudroyant*. He also said that the French out-sailed the British under their topsails and foresails.

Even Pope, as pro-Byng as anyone, could not but observe that in his journal Hervey was prone to exaggeration, an understatement to put it mildly. Ironically it was more than likely that the harder Hervey pushed on Byng's behalf the less likely he was to be believed.[94]

Next to be called was Captain Amherst of the *Deptford* and then Peter Foulkes, First Lieutenant of the *Phoenix*, who followed up Hervey's evidence with what he saw of the action and the signals made by Byng from *Ramillies*.

The witness that followed was very important as far as Byng and his defence was concerned. He was Captain Lloyd of the *Chesterfield*. He was stationed at the rear of the squadron, abreast of the *Culloden*. At first it did not seem as if Lloyd would aid Byng's defence, stating that the rear might have come up if they had made more sail. However, under cross examination by Byng he admitted that it was the *Revenge*, when she went to leeward of the *Intrepid*, which caused many of the problems. He also testified to the fact that at one point during this crucial period during the action it appeared as if the *Ramillies* had gone aboard of the *Trident*. So close was the *Trident* under the lee bow of the *Ramillies* that the latter had no alternative but to back topsails to avoid a collision.[95]

In fact, Captain Lloyd was pressed very hard on what actions Byng took about setting sails in his squadron. So heated did the exchanges become that the President of the Court Admiral Smith had to explain that he and the rest of the Court were not trying to trap him into giving a false impression of what he saw.[96]

When the court sat on 6 January 1757 it had been sitting for nine days and, given the perfunctory nature of much of the judicial system in the eighteenth century, it cannot be said that Byng's trial was rushed. Even allowing for the fact that not all of his witnesses had been brought home, Byng was going to be able to mount a sustained defence of his actions and an equally strong rebuttal of those charges laid against him.

The next series of questions were vital to both sides when the President of the Court asked Captain Young whether the loss of the *Intrepid's* 'foretopmast put any other ship in danger of being on board of you?'[97] To which Young replied: 'No, not that I could perceive'. The next question from the Court was: 'Did the loss of your foretopmast occasion any impediment to the Admiral and the rear division from going down and engaging the enemy close?'[98] This was the crucial question, but one which, given the lack of visibility and the fact that ships appeared only at a short distance and then from the topmast, Young could not give a cogent answer to. His reply was: 'Not that I could perceive'.

He was asked if he had seen any of the rear backing their sails after he had lost his foretopmast. His response was confusing: 'I did not mind the ships to the rear just then they were not backing: they were to windward of me when I bore down'. The President of the Court could make no sense of this and asked Young again the same question. Young answered: 'I did not then'.[99]

For a third time Smith asked the same question of Captain Young, and this time he was more forthcoming, saying that he had seen ships on his weather quarter with their topsails aback. He pressed him again as to whether he thought those ships might have come aboard him, to which he replied no.[100] The question on this subject became very detailed; could the rear have driven aboard his ship or not? He was forced to admit that Byng had passed to leeward of the *Intrepid*, but as to when the ship had passed Young he was somewhat vague – perhaps three quarters of an hour or maybe an hour. At this point one of the members of the Court said that he was feeling unwell and the Court was adjourned for the day.[101]

When the court reconvened on the following day Young was once again examined about the part his ship took in the action. He was asked again whether he had seen anything which would have stopped Byng's ships passing the *Intrepid* – he felt they had the same wind and weather as his ship and therefore there was no reason why they should not have passed him. Admiral Holbourne wanted to find out about the damage to his ship and if it was sustained from only one French ship. Young replied that it was from three French ships. When asked what the rear under Byng was doing, Young could not say, as he was: 'minding his own ship'.[102]

It was now Byng's turn to ask Young questions, and it was very much in his interest to get him to change his story, especially about the problems his ship had caused to those around him, as well as to the timing of the damage to his ship. Byng opened the questioning of the witness by asking about whether he, Young, had seen the *Revenge* brought-to or with her sails aback while the *Revenge's* boat was coming or going from his ship? Young replied that he did not see anything except that after her boat was gone *Revenge* passed him.[103] Byng returned to the same question as before, to which he got the same response as before. He then asked when the *Revenge* had sent her boat over to the *Intrepid*, as this was crucial, and what position she was in when she did so.

At this point Young said that the *Revenge* was right astern of him and on the lee quarter. The next question asked was in what position, and the answer was with her topsails, to which Byng asked aback or full (i.e. aback was setting her sails to take the wind so as they pressed against the mast, or full which was the normal way sails were set). Young answered that the sails were shivering, that is, just holding the wind but on the point of backing.[104]

The most important question Byng asked in this exchange was how, if Young did not see the *Revenge* from the time that the *Intrepid* lost her topmast until she came up, could he be in a position to say whether there were impediments to the rear coming up. In truth, he could only say that he made no impediment. He could not have seen what was going on and he knew it.[105] This was the final blow for Young's evidence as to what he had truly seen rather than just speculation.

The next witness was Captain Cornwall of the *Revenge*, who was one of those whose courage had been impugned. It was he who had not passed to leeward of the *Intrepid* and it was he who had held up the line and caused at least one other ship in the line to come so close that the second had put her jib-boom over his stern – the *Princess Louisa*. Prior to the near-collision, Cornwall had brought the *Revenge* to on the weather quarter of the *Intrepid*, but had not sought to pass her. This in essence was the nub of the problem – Cornwall did not think he had the authority to pass the next ahead of him. He said quite clearly that the *Intrepid* was the cause of his not going on. He thought that at any time Byng in the *Ramillies* would make the signal for him to leave the line. The episode demonstrates just how little initiative some captains would take – he had to pass the next in line to engage his proper opponent and yet he waited.[106]

He was questioned by Byng as to why he had not passed the *Intrepid*, either to windward or more sensibly to leeward. To the former question Cornwall bridled, saying that it was because he would be withdrawing from the enemy, which was something he would never do. As to passing more to leeward, he fell back on the trope that he had not been authorized to do so, and he felt he might have been between two fires. Pope points out that the *Revenge* did not have any casualties during the action nor did she receive any substantial damage. He also makes the valid point that neither Byng nor the Court followed this point up.[107]

Byng was keen to press Cornwall on why he had not passed the *Intrepid* and, just as importantly, why he had stood by the ship: 'What authorized you to lay by that ship? Was it by orders from the Admiral, or any signal by the Admiral?'[108] The answers he came up with are interesting in that Byng had not taken down the signal for the line of battle and that he had not made a signal for the *Intrepid* to leave the line, and his duty as per instructions was to aid ships in distress. Byng brought up Article XXIV, which in essence stated that no ship was to leave the line without telling the Admiral the state of his vessels; however, if it did so the next in line were to close up the line. His answer was that he had read the article on the day: 'I tell you, I thought it wrong that it was a breach of the article, that is if he had passed the *Intrepid* he would himself be in breach'.[109]

Byng would perhaps have liked to follow this point up, but he was prevented from doing so by the President of the Court interjecting that the Court had nothing to do with the question of Captain Cornwall's duty. This was strange as it was very much to the point as to whether Captains had followed orders given by the Admiral and to what extent they, not he, had caused the miscarriage off Minorca. Byng remonstrated with the Court that he had ordered another vessel, the *Deptford*, to come to the aid of the *Intrepid* and likewise he must be allowed to push the point as he was accused of not coming forward. However, if he could show that there was just reason because of the action of others he would be vindicated.

Cornwall's last remarks to the Court were to the effect that he had drawn the attention of two army officers aboard to look to the situation of the Admiral.[110]

This was the last evidence taken on that day's sitting and by and large Byng had come out of it quite well, but it would have been even more to his advantage if he had been allowed to continue to question Cornwall on his role in the whole affair. Failing that he would have to look to the next witness to fill the gaps in the evidence. The one gap which would not be filled was that there would not be any witnesses from the *Princess Louisa*, as none had been called home by the prosecution and Byng had not got any through on his list.

The *Princess Louisa* was the vessel which had passed so close astern of the *Revenge* that the former's jib-boom had crossed her stern. Witnesses from this vessel could well have added materially to Byng's defence, as they might give evidence as to why they carried out the manoeuvres the way they did. It was a missed opportunity, as no one from the ship was going to be examined and no written evidence was entered into the Court either.

The next day that the Court was to sit was 10 January and the witness called was Captain Durell of the *Trident*. The now familiar question as to whether his ship had been impeded by her next ahead, the *Princess Louisa*, was asked, to which he gave the equally familiar response: 'not at all'. Durell's evidence is of interest in as much as it shows two things. First is the distance between the two fleets when the action was joined at the van. Durell estimated that there was something like three and a half miles between the British rear and the French. The second is that he clearly stated that the rear would have to steer an even more oblique course than the van, with the wind about four points, or forty five degrees, abaft the beam. Tunstall felt that given this the *Trident* and the other ships of the rear could have gone to leeward of the *Intrepid*.[111]

Durell also gave a detailed description of how he manoeuvred his ship with regards to the *Princess Louisa*. He said both the *Princess Louisa* and the *Intrepid* were seen to be heavily engaged and taking damage and he saw that the *Revenge* was seen to be trying to pass the *Intrepid*. He stated in evidence that what he wished to do was come to the aid of these two hard-pressed ships and was sailing down between them and the French. To do this he turned to starboard to clear his next ahead, the *Princess Louisa*, which had brought up close to the *Revenge*.[112] What happened next, in the view of Pope, was extraordinary, as Durell said that having got into that position he backed his maintopsail.[113] Prior to this evidence the *Trident* had been thought to have gone aback because she was being obstructed by the *Princess Louisa*, and that that vessel was brought-to by damage. This meant that she, the *Trident*, brought-to before the flag ship was approximately two hundred yards astern.

The crucial point was taken up when Durell was asked the following question: 'Might not the *Ramillies*, in the heat of the battle have been liable to run on board you if she too had not backed her main-topsail?'[114]

As so often at a moment which seems to turn the world one way or another, it is the unexpected which precipitates them. Having both figuratively and literally put himself in the firing line, Pope feels that he had broken Article XXIV, albeit for benign reasons. He was rescued by Captain Boys, who at this vital moment interjected that: 'if you think it will hurt you do not answer'.[115] It has to be remembered that the right to silence was not then taken as an indictment of guilt, but the fact that Boys spoke in such terms shows that there was a danger of Durell indicting himself.

What perhaps is stranger still is the fact that Byng made no challenge to this. Here was a golden opportunity to prove beyond reasonable doubt that what he had ordered was necessary for the safety of the *Ramillies*, as well as the good order of the fleet, and he was thwarted and made no protest, at least none that was recorded.[116]

What Byng did do was ask Durell about the signal for general action, the red flag hoisted at the main which denotes that all ships should engage as the Admiral has prescribed. Byng was pressing the Captain about under what circumstances a ship could come to the aid of another and much more to the point that if any ship did go to the aid of another without permission of the Admiral it would disorganize his plan of attack.[117] Durell explained that he felt it was his duty to come to the aid of ships in distress.

Next to be examined was to be Captain Gardiner, Flag Captain of the *Ramillies*. He above all others was able to see how Byng had acted as the action started, and what his orders were and what advice he was, or was not given. He stated quite clearly that Byng wanted to close the enemy and get to close quarters with the French.

It was during this account that Gardiner went through the evidence about why the *Ramillies* could not get closer to the French. He said that it was Lord Bertie who had seen a vessel under the lee bow of the *Ramillies*, and that he, Bertie, thought it was British. He himself had not seen that ship but saw another under her starboard bow; this was the *Trident*, and at the same point the *Princess Louisa* was also very close by. Gardiner was also asked about whether it was right and proper that the undamaged ships should have chased the French: he felt that would not be correct as the French were mostly undamaged.

After Captain Gardiner had given his evidence it would be the turn of Lord Bertie whose regiment was aboard ship in place of the marines and who might have been landed in Minorca. The start he made was not propitious: when asked by the President of the Court whether he had any information relative to the action he responded that he knew nothing of sea affairs. However, he would be happy to answer questions. One of the members of the Court was less than impressed by this admission, saying that the Court would only deal with events concerned with the sea.[118] Another member of the Court did not take this into account and asked whether there was any 'accident that the Admiral judged to impede his engaging the enemy properly'.[119] Bertie said that the Admiral asked what the ships ahead were about. It was after this that Byng himself had a chance to examine Lord Bertie and he returned to the question as to whether Bertie thought that the number of men who could be put into the fort would have made any material difference. Bertie was emphatic that they would not be of any service ashore and much better to be kept aboard ship.[120]

Bertie's most important evidence was to the effect that he had seen a ship under the starboard bow of the *Ramillies*, and as such had rushed back to the quarter deck to warn Admiral Byng and Captain Gardiner. Byng, who wanted to make the point to the board, said: 'I think that implies his Lordship saw her'.[121] Byng next handed the President of the Court a list of questions which he requested that he might ask of Lord Bertie, this because they were concerned with his own behaviour and he felt would best be put by the Court. The President of the Court said that he would ask the questions.

The first question asked was whether Bertie was near the Admiral before, during and after the action, to which he responded that he had been. The second asked in a roundabout way whether Bertie perceived any backwardness in the Admiral or any marks of fear or confusion.[122] The answer that Bertie gave was that Byng gave his orders coolly and clearly and there was no mark of personal fear. The next question is worth quoting as it goes to the heart of the matter the Court was looking into: 'Did the Admiral appear solicitous to engage the enemy, and to assist His Majesty's ships that were engaged with enemy?'[123]

The simple answer was: 'Yes'.[124] Whilst this was a simple answer to the question, it should be remembered that Bertie, whilst in an excellent position to view Byng, had already admitted that he knew little or nothing of sea affairs, something the Court had already alluded to. The next question put by the President of the Court on Byng's behalf was to ask whether during or after the action Bertie had heard any discontent by officers about Byng's conduct of the action. Bertie said that he had not heard anyone of the *Ramillies* speak the least disrespectfully of the Admiral.[125] Again this is interesting for the fact that the criticism when it came did not start from the flagship but other vessels within the British squadron.

Byng was clearly trying to show that he was neither personally nor professionally a coward, but he was in danger of getting bogged down in the detail – some of which was essential – the big issue was whether he deployed the squadron to best effect and could he have done anything else.

Another army officer, Colonel Smith, was called to give evidence but added little to what Bertie had said: Byng acted coolly and decisively.[126]

Next an equally-important witness was called: this was Captain Ward of the *Culloden*, which had been next astern of the *Ramillies*. His statement was to the effect that his ship was astern of the flagship, by about one hundred yards. The ship had hardly engaged the French, nor was the *Culloden* damaged by the French. Pope is very anti-Ward, asking how it was that she could be in close proximity to both the *Defiance* and the *Intrepid*, both of which took a battering, and yet she received no damage whatsoever. He also asked why it was that the Court did not follow this point up, the clear implication being that it would have been inconvenient if they did so.[127]

What followed after this was an examination of the first lieutenant of the *Culloden*. This showed up how logs and journals, sometimes one and the same thing, were kept during this period. It might be thought that there were just one or two logs kept aboard ships. However, there could be on a large ship such as *Culloden* up to nine journals being kept simultaneously. All Lieutenants had to keep a journal, partly as proof of service; the Master of the ship also kept a journal, as did the Captain. All of these were bound to keep a journal and hand them over at the end of each voyage. The other point to make was that journals were often 'made up'; that is, completed after the events recorded – sometimes days after the event – and there is some suspicion that as far as Lieutenants' logs are concerned a certain amount of copying between officers took place. It should also be remarked that Masters' logs often have great detail of sailing and navigation instruction, as the Master was charged with these matters. The Captain would also have some of this detail but also more general observations of events aboard ship and what other vessels had been doing. All of this has a bearing on the evidence given by Worth, the First of the *Culloden*. Byng asked him whether he had made any comments in the ship's log about the situation ahead of the *Ramillies* and more particularly of what was happening with the *Revenge*. At this point Worth said that he had made a copy of some of the remarks made in the ship's log, that is the Master's log.[128]

There followed an exchange between Byng and Worth as to who had ordered the remarks to be recorded. Worth thought that Ward had given such direction to the master to note particular events. Captain Moore, a member of the Court, asked Worth when he had seen the log – was it on the day of the battle? Worth said no, not on the day, some days afterward. Moore followed this up with a question as to when the log had been completed for 20 May. Worth could not be sure as to when that might have been.[129]

The whole reason for this is something again which Pope makes much of – that there was a suspicion that the Master's log of the *Culloden* was a verbatim copy of the Captain's log of the *Trident*.[130] And it is a fact that they are. Pope quotes the relevant sections; look at the logs and although they are obviously written by two different people the information is identical right down to the wording.[131]

It would not be unusual for copying amongst officers aboard, but not so between ships. It is impossible to substantiate Pope's claims that it was done because of the criticism of Ward both by Byng and West: it is mysterious but perhaps more indicative of the sensitivity of all of those involved in the action off Minorca in May 1756, and of how it might affect their careers. This is almost certainly why there was so much obfuscation by those giving evidence: it is difficult to be open and honest when what happens to your Commander-in-Chief reflects upon you.

With this left as a historical mystery the Judge Advocate said that after one more witness, and seventeen days into the trial, there would be no more prosecution witnesses called. It is easy to say that all of the witnesses were either neutral or against Byng, but this was not a quick procedure: very few civilians would have had the chance to examine witnesses in such great detail as Byng had. If Byng had a fault, given he was a sea officer not a lawyer, it is that he got bogged down in the detail. Sometimes this was important, but he was trying to prove an intangible; whether he had done his utmost to take and burn or destroy the enemy.

This was more about the dynamism of how he went about things. Whilst ships getting in the way were important, it was the whole tenure of how he did the thing, which was very deliberate and something which was difficult not to reflect on when he was cross-examining witnesses at the Court. It is difficult for anyone to change their nature, and Byng would perhaps not have been able to project a dynamism which was not part of his personality. This does not imply he was plodding or slow, just that on occasion he deliberated too much when action was required. This was as true in the Court as it was when Byng was in command of the squadron in the Mediterranean: in fact it was more so in the Court.

It was now time for Byng to present his defence. This he was to do in writing in the first instance, followed by cross-examination of a few witnesses. He started to compose the final version when the Court rose on Friday, 15 January. Byng would work on this defence over that weekend and, with the leave of the court, throughout Monday.

When the Court reconvened on Tuesday, 18 January Byng had a request to make of the Judge Advocate: given that Byng was still suffering an inflammation of the eyes, he requested that his written defence should be read to the Court.[132]

The Court acquiesced to this request and it was the Judge Advocate who read it out. It started with a reproach to those who sought to blacken his name and character before the public and that they, the unseen power, that is the ministry, were seeking to crush him. He reprised the arguments against him that it was down to his misconduct that Minorca was lost. He was also dismissive of the other charge which was set against him, as he saw it, that the failing off Minorca was down to his personal cowardice. His whole approach to this opening was couched in the same manner as the rest of his questioning of the witnesses – somewhat circumspect, almost apologetic in tone when he said in effect that to prove his innocence he would have to prove their guilt.

What followed was a retelling of why he had been sent into the Mediterranean. It was his duty to relieve Minorca; the French squadron had retreated from the British and, according to Byng's written defence, this was the first time that someone had forced an enemy to retreat and then been accused of failure.

The next part of his defence was to play the numbers game, that in both men and material his squadron was inferior to the French which he met. He also tried to show that his instructions were drawn up with the implicit thought that there would be no substantial French fleet. To add weight to the latter part of the argument he showed that the lack of frigates, fireships and hospital ships was a sign of how little opposition the Admiralty, and hence the ministry, thought there would be.[133] He reiterated his point, made in some of the cross-examination of the witnesses, that his squadron was the worst found – that is, manned and in bad condition – in the whole of the fleet.

He went further, showing that part of his instructions were phrased as if the French, such as there were, would be going to America, not the Mediterranean, as per his instruction to detach West and send him in pursuit. Next and perhaps most riskily he baldly stated that when he got to Gibraltar and was informed that Minorca had been invaded he said that every person concluded that the place was lost.[134] It was true that Fowke and the Council of War had protected themselves before doing the King's service, but as far as Byng's instructions were concerned a Hawke or Boscawen would have acted first and consulted later.

There was an ineluctable logic to how Byng set out his defence; speaking of the battle he felt he had done as much as it was humanly possible to do and in like manner if he had re-engaged the enemy, given the state of some of his squadron, he would have been defeated. If he had been defeated the only place to go inside the Mediterranean would be Gibraltar, and if there was not a sound British squadron there they would most assuredly be at great risk of being besieged themselves. This was dangerous, as many a sea officer sitting round the table in the great cabin of the *St George* might well have taken the view that his main duty and one which he, above many others, should have known, was the protection of Port Mahon and Minorca, as much as anything else because of the years he had spent in the Mediterranean when a junior officer.

Byng in this opening statement made it plain that he had wished to call other witnesses and that this had been refused; he brought to the Court's attention the letter from the Secretary of the Admiralty refusing his request. He pointed out that amongst those he wished to call were officers from the *Captain* and the *Princess Louisa* who could shed light on the manoeuvring which had to take place because of the damage at the head of the line.

Byng went to great lengths to excuse his attacks on his enemies, however, saying this was because of the great oppression he was under and that there was little else he could do. He felt, rightly, that he had been libelled and traduced and misrepresented, all of which was counter to the spirit of justice. With these fine flourishes his written opening statement came to an end.[135]

The first witness that Byng recalled to give evidence on his behalf was his Flag Captain, Gardiner. From the verbatim transcripts he added nothing of any great pith or moment to his previous testimony. It was now late in the day and the Court adjourned until the Wednesday. When the Court was back in session Byng only called his Secretary, George Lawrence, who had been by his side throughout the action, and who gave evidence as to why the Admiral did or did not carry out certain manoeuvres. With this, and rather suddenly, Byng's defence closed. Hervey, in his own way, thought it was because of some split between Byng and Lieutenant Cook. However, this does not appear to be plausible: it is more than likely that Byng had travelled over all the ground he could with the witnesses and had nowhere else to go.

The Court could now read through the evidence, which they did on 21 January, and there would be a further six days before they would bring in their verdict.

As might have been expected the trial caused a great deal of public interest. Horace Walpole took a keen interest in events: by and large he thought things were going against Byng. However, Walpole thought that Byng would not be too severely censured by the Court.[136] Lord Morton also felt that the evidence against Byng was strong but thought it would be wrong to pronounce on it until after the verdict. Others again saw that some of the Court had acted with great propriety and asked sensible questions of the witnesses. Others again thought that Byng should not be allowed to recall witnesses, however as Tunstall points out very few were listed for recall and as it turned out only two were eventually re-examined by Byng.[137]

As might also be expected there were rumours aplenty, most of which circled around the issue that this was not a straight-forward action – or lack of it – at sea. It was a joint operation, and how was Byng to be condemned for breach of Articles which in and of themselves made no mention of such operations. Nor was this trying to count angels on the head of a pin; he had not carried the joint operation, yet there was nothing within the Articles which would encompass such a failing. That left a dilemma that they were to resolve. This was likely to have been one of the reasons why it took them six days to come to a verdict. The other was the sheer mass of evidence which they had to go through to make certain that everything that had been brought to the Court was given due attention.

Chapter Eight

A Proper Object of Mercy[1]

Whilst the trial was coming to a close there was strange twist and from an unexpected quarter. This was from a man of letters and an ardent anglophile, Voltaire, who in turn had somehow persuaded the Duc de Richelieu to write a testimonial on Byng's behalf. This might be seen as the magnanimity of the victor. Yet this was also the gentleman who was supposed to have said, when he heard that Byng had withdrawn from Minorca, that: 'now we can continue our siege in our carpet slippers'.[2] Be that as it may, he did write a testimonial and Voltaire wrote from his home in Geneva, where he was in exile, enclosing the Duc's letter. The letter was dated 2 January 1757. Voltaire says little or nothing of Byng in what is in fact a covering letter for the Duc de Richelieu's letter. The letter is in many ways a glowing testament to a beaten opponent, and as such is worth quoting in full:

I greatly pity the fate of Admiral Byng. I do assure you all that I have seen or been informed of concerning him ought to rebound to his glory: his reputation ought not to be attacked for being worsted, after having done everything that could be expected. When two men of merit contend, one of them must have the disadvantage, without necessarily implying dishonour to the other.

'All the measures taken by Admiral Byng were admirable. According to the unaffected accounts of our sea officers, the strength of the two fleets was at least equal, though the English had thirteen ships, and we but twelve, with a greater number of men and fresh out of port.

'Chance, which has so great a share in all battles, especially those at sea, favoured us in directing a greater number of our shot to strike the English masts and rigging: and it appears to me generally acknowledged that if the English had obstinately persisted, their Fleet must have been destroyed, so that never was a more flagrant injustice than what is attempted against Byng, and every man of honour, and in particular every military man, ought to interest himself.[3]

It is interesting, looking to the content, that Richelieu makes no bones about the fact that the French ships were firing high, and uses the phrase: 'directing a greater number of our shot to strike the mast and rigging', showing that in fact the French Admiral was seeking to disable Byng's squadron.[4] Notwithstanding what the Duc said it was more than likely, given La Galissonnière's instructions, that that is all he wished to do. The destruction of the British squadron would have involved too much danger of serious damage to the French squadron and disruption to the siege of Fort St Philip.

The letter did not arrive in London until 19 January, addressed to M. L'Admiral Byng, Portsmouth. It was intercepted at the post office and taken to one of the Comptrollers, who in turn sent it on to the Secretary of State for the North Department, Lord Holdernesse. As was often the case with foreign mail he had the contents copied and the packet closed, an operation which the government had been undertaking for certain mail since the reign of Charles I.

A copy of the letter was taken to the King and the original was sent back to the post office for onward delivery to Admiral Smith, the President of the Court. Smith would receive the letter on the twentieth, showing how quickly the government could act, in these matters at least. Smith was at a loss as to why the letter had been sent to him as it was addressed to Byng, and he therefore sent it back to London to the First Lord, Lord Temple, who took it to his brother-in-law, William Pitt Secretary of State for the Southern Department.

Pitt read the letter and according to Pope was very angry that the post office should have intercepted it.[5] It was sealed again, for the second time, and sent back to Admiral Smith, this time with a covering letter from the Board of Admiralty ordering him to deliver it to Byng.[6] The tenor of the letter was that Byng might make what use of it he thought expedient.[7] It would seem that copies of the letter were in fairly wide circulation; it is certain that the Duke of Newcastle knew of it, as did Admiral Lord Anson, who is supposed to have said to: 'sink them as they would harm the court martial'.[8] In many ways the letter is an interesting historical digression; the order to Smith to deliver it was not received until 23 January 1757. Four days after the Court had finished taking evidence, what use could it possibly be to Byng?

John Cardwell has shown quite convincingly that given the current state of the public mood it was unlikely that any letter from any Frenchman, however distinguished, would be taken seriously, and in fact quite to the contrary that it would be taken ill by the public. To back this opinion up Cardwell quotes from at least one poem which showed the public temper:

But what Sort of Defence is it you now advance!
Our Isle won't suffice, you'll have Witness from *France*,
We must be convinc'd by such Evidence rare.
Produc'd by the decent, unspotted *Voltaire*.[9]

Against such a tide, and with the Court discussing what its verdict should be, the letter would most likely have been cold comfort as Byng awaited the verdict. As Pope points out quite cogently, it was around this time that Hardwicke commissioned Phillip Carteret Webb to write a detailed defence of the previous ministry, which was helped by the fact that one of the assistant Secretaries to the Board was Mr Stephens, who at one time had been Anson's secretary, much in the same way that Corbett had been George Byng's secretary before he was at the Admiralty. This gave him access to both the former Lord Chancellor's papers plus those at the Admiralty.[10]

There was, according to Pope again, some mystery about a letter quoted in a copy of Webb's defence, which was supposedly written by Byng in 1755, to the affect that there was nothing to worry about in the Mediterranean as far as the intelligence from there showed. It is again one of those oddities which might preface much but with little evidence one way or the other is like Voltaire's actual letter; at best a distraction from the main point which is that no one on either side knew what verdict the Court was to bring in.[11]

The British press were all agog to see what verdict the court might bring in and the longer the deliberations took the greater grew the speculation as to what was happening. Aboard the *St George* were the thirteen members of the court, where they were obliged to remain until they had brought in their verdict. The Court were supposed to be split, according to the papers, with five for condemning him, four for breaking him and four for acquitting him. Given the secrecy which obtained as to their deliberations, such speculation was to be expected.[12]

Byng and the rest of the country would have to wait until 27 January for the court to come to a decision. At 2pm the *St George* fired one gun and hoisted the signal for all to attend the Court. The ritual was well worn by now of the marine guard arriving outside of the Boatswain of the Yard's house, followed by the short march to the edge of the yard and into the cutter which would take him and his entourage out to the *St George*. Then into the great cabin with the long table athwart ship and the thirteen members of the Court sitting in the order they had always done.[13]

Pope gives an affecting account of how Byng, waiting just prior to his going into the Court was told by one of his party that he himself had been warned by a member of the Court that the verdict was against him. This is based on a pamphlet, 'A Letter to a Gentleman in the Country from his Friend in London', published in the later part of 1757. Who the author was

saying little more than if the King thought it proper to refer the sentence to the cabinet he would look favourably upon such a request. One can only imagine that this was not what Sarah and the rest of the extended family wanted to hear. Sarah was to write again to the Duke of Bedford and let slip something which perhaps the powers that be would have wished to have kept to themselves. This was the fact that one of the current members of the Board of Admiralty had refused to sign Byng's death warrant.[34]

The Board of Admiralty had met on 9 February to look into the findings of the court martial. The whole reason why this had come about centred around whether the charge of negligence, which was the part of Article XII under which Byng was condemned, could be implied from the evidence which was given to the Court. The Board put it thus: 'doubts having arisen with regard to the legality of the sentence, particularly whether the crime of negligence, which is not expressed in any part of the proceedings, can, in this case, be supplied by implication'.[35] All of this caused them to give pause and as such they wanted the legality of the sentence confirmed. To that effect they sent the sentence and the thirty seven resolutions, plus a petition from Byng's nephew the current Viscount Byng, to the King.[36]

According to Pope the Board of Admiralty gave the King a loophole which meant that it was all but certain that he would be shot rather than pardoned. The reason Pope adduces for this bleak assessment of the Board's intervention came about because they asked about the legality of the sentence. Pope felt that if they had merely passed on a plea for mercy the King could not have ignored it and would have given a straight yes or no. However, as they asked for a legal opinion he could pass this on to a panel of Judges to decide on this question.[37]

Pope is excoriating in his condemnation of the Board of Admiralty, saying that it would not take long for twelve judges to see that the sentence was legal. He points out that what they should have been asking was whether or not the verdict was legal.[38] He is also indignant that the communication from the Board to the King made no mention of mercy or for asking the King to exercise the Royal prerogative and grant Byng clemency.[39] There may well be some justice in this, but it is possible to see that what the Admiralty was seeking to do was vary the draconian measure of Article XII and allow a certain amount of latitude in the sentencing of Byng.

Be that as it may, what happened was that on receipt of the petition from the Board of Admiralty the King passed it on, with the supporting material, to twelve judges. The most senior of these was Lord Mansfield, the former Attorney General William Murray who had plagued Newcastle for preferment. The next was Sir John Willes, who had been a legal advisor to the Duke of Newcastle. These two plus the other ten judges were to meet on Monday, 14 February in Lord Mansfield Chambers.

The judgment that they came to is recorded on a quarter sheet of paper and merely states that the sentence was legal. The response of the Privy Council was made on 16 February: they simple stated that the findings of the judges should be sent to the Board of Admiralty.[40]

So far those who were seeking to gain any sort of pardon for Byng were not having any kind of success. It is not at all certain that the Board was seeking to do such by referring the matter for outside arbitration; those who are cynical might see a degree of blame-shifting taking place, giving all the appearance of doing something whilst at the same time letting things tick over as they are.

When the Board met on the sixteenth they were faced with the letter from the Privy Council, which signalled the Kings pleasure that the sentence on Admiral Byng was to be carried into exaction.[41] The Board minutes record in all their official quietness the outcome of all of these deliberations: 'Ordered that Vice Admiral Boscawen, or the C-in-C of His Majesty's ships at Portsmouth for the time being, do carry the aforesaid sentence into execution on Monday 28th Instant'.[42] The minutes go on to outline that Byng was to be shot aboard such ship as the C-in-C at Portsmouth thought fit and that a warrant was to be prepared accordingly. The warrant would later on cause some degree of stress, as its contents were to be used by Boscawen to say that Byng should be shot on the foredeck of the *Monarch*. However, the warrant makes no mention of the place aboard the ship where Byng would be executed and in fact it was left down to the Admiral at Portsmouth to appoint not just the ship but also the place aboard.[43]

But all of this would be sometime in the future. It would be at this point that Admiral Forbes would make his stand against the Death Warrant. He had already stood out against the death sentence, now he refused, notwithstanding the opinion of the judges, that the verdict was illegal and he would on those grounds not sign the Warrant. Forbes wrote a careful letter as to why he was not prepared to sign the Warrant. He said in effect that the Court had acquitted Byng of cowardice and disaffection and does not explicitly mention the word negligence, so how could he be condemned under Article XII of the Articles of War? In Forbes view he could not.[44]

Despite Forbes view on the verdict and sentence he was a lone voice on the Board, even allowing for Boscawen being in Portsmouth as temporary Commander-in-Chief, there were enough members willing to sign the warrant to make it legal. The members of the Board who signed Byng's warrant were First Lord Temple, and members Hay, Hunter and Elliott; it was only necessary for three members to be present for it to be legal. With all of this activity going on in London for and against Byng, he himself was now confined aboard the *Monarch*, with only his detachment of marines as a guard.[45]

In this he was a strange and detached figure, who was not averse to escaping his fate yet at the same time oddly acquiescent in the whole proceedings. It is perhaps a reflection of his character that despite the verdict, which must have come as a great shock to Byng, he was almost stoic in accepting his fate. This attitude seems to be reflected when the Board of Admiralty wrote to Admiral Boscawen to advise him of the date of the execution. Boscawen informed Captain Montagu of the *Monarch* to tell Byng that he was to be shot to death on 28 February.[46] He is reported to have said: 'His Majesty's pleasure must be complied with'.[47]

There were other procedural matters which needed to be gone through; as Byng was a Member of Parliament, the House had to be informed that one of its members had been sentenced to death. Thomas Hunter was the chosen conduit from the Admiralty to the House of Commons.

The Speaker of the House seemed overly concerned that if Byng were executed this would reflect poorly on the House. To prevent such odium descending he cited precedents as to why Byng, who sat for an Admiralty seat, should be expelled.

A number of Members of the House thought that this was remarkably precipitous and that to expel one of their number precluded the possibility of mercy being exercised. Horace Walpole reported that some took this up very strongly, pressing the Speaker on Byng's behalf while denying they had any direct connection with him, Byng. They moved that the Court's plea for mercy should be put before the House. Fox, amongst others, opposed this, saying that if this were done it would be seen as a criticism of the proceedings of the Court; in the event this motion was defeated but this was just the start of Parliamentiary manoeuvring on Byng's behalf.[48]

This was not, however, the first movement on the floor of the House. Earlier in the week the formal motion was placed before the House for an inquiry into the loss of Minorca. This would have no doubt started a great deal of work in all the great offices of state to copy documents and make ready papers for this enquiry. Pope is once again harsh in his judgements of this process, stating quite boldly: 'However, since the former ministers still had friends like Cleveland at the Admiralty, Barrington at the War Office and Holdernesse as Secretary of State for the Northern Province, it was unlikely that a single paper damning the late Ministry was left in the files; in any case Philip Carteret Webb had already been through them and prepared the collective alibi'.[49]

In fact it was not unusual for ministers who were dismissed from office to treat Government papers as their own. Furthermore, it was not until the reforms of the middle of the nineteenth century that official records across the Government were kept; and it would take until the onset of the First World War for cabinet records to be kept.

In the British National Archives there are digests of papers kept by the Admiralty which are concerned with the Minorca expedition. It is true that by and large they are to do with operational matters or victualling rather than grand strategy. Nonetheless they do show quite clearly that the Admiralty was facing difficulty in manning the ships then in commission in the winter of 1755–56, including the stark admission of the fact that Boscawen's squadron had lost over 2,000 men by the time of its return from Newfoundland. They further show that there were also problems with other stores for the ships. [50]

There were also the official minutes of the Board, which however prosaic gave a trail of decisions taken and orders issued, and just as importantly who was present when such decisions were made at Board level. [51]

This is not to say that no papers disappeared; however there were plenty in the State Paper Office, at the Admiralty and elsewhere to give a pretty good idea of what had occurred prior to Byng's sailing. However, the papers of Lord Hardwick and the Duke of Newcastle, which mix business and pleasure together, would not have been open to Parliamentary scrutiny for the simple reason that they were their papers. As was pointed out already there was nothing venal or corrupt in this: that was the way of the world in the mid–eighteenth century. It did have the useful, to them, corollary of keeping from public and Parliamentary view the inner-workings of the ministers of the Crown. It would only be when the papers of these two men, plus others, were published that a more rounded view of what had gone on would come out. This would never have been the case in the eighteenth century.

While all of this was going on at the official level, Byng's eldest sister Sarah was writing to anyone who she felt might be able to intercede on her brother's behalf. She wrote to the new Secretary of State of the Southern Department asking that he might petition the King for mercy. [52]

She wrote a long and eloquent letter to the Board of Admiralty pointing out the contradiction between the fact that the Court condemned him on the one hand and yet on the other thought him a proper object of mercy. Sarah ended her letter thus: 'I hope your Lordships will not think he ought to suffer, either under a law unexplained, or doubtful, or under a sentence erroneously passed'. [53]

The question of the King's attitude is also a contentious one. According to his latest biographer his view on Byng's verdict was coloured by the court martial of Lord Henry Powlett, son of the Duke of Bolton, who left his blockading squadron and brought his ship into port for refit without orders from his Commander-in Chief Admiral Hawke. Powlett was acquitted by the court martial and with the support of Newcastle was eventually promoted to Vice Admiral. However, George II was so disturbed by what he thought was Powlett's lack of courage that he made certain that he never held command again.[54] It was this that made George so obdurate when it came to Admiral Byng and any question of mercy, though it should be noted that he took a lot less interest in the Navy than he did in the Army. His own courage had also been called into question in the past: as the last British Monarch to lead his troops into action, this was a very sensitive subject and not one about which he could be objective. Captain Augustus Hervey put it most succinctly, describing George II as: 'such a hardened brute that he was determined Mr Byng should not escape'.[55]

On occasions those who sought to intercede on Byng's behalf did not help the cause by the manner in which they approached the task. This was particularly the case with the new First Lord of the Admiralty, who got into the King's face when he argued for clemency on Byng's behalf. He was shouting at the King and as such breached every protocol that informed contact with the King and wrecked any hope of a pardon via that route.[56]

While William Pitt was in office he did not have true authority, as he lacked support in the House of Commons. Political manoeuvring had put him, under the Duke of Devonshire, as Secretary of State for the Southern Department. Pitt had a vision of how to fight the war; what he did not have was the backing of the King to carry forward his schemes. The former ministers, and in particular the Duke of Newcastle and Henry Fox, were biding their time while others of the old ministry who had kept their jobs were hostile to Pitt and quietly worked against him. Two of the most prominent of these critics who were still in office were Lord Holdernesse, Pitt's opposite number as Secretary of State for the Northern Department, and Barrington who remained as Secretary of War.[57]

What Pitt would most likely have liked to have done is attacked Newcastle and Fox out of office, as he did when they were in. However, given his fragile coalition, this was not something that he could do. Pitt was sympathetic to the plight of Byng but he had limited room to manoeuvre. If Pitt attacked both Newcastle and Fox he might inadvertently drive these two, who were known political enemies, together and thus undermine his own position.[58] He was also hemmed in by the knowledge that the King was opposed to Pitt being in power. The King was known to be against Pitt because of his almost implacable opposition to George's German business, as it was called: in fact it was his and his German ministers' concern with what would happen to Hanover in case of a general European war.

By 25 February it seemed as if there was little or no hope of saving Byng. Even so, an event which had been set in train two days before might yet give him and his supporters hope. On 23 February three of the members of the Court, Keppel, Moore and Denis, went to see First Lord Temple and spoke with him about the Board, asking the King once more for mercy on Byng's behalf. It is not known whether they knew at this point of Temple's angry exchange with the King or not, but they did not receive an encouraging response.[59] Also very active at this moment was Hervey, who, if his Journal is to be believed, was one of those pressing the likes of Keppel to break their silence.[60]

On the twenty fifth of the month Admiral Norris approached George Grenville, saying that he had something on his conscience which he wished to be able to discuss openly, but he was bound by the rules of the Court not to do so. He wished Grenville to have a motion put before the House which would release them from their oath and allow them to speak freely; though Grenville was not prepared to do so.[61]

It was then that the matter was once again brought up at the Board, but the three officers still received no satisfactory response to their plea. They turned instead to Horace Walpole, who had been a Member of Parliament but had just stood down from his seat so that he could be reselected for a new one in the place of his cousin. Notwithstanding this, Walpole at first tried to get Keppel to bring in the motion himself, which he declined. They then spoke with Henry Fox, at Walpole's urging – a strange choice, given what we know of his part in the affair – and he also was in a quandary as to whether or not to put the motion forward on the day's order paper.[62]

In the end it was neither Captain Keppel not Henry Fox who put the motion before the House, but Sir Francis Dashwood. According to Walpole's memoirs, Dashwood hurried into the chamber of the House and as the paper was being read out by the Speaker stood up and told the Speaker of the House of the desire of some of those who sat on the Court to be released from their oath. What adds even more drama to this, even allowing for a certain amount of embellishment in Walpole's account, was the fact simple fact that 25 February 1757 fell on a Friday: Byng was to be shot to death on the following Monday, so if any kind of stay of execution was to be moved and then signalled to Portsmouth, it had to happen on that Friday.

There followed a debate on the floor of the House during which Pitt urged Keppel to break his silence and speak. In the end he did so. After Keppel had spoken other Members of the house said they had been approached by members of the court martial who wished to be released from their oath, among those approached was Sir Richard Lyttelton who read a letter from the President of the Court Admiral Smith.[63]

Lord Strange was reported by Walpole as saying that at first he had been against Parliament being involved, but as the judges wished this it would be difficult to refuse them dispensation. What is significant is that the factions who followed the Duke of Newcastle sat in total silence whilst this matter, which might have a great bearing on their leader, was debated.

George Grenville and Lord George Sackville thought there was no need for a bill to be passed, as the oath only stopped the members from divulging the opinion of any single man. As the debate drew to a close Pitt assured Keppel that the House would in fact sit the next day.

Pitt went to the King on Saturday the twenty sixth, and on this occasion he went on behalf of the whole House of Commons. He was rebuffed as to the pardon. It was resolved that they respite the sentence, after the King had been informed that a member of the Court wished to be released from his oath, until 14 March. This had been resolved upon by the inner cabinet meeting at Devonshire House. Pitt sent orders to the Admiralty to inform them of the stay of execution and further ordered them to send orders to Boscawen put it into effect. One set of these orders was sent by messenger at 7pm on that Saturday, another by a second messenger shortly afterward, and a third by the post. In those orders Boscawen was told that he must acknowledge their receipt by return.[64]

This was not the only business which the Board transacted on that Saturday: as part of the process they sent orders to all member of the Court to be present in London on Tuesday in the evening so that they could be examined. Because of the time of the year all of the members of the Court were still ashore in this country; had the court martial taken place in the middle of the year, many of them would have been back at sea.

Pitt had to attend the House that Saturday morning to inform them of what was going on. One thing which was certain was that the King was still opposed to granting Byng a pardon. It was, however, not totally without hope as he, the King, had been informed by Pitt that one of the members had asked to be released from his oath, and the King had agreed to respite the sentence until the fourteenth of the following month. As this was the royal will, Pitt told that House that orders had been sent accordingly to the Commander-in-Chief at Portsmouth, Admiral Boscawen, to stay the execution until the fourteenth of March.[65]

The business of the House that Saturday was passing a Bill which would enable the members of the Court to be released from their oath. Given the King's opposition it would be difficult to see what the Bill would achieve unless the members of the Court had something genuinely material to say. It was against this background that the Bill was put through its first two readings on that Saturday, then it went to the committee stage. When the House rose the Bill was well on its way.

On the Sunday all of this progress seemed to come to nought. The cause was a rumour that some of the officers who had asked to be released from the oath had now recanted. It was said that Rear Admiral Norris and Captain Moore were supposed to have gone back on their word and were supposedly not interested in being released from their oath. This brought into question the whole basis for the Bill in the first place

The result was a flurry of activity on behalf of those who were seeking the bill to find out exactly what was happening. Amongst those who were central to this was Horace Walpole. He was seen to be criss-crossing London, going from Mr Fox, to Sir Richard Lyttelton, to Mr Pitt, to the Speaker's House. In the end it turned out that it was not to all four of them, but just two: Captain Holmes and Geary. The two who had the finger pointed at them were in fact staunch in their support of the Bill and wrote to Keppel. They said: 'The world says we have varied, but we desire to adhere to what we told you'.[66]

Of those who were of the contrary opinion, Geary gave the most honest answer when he said that it would hurt his preferment in the service to tell.[67] If any of the officers were to speak out they might well affect how or if they were employed in future. It would seem to be anachronistic to say so, but both Geary and Keppel, on opposite sides of this argument, would be employed in future and of the two Keppel would end his not-untroubled career as the professional head of the service.[68]

What was to happen next was the playing out of the Parliamentary opposition. When the House sat on the Monday for the third reading, and just as that reading was about to be moved, Fox spoke to the effect that someone had more information for the House. This was a remark designed to bring Keppel to his feet to explain who, if anyone, of the Court wished to be released. Keppel had to say to the House that Holmes was 'easy in his mind' and therefore did not support the Bill.[69] Captain Geary on the other hand was neither for nor against it, but would speak if called to. However, Admiral Norris and Captain Moore, as well as Keppel, wished to be released. Fox sought to play the numbers games by arguing that of the seven members of the Court then present a simple majority were content and therefore the Bill should be withdrawn. However, in the end the Bill was voted through by 153 for and 22 against.

Having passed through the House of Commons it was going to the House of Lords; it would be much more difficult for the Bill to pass through the Upper House. Lords Mansfield and Hardwicke were to be amongst those who would seek to slow down or derail the Bill in the Upper House. Given that Hardwicke was Lord Chancellor under the old ministry and that Lord Mansfield was the most senior of the Judges who had ratified the legality of the sentence, the outlook was propitious. One of the ways that the Lords overpowered this Bill was that at the second reading the Lordships wished to question each member of the Bill individually.

For commoners to appear before the Lords was usual and they would be called to the Bar of the House, yet as Pope himself says this would be a very intimidating process. This would be a clash of professional sea officers and some of the most senior judges in the country. When the witness was brought to the Bar he would be asked a series of questions. The questions themselves or their outline was as follows: the first was; 'Whether you know of any matter that passed previous to the sentence on Admiral Byng to show it to be unjust?'; and second; 'Whether you know any matter that passed previous to the sentence which may show that sentence to have been given through any undue practice or motive?'

If there was a 'yes' to either of the first two questions they would be asked two further questions. The first of these was: 'Whether you apprehend you are restrained by your oath from disclosing any such matter?'; and the fourth was; 'What kind of the matter or things you apprehend you are restrained by your oath from disclosing?'[70]

One of the other parts of this drama, for that was what it was, was that the Lords would read each member of the Court the oath of secrecy as if they were to sit again at the Court. The first of those to be called would be the President of the Court Admiral Smith. Walpole and Hervey thought, correctly, that Hardwicke and Mansfield were indulging in politicking of the worst kind and that most of the officers who were to be examined would not realize this.[71]

Walpole, never the gentlest of critics, felt that Smith was a man of no capacity, of no quickness of comprehension. He would be questioned by Lord Mansfield, the former Attorney General. His, Mansfield's, first question opened up the attack on the Bill. He asked whether Smith knew of anything that had happened, before the sentence was pronounced on Byng which would show it to be unjust? Smith fell into the trap by answering he did not. The next question was very precise and well worded: 'Did he know of anything which might show the sentence to have been given through any undue practice or motive?'[72] To which Smith gave the same reply as he had previously.

He was asked by Mansfield whether the Bill now before the Lords should be passed into Law. To this he is reported to have said that he had no desire for himself but if it gave relief of conscience to any of his brethren it would not be disagreeable to him.[73] He was asked whether he had any further information about the case or the sentence necessary for the King to be inclined to Mercy. This in many ways was the killer. He could only answer that he did not over and above that which had caused him to write the plea for mercy in the first instance.

Smith went on to say that he had written to his brother, George, a Member of the House, in terms which meant that if required all members of the Court would have come to the House, if they had been required to do so, to explain their reason for their recommendation for Mercy. In the House of Commons earlier there had been much debate, and in some cases fierce opposition, to any such intercession in the workings of the court martial: now it looked as if it was going to fall at the second hurdle.

There was little else that Rear Admiral Smith could have said. He, and all of the members of the Court, were basically decent and honourable men: they had sifted a great deal of evidence and come to a decision. Now they were faced with revisiting those events within the full splendour of the House of Lords. These sea officers, some of whom sat in the House of Commons, were faced with the most senior law officers, or former law officers, of state. There was likely to have been only one outcome in this encounter.

After Smith had been given leave to withdraw the next member of the Court called to the Bar was Rear Admiral Holbourne. He in turn was asked the first four of the questions on the list. To all of these four questions Admiral Holbourne replied no. With that, and given the nature of the series of questions, Holbourne was allowed to withdraw.

The next officer who was to be called into the House of Lords was the third flag officer, Rear Admiral Norris. According to Pope, who himself was quoting Horace Walpole, he of all of those summoned was, as they both saw it, the most abject in the face of the questions put.[74] Pope in fact goes further than Walpole, quoting back what the Admiral had written a day or so before about adhering to what they had told him, the 'him' being Augustus Keppel.[75] Perhaps what Pope and others who have taken a tilt at this windmill should have looked at was the whole issue of military tribunals and how they fitted into the general concept of justice in the eighteenth century. The one historian who has done so recently, Markus Eder, has examined this in great detail. He takes a middle view between the two extremes, as he sees it, of the hanging and flogging view of justice a century ago and the more modern research which sees it as an analogue of what was happening ashore.[76]

This of course did not help the supposedly hapless members of the Court as they were brought before the Lords. It is important for historians to pause and look at what the legislation to relieve the members from their oath would have achieved if it had been passed into law.

The whole point would have been to allow the members to speak of their problems with the Articles of War as they pertained to this verdict in particular. It is difficult to say what was going on in their discussions, as has already been touched on, but for there to be any effect on the sentence there would have to be something material which would persuade the King that Byng was a proper object of mercy. Therein lays the problem: what could it be that would have been discussed between the members which would move the King to clemency. They seem to have to have been split, some for convicting, some for acquittal, and some who wavered between the two. None of this seems fertile ground for moving the sovereign to pardon Byng unless they could say that they themselves had miscarried in their execution of Justice, which would have taken more courage than facing their Lordships in the Upper House.

So when Norris is accused of being hapless and hopeless it may well be true, but it obscures a broader point: what, in legal or other terms, was it that would turn this trial on its head? They had deliberated for six days; they had all of the written evidence; nothing in the process was incorrect excepting only the Admiralty's somewhat grudging attitude to witnesses.

So when Norris was dismissed by their Lordships it was the turn of Rear Admiral Broderick to come to the Bar and be put to the question. To all four of the first series of questions he answered no. This was to be the case for two others of the Court, Charles Holmes and Francis Geary.

Captain Moore was for the Bill, as was the instigator Captain Keppel. In all only two of the thirteen members of the Court wished to be absolved from their oath. In truth, two would have been more than sufficient had they something material to say on the subject. However, it is doubtful if what they could have brought forward would have moved the king to clemency. More to the point they were unable to persuade the Lords to pass the Bill.

Hervey and Walpole took a dim view of the proceedings in the Upper House. Hervey was excoriating in his condemnation of the goings on: 'most people imagine there was some compromise between the late and present administration to screen those most famous delinquents, Lord Anson, Mr Fox and the Duke Newcastle'.[77]

Hervey was half-right but for the wrong reason. Pitt would have found it very difficult to have kept together the fragile alliance under Devonshire, which would most likely have fallen apart. This does not, however, absolve the likes of Hardwicke and Mansfield from using the full majesty of the House of Lords, as well as very sophisticated questions, to brow-beat the members of the Court. This was a potent mix of two opposites, with Byng's fate being held in limbo between the two opposing parties.

Pope picks out the President of the Court Admiral Smith for particular criticism. In Pope's view Smith had said that the Court was willing to go before the Privy Council to be interrogated on the discussion of the Court.[78] However the methods available for clemency were few and far between and it would be unlikely that there would be a unanimous view from the members of the Court.

The wheels of justice may grind slow but they do not stand still and after the Bill had failed to pass through the Lords the Board of Admiralty met, and during this meeting a new warrant was issued for the execution of Byng on 14 March.[79] Once again this was despatched to Admiral Boscawen at Portsmouth. In the despatch Boscawen was warned not to allow Byng to escape, notwithstanding that he had never once shown any sign of even thinking of fleeing, and to this end was to make sure that there were sufficient guards aboard the *Monarch* for that purpose. He was to give orders to the Captain of the *Monarch* and his officers to make sure that everything was in place and that the admiralty marshal was extending all possible facilities.[80]

All of this was set in motion just three days before the day that Byng was due to be shot, this was on Friday, 11 March. Once again this warrant made no mention of where the execution was to take place aboard the ship, and also aboard which ship in the harbour: that was left to the Admiral at Portsmouth to decide. Thus all was in place; the prisoner aboard the Monarch and those who had sent him there waiting for a chance for a recall to power. None of them realising that when Newcastle did return to power, it would be as part one of the most unlikely coalitions of the eighteenth century. All the while Byng's friends and family were waiting for noon on the fourteenth, after which all of this would be academic in any case.

Chapter Nine

Death of an Honourable Man[1]

The Bill to remit the oaths had fallen and there was no prospect of the King being moved to sudden clemency: Byng would not be saved. He had been on the brink once before when the king had remitted the sentence. Now that stoic quality which seemed to underlie much of what Byng did as an adult was to the fore. Aboard the *Monarch* the daily routine would continue: the only difference would be that Byng was to remain aboard until his execution. To that end, once the second warrant was sent to Admiral Boscawen Byng would be guarded almost as closely as he had been when he was confined at the Seaman's Hospital. He would have his own company of marines who would stay aboard, separate from the ships marines, whose sole purpose would be to guard the Admiral, and when the time came they would carry out the execution.[2]

Given the size of the vessel Byng was aboard the marines would only have to patrol the quarterdeck, the stern galleries and outside the door of the great cabin where Byng was held, although he himself had access to a day room and could walk on the quarterdeck.[3] These anonymous men were in many ways to be those closest to Byng in the last days of his life, yet it is doubtful that a single word would have been passed between them and perhaps, with the exception of the sonorous cries of 'all's well', Byng may have hardly noticed them, such was the gulf between the Flag Officer and the ordinary marine.[4] It was almost a well-worn routine in which Byng took part. He would have visitors every day and their time of arrival and departure was noted in the master's log. In many ways this was even more stringent than anything which Isaac Townsend had placed in the way of Byng at Greenwich.

However, there was to be an increase in the number of marines who guarded Byng. On 6 March, just eight days before his execution, Admiral Boscawen ordered an increase in their numbers.[5] He also stipulated that Byng had to be attended by officers of the ship at all times. Four lieutenants where chosen for this task; Brograve, Lambert, Shirley and Uvedale. They would take four-hour watches and note down all the names and times of arrival and departure of Byng's visitors.[6] As at Greenwich all visitors had to leave before dusk, approximately 6.30pm, and once they had left one of the ship's boats was to be manned and used as a guard boat, much as it would be when in foreign ports to stop desertion, in this case to stop Byng escaping or any of his friends trying to spirit him away.[7]

This idea was not as far fetched as it might seem: there was one member of Byng's circle, Augustus Hervey, who had just that idea. Nor was it just talk: according to his journal, Hervey was determined to help his friend escape if he could.[8] To this end he had sets of horses left on the way down from London to Portsmouth, at Ripley and on the South Downs just outside Portsmouth. It would cost Hervey £3-00 a day for livery for the animals, but it appeared to be a bargain if it allowed the escape of his friend.[9] His idea was that once Byng was ashore he would be taken to London. From there the plan is a little less well-thought through, if any of it was properly thought through in the first place.[10] However, all of this came to nothing, as when Hervey arrived at Portsmouth he found that Byng was under close arrest aboard the *Monarch*.[11] Notwithstanding what Pope has to say on the subject – in his view the measures were a 'ponderous absurdity'[12] – it does seem that the much-maligned Boscawen had a point when he had these measures put in place for guarding the prisoner. At least one person had planned to engineer Byng's escape and had acted upon it.

Because of the record of the comings and goings aboard the *Monarch* there is some objective record of how Byng spent his last week. He would rise at 7am and be washed and shaved. Byng would then have his breakfast. At 8am the guard would be changed and at 8.30 the first boat would come alongside the *Monarch*.[13] Hervey visited Byng twice in the *Monarch* and he himself told Byng of his plans to help him escape. If this is the case – and we only have his record written in his journal to attest to it – it shows that the lieutenant who was supposed to be present at all times seems to have withdrawn from the great cabin at this point or else does not appear to have been listening, which given the circumstances seems hardly likely.[14]

With thoughts of escape firmly banished there was the more straightforward and material to deal with: the disposal of his worldly goods. To this end Byng not only drew up his will, but also set up trusts and ratified settlements which he had made as long ago as 26 and 27 October 1756.[15] He placed in the hands of his trustees the bulk of his monies and some of his property. Whilst Byng may have had lavish tastes, as those who mocked him so cruelly pointed out, he was also prudent in as much as he had at the time of his death £12,000 in three-percent bank annuities and a further £4,000 in three-and-a-half-percent annuities.

At first glance it might seem that he had that money tied up for a low return. However, the way that Bank of England annuities worked was that the interest was paid in perpetuity and it was paid twice a year. In Byng's case that would mean that combining the two stocks, as they were called at the time, would have given him an income of £1,000 per annum just from these investments. His pay as an Admiral on active service would have been £3-10s pier diem, or £1277 per annum.[16] Given that Byng was not struck from the list of officers all of the time that he was on trial and awaiting execution, he would have been entitled to his half pay of £1-15s per day, equal to £638 per annum, all of which would have had to have been drawn on the Navy by his executors after his death. It is difficult to estimate his annual income from all sources given the condition of the records available, however on a conservative view when he was on active service he would have had well over £2,277-0-0 and perhaps closer to £3,000 per annum. When on half pay he would have still had approximately £1,600 per annum. Given how much Jane Austen's character Mrs Bennett raved about Mr Bingly having £5,000, Mr Byng was very much in the mode and manner of a country gentleman in terms of his income.[17] If he did not exceed the likes of the Cavendish family, which had upwards of £80,000 invested in Bank of England annuities, he was still a man of means.

Byng also had land at South Mimms, already alluded to, which was also to be held in trust under the agreements of 26 and 27 October.[18] The rents from the farms and also from the land at Wrotham Park would be left to his nephew George.[19] He gave to another of his nephews, the current Viscount Torrington, both the principal and interest on a mortgage held on a property and lands held in Southill, near the family seat in Bedfordshire.[20]

Pope focuses on the things which Byng had, rather than seeing them as accoutrements of what he was, which was a well-connected sea officer and a gentleman. The fact that he had in his possession a portrait of the King of Sardinia set with diamonds shows how long he had spent in the Mediterranean and the gratitude of some at least for services rendered.[21] In the same vein is the gift of a blue-enamelled snuff box, given to him by the Marshal Duc de Bellisle, which also went to his nephew the Viscount Torrington. Given the somewhat tempestuous nature of their dealings in the last war, this attests to the esteem in which Byng was held by the marshal.[22] As might be expected from a man of property, his will runs to four pages, giving in some detail his principal passions as well as some small items. The one thing which the will does not do is give a clear view into the personal life of the Admiral, notwithstanding that is how Pope has used it.[23] Most semi-successful sea officers would have had similar items in their possession.

All of the items were listed as was the norm in wills of the eighteenth century. His china, his plate, his pictures, his rugs – Persian and Turkish – bust and statues, all are sent out for division amongst his family and his closest friends. He forgave the debt of those who owed him money – one of his tenants and his valet – as any good Christian should do on their death.[24]

Byng wrote on the same day that he made out his will, 12 March, to his eldest sister Sarah Osborne, thanking her for all of her efforts on his behalf: 'I can only with my last breath thank you over and over again for all your endeavours to serve me in my present situation. All has proved fruitless, but nothing wanting in you that could be done. God forever bless you in the sincere prayer of your most affectionate brother, J. Byng'.[25]

It is by turns both effusive and restrained, in the same manner of the letter he had written to Admiral Temple West after the battle off Minorca. It showed concern with others whilst being mixed with a degree of piety. There is little except this and one or two other letters on which to judge Byng's private feelings on religion. Publicly he would have been a professing member of the Church of England, but other than that little can be said with any confidence.

Once these matters were attended to Byng continued to receive visitors, both on Saturday 12 and Sunday 13 March. It was on the Sunday when Byng was informed that Admiral Boscawen had received the warrant from the Board of Admiralty to carry out his execution. It was the duty of Admiralty Marshal Brough to inform Byng of it. The warrant informed Byng, who already knew the appointed day and manner of his death, in official terms of how all was to be carried out: 'the said John Byng to be shot to death by a platoon of Marines on board such of His Majesty's ships in Portsmouth Harbour as he (Boscawen) shall think proper'.[26]

As has already been mentioned, there was no mention in any of the official correspondence or in the warrant specifying upon which ship or where aboard the chosen ship Byng would be executed. It should be remembered that seamen who suffered the death penalty were hung from the foreyard arm, off the forecastle. This was important as an officer, and more importantly a Flag Officer, was not to suffer the execution of a common seaman: he was to be shot instead of hanged. Of equal concern was the fact that his place aboard ship was the quarterdeck, not the forecastle, which was the preserve of the seaman. If he was to be shot it should be on the quarterdeck.

The ship which Boscawen had chosen was his current place of incarceration, the *Monarch*. What was an insult to his dignity as an officer was that the he was to be shot on the forecastle. Whether this was a studied insult to Byng by Boscawen, who was all for his execution, or merely an unthinking act is difficult to say at this distance from events and without documents to back any assertion.

However, Boscawen could not be unaware of the significance of the place of execution, as well as the manner in which it was to be carried out. He himself was a Flag Officer and would have taken it hard to be so dealt with, so there may just have been an element of spite in that order. Be that as it may, the order was soon rescinded, most printed accounts putting this down to the intercession of Edward Bramston, Byng's cousin, who remonstrated with Boscawen aboard his flagship, the *Royal George*, after visiting Byng on the Sunday. The time and place were now set: 12 noon on the quarterdeck of His Majesty's Ship *Monarch*. All that was wanting was for the new day to dawn.

March is a cold, hard month, and until recently it had presaged a new year – under the old calendar – and 14 March was no different. The wind was in the north-west and blowing a small gale. At 7am a boat came alongside. Aboard was the last piece in this macabre jigsaw: it was Byng's coffin. The *Monarch* master's log describes its arrival straightforwardly: 'Mr Byng's coffin was brought aboard'.[27] The marines were already aboard and those who were to form the firing party had been told off for that duty. Byng himself had risen early at 5am, at least according to the pamphlets published after his death which purport to give an accurate description of events.[28] According to Pope it was a triple-lined coffin with the inner coffin of wood, surrounded by a lead lining, with an outer wooden coffin.[29] On the lid was a simple inscription: 'The Hon John Byng. Esqr Died 14th March 1757'.[30] Few except the condemned know the day and time of their death so intimately, yet Byng does not appear by all accounts to have been phased by this at all.

There was, according to the pamphlet quoted above, another incident. After Byng had taken breakfast with Mr Brough, the admiralty marshal, he changed his coat and at the same time mentioned to his servant that he, the servant, might have his buttons. In the will it mentions that Byng's clothes were left to his valet, lest it be thought that he had stolen them from the corpse after the execution. To prevent any such allegations being made, Byng had the exchange witnessed by the marshal. Byng had stipulated that he was to be interred in the clothes in which he had been executed.

The weather continued inclement as noon approached; the wind was at west-north-west, blowing hard. The signal was made for all ships then in the harbour to send boats to witness the execution. The *Monarch* was moored sufficiently high up the harbour as to make it difficult for the boats to make against the wind and the tide, which was on the ebb.[31] Byng had dressed, not in a sea officer's uniform, but according to the pamphlets in a light grey coat, a white waistcoat, white breeches and white stockings and a powdered wig.[32]

Byng received visitors that morning. Many of them had been visitors since he had been placed on trial. What they spoke of has not come down to posterity, though one subject has been recorded and it concerned his execution. It fell to his cousin to broach the subject of how Byng should face the firing squad: Byng himself wished to give the signal and he wished not to have a blindfold.[33] However, the commander of the platoon of marines asked that he wear a blindfold as the range was so short that his men would be staring straight at his face and this might disturb their aim. It should be remarked that the distance, allowing for artistic license in the well-known picture, would be extremely short: less than six feet from the front rank to Byng. At that range they could not help seeing his face. According to the letter to a Country Gentleman, a discussion ensued between Byng and his cousin as to whether he would or would not wear the blindfold, Byng being strong for looking his executioners straight in the eye.[34] In the end his cousin persuaded him that wearing a blindfold would steady the nerves of the firing party and have no reflection on him whatsoever.

He even contemplated, as is recorded in the same source as just discussed, as to whether he should take off his coat, the purported reason being that he might be reported as being afraid to receive the blow and feel the bullets. This is the reverse of how Charles I went to his execution, with two shirts so that he did not shiver and give the impression he was afraid. Once again he was persuaded that taking off his coat was unnecessary, this time it appears by the admiralty marshal.[35] Byng also insisted that he be told the details of the proceeding as he did not want to make any mistakes.

The supposed conversation between Byng and his friend has often been repeated: sufficient to say that as he waited for noon he acted with great dignity and calmness, and just before the hour he gave the marshal a paper which he said contained his thoughts on the matter.

While all of this was going on below deck, on the quarterdeck boards had been lashed to the railing on the port side and almost amidships a cushion with sawdust around it sat incongruously waiting for Byng to kneel on it. As noon approached the firing party was mustered on the starboard side, while the rest of the crew of the *Monarch* were mustered in the waist of the ship to witness the punishment.[36]

After a few minutes alone in his sleeping cabin Byng walked on to the quarterdeck escorted by Marshal Brough and his cousin Bramston. He had with him two handkerchiefs: one he would use as a blindfold, the other was to be dropped from his right hand as the signal to fire.

The marines were drawn up in three ranks of three and were ordered to prepare. The front rank knelt on the deck, the second crouched behind them, and the third stood with their arms at the present: their job was to fire if Byng was not killed by the first volley. At an order from their captain they cocked their flintlocks as Byng tied the handkerchief around his eyes. Once it was in place the captain ordered present, Byng raised the second kerchief and then let it fall, to be snatched at by the wind, followed by the report of six muskets as they discharged at point-blank range into Byng's chest, one ball missing him even at that range. He fell on his side quietly 'as if to preserve decency and dignity even in his fall'.[37] More prosaic was the description in the *Monarch's* master's log, used by Pope as the title of his biography: 'At twelve Mr Byng was shot dead by six marines and put in his coffin'.[38]

At 9.30pm Byng's body and his baggage was rowed ashore and taken back to the Boatswain of the Yard's house, there to await its final journey back to Bedfordshire, where he would be buried, as was his brother, in the family vault.

While his mortal remains were treated with the respect they were due, those who had satirized him in life could not let his passing go unmarked. His ghost was made to haunt those who, it was thought, had sent him to his death, and in particular Newcastle, who was seen as the main culprit. In one poem he confronts Newcastle in his bed chamber:

> Else, I will, ceaseless, sting your soul:
> Till you repent, and clear the whole
> To a Deluded King
> Each Night, in Person I'll appear!
> Each Day, I'll thunder in your Ear
> The Name of murdered Byng.[39]

Byng would find no rest whilst there was tension between the old and new ministries. The irony – one of many – was that Pitt and the Devonshire ministry would not long outlast Byng. Pressure from the old ministers, the dissatisfaction of the King over Pitt's handling of the German question, and opposition from the King's son the Duke of Cumberland, meant that by early April the end was in sight for his first term in high office. The First Lord of the Admiralty Lord Temple was dismissed on 5 April and when Pitt did not follow by resigning he too was dismissed on 6 April 1757.

The greater surprise was that in the end it was neither Pitt nor Newcastle who would single-handedly direct the war to its triumphant conclusion: it would be both of them harnessed together as the Great Commoner and the Neurotic Duke. Separately, they could not succeed: together, and despite their very real differences, they were a winning combination.[40] None of this mattered to Byng's family, who summed up their feelings with the inscription which was placed on his tomb:

To the perpetual Disgrace of
Public Justice
The Honourable John Byng
Admiral of the Blue
Fell a Martyr to
Political Persecution,
On the 14th March in the Year 1757:
When Bravery and Loyalty
Were insufficient Securities
For the life and Honour
Of a Naval officer.[41]

Their feelings were, and two hundred and fifty one years later still are, of outrage at an injustice done. However the historian must stand back and as far as is possible take a dispassionate look at what happened and why.

Byng's career was not unusual, except in its ending. He entered the Navy at fourteen, some three years after others might have joined their first ship, and his move through to Lieutenant was steady but not meteoric. It should be remembered that Byng's father was out of office from 1722–27, and he only returned as First Lord of the Admiralty in the latter year. As first Lord, George Byng could influence how and where the younger Byng served. This is not to say that he gained no benefit from his father's position: that would not be reasonable. In 1727 Byng resigned his commission so that he did not have to go to the West Indies, yet he was able to gain employment almost immediately afterward, and this coincided with George's return to the Admiralty. After 1733, when his father died, he seems to have had a steady but unspectacular progress through to 1745 when he was appointed Flag Officer, and from all the surviving evidence this was on seniority: by that time he had been a Post Captain for nearly eighteen years.

Already in his early career some of those traits he later displayed were manifest: his punctilious attention to detail and his views of the roles and rights of a sea officer were on display with his dispute with the Minister in Portugal, which ended with the flurry of correspondence and the request from the Minister that Byng not serve on the Lisbon station again. Byng showed himself to be self-possessed and certain of his authority, but also unwilling to take a flexible approach. This does not mean that he was overbearing; if that were the case, why did he acquiesce in the decision of the Council of War at Gibraltar not to give him more men? It does not make sense unless he is classified, somewhat crudely, as a bully who when confronted with someone who stands up to him backs down.

However, this does not seem to fit the known facts. He was aware of his authority, but he also seems to have thought through problems without coming to a clear determination of the solution.

Therein seems to lie many of Byng's problems: he knew, on most occasions, what he was supposed to do; what he could not always do was find the means to do it. He has been criticized by some historians for his tenure in the Mediterranean at the end of the War of the Austrian Succession; however, even Sir Herbert Richmond had to concede that Byng was trying to implement a plan with too few ships, and it was not just greed and the placing of what ships he had on lucrative cruising stations which hindered it.[42] It was the fact that there were a reduced number of ships on station and the war itself was slowly winding down.

Prior to his appointment to be Second-in-Command in the Mediterranean Byng had acquitted himself very well when he was off Dunkirk, blockading the port against the escape of Jacobites. In a similar vein he operated very well when he followed his orders, which said he should follow any suspected reinforcements north. This he did without question and cooperated with the military forces ashore, as per his orders. All of this tends to the view that Byng was an efficient if unspectacular sea officer. Although still punctilious about his own authority he was no more overbearing than any other sea officer of that generation, and the evidence seems to suggest that he had cordial relationships with the military during the 1745 rebellion. By the end of the War of the Austrian Succession Byng had made prize money, as had Anson and many others. In that he was not unusual: his father had also done well from prize money. In fact, from the surviving evidence Byng's prize money was nowhere near the stellar amount that Anson received for the Manila Galleon and his share in the proceeds following the Battle of Finisterre in 1747. For the latter he, Anson, received something close to £300,000.[43] Byng probably made approximately £9,000 during the war. This would put him well up the rankings but not at the top of those who looked to prize money to better themselves – something that many if not most sea officers sought to do.

Prize money has been touched on earlier, but it needs to be pointed out that the pursuit of prize money was not an aberration which only venal and incompetent officers pursued without regards to anything else. Most officers in the Georgian Navy wanted to capture prizes and thus enrich themselves: they did not see that there was any inherent contradiction in doing so and at the same time doing the King's service. One of the rewards for what could be a dangerous career was the lure of prize money. In this as in much else in his career Byng was following a well-worn path, and not necessarily to the extremes which his critics such as Sir Julian Corbett have suggested.[44] If Byng had a steady if unspectacular War of the Austrian Succession, what was it that went wrong in the first full year of the next war?

There has been a tendency in most works which mention Byng to either blame or excuse him to the exclusion of any other view. What happened after

1755 and Byng's successful cruise in the Channel – during the late part of the season: he did not come in until November – would seem to follow the pattern set earlier in his career. Byng was more than capable of following orders, even if on occasions he was a little over-zealous in interpreting them, such as in the incident in Portugal.

He was also able to interpret his orders correctly, such as when he was off Dunkirk and the North of Scotland. When he gained a command at the end of the War of the Austrian Succession he made good use of the forces under his command. However, it did also highlight another weakness which Byng had, in all likelihood, from the start; that of over-analyzing and worrying about situations, especially when they were his to resolve. In the classic phrase, he could not always see the woods for the trees. This can be a major drawback when confronted with a situation such as the one in which he found himself in the spring of 1756.

His ability to see where there were deficiencies was more than admirable, but the concomitant of that is being able to see that in the case of the relief of Minorca the effect of sea power could be used at one remove. It was not the troops which could be landed: it was the presence or otherwise of his and the French squadrons which would dictate the outcome. Disrupt the French supply lines and the siege would in all probability have collapsed under its own weight. That is what the battle off Minorca was about and Byng knew that part. What he could not see was that even the presence after the action of some of his ships could have disrupted the French, as they could have been detached and harried the ships carrying troops and supplies. This would have forced the French admiral to split up his squadron to act as convoy escorts. Given how often the British had convoyed ships over the previous eighty years to and from the Mediterranean, including by Byng's own father George, it is a little surprising that he could not see that.

What he also seemed to lack, at least to the same degree, was his father's instinct for politics. This mattered when he faced the situation when he was relieved of command and sent home under arrest: a situation he seems, from his official correspondence, not to have understood. This is not to say that the Newcastle ministry did not use him as a scapegoat, which they most assuredly did, just that Byng seems not to have comprehended just what was at stake politically as well as militarily off Minorca. The firestorm which broke over his head seems to have caught him totally unawares, and although he does appear to have joined in the game of pamphleteering, he was outgunned – at least to start with – even allowing for the intercession of friends such as Augustus Hervey and, later, Horace Walpole.

It is not surprising then that when in that kind of situation Byng would revert to type and worry excessively about the details of his case. When it came to the court martial, his trial lasted from the end of December through to January of 1757, and it sat six days a week between dawn and dusk. What is interesting is that Byng himself, notwithstanding the fact that he seems to have found some of the behaviour of his Captains during the battle reprehensible, took no formal action by instituting court martial proceedings against any of them, even when he returned to Gibraltar.

During Byng's court martial there were surprising omissions: for example, why was no one from the *Princess Anne* called? However, the mere fact that it took six days to come to a verdict shows at the very least that they weighed a considerable amount of evidence with some degree of care.

The agony of mind that they, the members of the court martial, suffered may have been both political as well as real. Given that there was no leeway in the verdict if Byng was found guilty of any offence under Article XII, some at least realized that Byng had made an error of judgement with his withdrawal to Gibraltar. Yet others had made, and would make, similar mistakes and would not suffer the death penalty. It is interesting that one of the supposed conversations which Byng had went along the lines of 'they have broke me'.[45] He had some idea that he might be dismissed, but he must also have known that after 1749 and the change in the Articles of War the penalty was death with no mitigation. Was he guilty under the Articles of War? No. Was he was guilty of a lack of judgement as to the real strategic priority within the Mediterranean? Yes – for which in all likelihood he should have been dismissed but not shot.

What of the man? Byng was self-contained and seems to have had few close friends, although this judgement must be tempered by the lack of personal as against official material which survives. He had good taste – notwithstanding Fanny Boscawen's jibes about his mode of dress and speech – and his activities as a collector of porcelain, as well as Persian and Turkish rugs, adds to this view. His letter to Temple West after the battle illustrates quite an emotional man, as do his outbursts over his authority. However, for most of the time all of these were kept behind the mask of a polite and polished gentleman. The fact that he never married and only seems to have taken a mistress late in his life, with whom he was very happy, and even that was to be cut short by her death, seems again to point to a shy man, and perhaps even that judgement is stretching the evidence very thin indeed.

What can be said with certainty is that John Byng was an honourable man, in every sense of that word, and both in his life and the manner of his death he bore testament to that fact.

Notes

Prelude

1. British Museum Additional manuscripts (Hereafter Bl Add) 3359.
2. *Ibid.*
3. The Church Service attended by 250 member of the Byng Family 14th March 2007 attests to this.
4. Bl Add 3359.
5. *Ibid.*
6. *Ibid.*

Chapter One

1. Ware, C. 'George Byng Viscount Torrington', in *Precursors of Nelson*, ed. Harding and La Fevere (London 2000).
2. Ware, *Precursors...* p.95.
3. *Op Cit.*
4. Davies, J D. *Gentlemen and Tarpaulins* (Oxford 1991) pp.213–15.
5. George Byng, *New Dictionary of National Biography* (Oxford 2003–2008) http://www.oxforddnb.com/ Accessed July 2007.
6. Ware, *Precursors...*, Op Cit.
7. TNA ADM35 Muster and Pay book Superb.
8. Streynsham Masters, *New Dictionary of National Biography: Vol 8* (Oxford 2003).
9. Black, J. *Natural and Necessary Enemies, England and France in the Eighteenth Century* (London 1986) pp.23–50.
10. *Op Cit.*
11. Black, *Natural...*, *passim.*
12. Hatton, R, *George I* (Thames and Hudson 1978).
13. Black, J. 'Hanover and British Foreign Policy, 1714–1760', in *English Historical Review* 120:486 (2005) pp.303–330.
14. Hatton, *George I* Chapters 2–3.
15. Simms, B. *Three Victories and a Defeat, the Rise and Fall of the First British Empire* (Allen Lane 2007) pp.140–4: Kamen, H. *Charles V* (Yale 2006) Chapters 2–4.
16. Ware, *Precursors...* pp.80–99.
17. Eherman, J. *The Navy in the War of William III* (Cambridge 1953) pp.496–4.
18. Ware, *Precursors...* p.8.
19. *Op Cit.*
20. Owen, J. *War at Sea under Queen Anne: 1702–1708* (Cambridge 1938) pp.98–103.
21. Baugh, D. *British Naval British Administration in the Age of Walpole* (Princeton 1965) p.35.

22. Richmond, H. *Byng and the Loss of Minorca* (London 1911) p.16.
23. Kamen, H. *Op Cit* Chapter Three.
24. Simms, *Three Victories...*, pp.137–39.
25. Simms, *Op Cit*.
26. *Op Cit*.
27 Defoe , D. quoted in Simms, *Op Cit*.
28. Simms, Op Cit pp.138–40.
29. Tunstall, B. 'Pattee Byng's Journal' *Navy Records Society 1928* Introduction.
30. Corbett, T. *Account of the Expedition of the British Fleet to Sicily under Sir George Byng* (London 1739).
31. Williams, B. *Stanhope, a Study in Eighteenth Century War and Diplomacy* (Oxford 1932) p.302–5.
32. Ware, *Precursors...* pp.94–9.
33. *Op Cit*.
34. Ware, *Precursors...* p.95.
35. Graham, J. *Annals of the Viscount and 1st and 2nd Earls of Stair: Vol 2* (1875), p.7.
36. Ware, *Precursors...* p.95.
37. Ware, *Precursors...* p.95.
38. *Passim*.
39. Simms, *Three Victories...* pp.139–144.
40. Hatton, *George I* pp.230–3.
41. Ware, C. 'George Byng and Cape Passaro', (unpublished paper 1995).
42. Ware, *Precursors...* p.9.
43. Rodger N, *Command of the Ocean* (London 2004) p.228.
44. *Op Cit*.
45. Simms, *Op Cit*.
46. Tunstall, B, 'Byng Papers' *Navy Record Society 1928 Vol III passim*.
47. Ware, *Precursors...* pp.49–95.
48. TNA ADM 35 Muster and Pay Book Superb.
49. Rodger, N. *The Wooden World: the Anatomy of the Georgian Navy* (London 1986).
50. Rodger, *Wooden World...* Chapters 2–5.
51. Streynsham Masters, *New Dictionary of National Biography* (Oxford 2008).
52. *Op Cit*.
53. *Op Cit*.
54. Rodger, *Wooden World...* pp.255–59.
55. Lloyd,C. *The Navy and the Nation* (London 1947) Chapter 3.
56. Rodger, *Op Cit*.
57. Eherman, *Op Cit*.
58. Horstein, S. *Trade in the Mediterranean* (Scolar Press 1989).
59. Corbett, J. *England and the Mediterranean: Vol. I* (London 1930) *passim*.
60. TNA SP89/35 Letter dated 16 June 1728.
61. TNA SP89/35 Letter dated 2 July 1728.
62. TNA SP89/35 Letter dated 4 July 1728.
63. TNA SP89/37 Letter dated 19 July 1732.
64. Woodfine, P. *Britannia's Glories: the Walpole Ministry and the War With Spain* (the Royal Historical Society 1998) pp.116–18.
65. *Op Cit*.
66. *Op Cit*.
67. *Op Cit*, pp.90–91.
68. *Op Cit*, pp.90–91.

Chapter Two

1. Richmond, H. *The Navy in the War: Vol. I; 1738–1749* (Cambridge 1920) pp.66– 72.
2. Richmond, Op Cit, pp.68–69.
3. *Op Cit.*
4. *Op Cit.*
5. *Op Cit*, p.151.
6. *Op Cit.*
7. *Op Cit.*
8. Spinney, D. *Rodney* (London 1968) *passim.*
9. Winfield, R. *British Warships in the Age of Sail, 1714–1792* (London 2007) p.115.
10. Richmond, *Op Cit*, p.170.
11. McLynn, F.J. *Charles Edward Stuart* (London 1988) *passim.*
12. See Prelude.
13. Richmond, *Op Cit*, p.170.
14. TNA SP36/60, letter dated 1745.
15. TNA SP36/72 letter dated 25 Oct 1745.
16. Richmond, *Op Cit*, p.175.
17. TNA SP36.72 letter dated 31 October 1745.
18. Williams, G. *The Prize of all the Oceans* (Yale 1999).
19. Luff, W. 'Mathews v Lestock: Parliament , Politics and the Navy in the Mid-Eighteenth –Century England', in *Parliamentary History* Vol 10; pt 1 (1991).
20. Luff, 'Mathews v Lestock ...' *Op Cit* pp.58–62.
21. Luff, 'Mathews v Lestock ...' *passim.*
22. Pope, *Op Cit*, pp.41–44.
23. Richmond, *Op Cit.*
24. Richmond, *Op Cit*, Vol III, p.165 et seq.
25. Richmond, *Op Cit.*

Chapter Three

1. Dull. J. *The French Navy* (University of Nebraska 2005) pp.29–31.
2. Simms, B. *Three Victories and a Defeat, the Rise and Fall of the First British Empire* (Allen Lane 2007) pp.140–4: Kamen, H. *Charles V* (Yale 2006) pp.350–52.
3. Dull, J. *The French Navy Op Cit.*
4. Dull, *Op Cit*, p.29.
5. *Ibid.*
6. Dull, *Op Cit*, p.31.
7. *Ibid.*
8. Rodger, N. *Command of the Ocean* (London 2004) p.263.
9. Simms, *Three Victories ...* Chapter 15.
10. Bl Add 17956, F 23..
11. Simms, *Three Victories ...* pp.350–4. See also Rodger, N. *The Insatiable Earl: A Life of John Montagu, 4th Earl of Sandwich* (Harper Collins 1993) for a contrary view to Simms..
12. Simms, *Three Victories ...* Chapter 13.
13. *Ibid.*
14. Simms, *Three Victories ...* p.359.
15. Quoted in Simms, *Three Victories ...* Op Cit.
16. *Ibid.*
17. Quoted in Simms, *Three Victories ...* Op Cit.
18. Anderson, F. *Crucible of War* (Norton 2000) Chapter One.

19. Anderson, *Crucible* ... pp.94–107.
20. Bl Add 32848 f 147 Duke of Newcastle.
21. WWW.bluepete.com/hist/glous/minorca, accessed 12.5.2008.
22. Dull, J. *The French Navy* p.31.
23. TNA ADM1/55116/2, digest of papers disposition and manning of HM ships 1756.
24. Dull, J. *The French Navy* p.38.
25. *Ibid.*
26. *Ibid.*
27. Black, J. *George II* (Exeter University Press 2007) Chapter Nine.
28. Dull, J. *The French Navy* pp.32–38.
29. *Ibid.*
30. *Ibid.*
31. Dull, J. *The French Navy* p.39.
32. *Ibid.*
33. Dull, *Op Cit.*
34. Richmond, H (ed) 'Papers Relating to the Loss of Minorca' *Navy Records Society* 1911 p.xxxi.
35. *Ibid.*
36. Wilkinson, C. *The Royal Navy and the State in the Eighteenth Century* (London 2006) pp.99–106.
37. Wilkinson, *Op Cit*, pp.100–106.
38. Op Cit.
39. TNA ADM 1/51116/2, digest of papers.
40. Dull, J. *The French Navy* p.47.
41. *Ibid.*
42. Bl Add 31959.
43. Richmond, '... Minorca' *Op Cit.*
44. Richmond, '... Minorca' Advices No10 B 2, p.23.
45. *Op Cit*, No79 P, p.25.
46. Richmond, '... Minorca' No181 P, pp.27–28.
47. *Op Cit*, '... Minorca' No169 P, p.28.
48. *Op Cit*, pp.28–35.
49. *Op Cit.*
50. Baugh, D. *British Naval Administration in the Age of Walpole* (Princeton 1965) pp.356–58.
51. *Op Cit.*
52. Lind, J. quoted in Baugh, *British Naval Administration* ... p.356.
53. Tunstall, B. *Byng and the loss of Minorca* (London 1928) p.90.
54. George Anson, *New Dictionary of National Biography* (Oxford 2004).
55. *Op Cit.*
56. *Op Cit.*
57. *Op Cit.*
58. *Op Cit.*
59. Bl Add35387, Vol 36, Elizabeth Yorke.
60. Richmond, ... *Minorca* Table on p.xxxi.
61. *Op Cit.*
62. Black, *George II Op Cit*, Chapter Nine.
63. Bl Add 31959, No 8 C 21st Jan 1756.
64. Tunstall, ... *loss of Minorca* p.37.
65. Bl Add 31959, No B 3 3 Jan 1756.

66. TNA ADM 1/4120, Barrington to Admiralty.
67. TNA ADM 3/64 meeting 9 March 1756.
68. Professor Daniel Baugh in conversation with author, May 2005.
69. Bl Add 32996 folio 373.
70. Bl Add 32996 folio 373.
71. *Op Cit.*
72. Bl Add 32996 folio 375 quoted in Pope, D. *At Twelve Mr Byng was Shot* (London 1987) p.77.
73. TNA ADM 2/13331.
74. TNA ADM 3/64 Board of Admiralty minutes 17 March 1756.
75. Tunstall, ... *loss of Minorca* pp.49–51.
76. Bl Add 35895 folio 321.
77. Each vessel had a muster and pay book – in fact a series of them – and the men aboard were mustered at regular intervals, for the purpose of pay amongst other things..
78. *Op Cit.*
79. *Op Cit.*
80. Tunstall, *Op Cit*, p.54.
81. Bl Add 35895, folio 333–5 copy of Keppel's instructions.
82. Bl Add 41335.
83. Tunstall, ... *loss of Minorca* Op Cit.
84. TNA ADM 2/516 quoted in Pope, *At Twelve ...*, p.81.
85. Bl Add 35895.
86. Pope, *Op Cit*, Appendix 2.
87. Pope, *Op Cit*, p.51.
88. See Chapter Four.
89. Bl Add 32863 folio 140.
90. Pope, *At Twelve ...*', p.84.
91. Tunstall, ... *loss of Minorca* p.56.
92. Pope, *At Twelve ...*', p.81.
93. *Op Cit.*
94. TNA ADM 2/1331.
95. TNA ADM 2/1331.
96. *Ibid.*
97. *Ibid.*
98. TNA ADM 2/1331.
99. *Ibid.*
100. Pope, *At Twelve ...*', p.89.
101. Dull, J. *The French Navy* p.51.
102. *Ibid.*
103. Pritchard, J. *Louis XV's Navy 1748–1762* (McGill-Queen's University Press 1987) p.83.
104. Pope, *At Twelve ...*', p.92.
105. *Op Cit.*
106. Pope, *At Twelve ...*', p.95.
107. *Op Cit.*
108. Entick, J. *History of the Late War* (London 1765) p.251.
109. Pope, *At Twelve ...*', p.114.
110. *Op Cit.*
111. Coad, J. *The Royal Dockyards 1690–1850* (Scolar Press 1989) p.116.
112. *Op Cit.*
113. TNA ADM1/83/4/5/1756 quoted in Coad, *The Royal Dockyards*, Op Cit, p.317.

114. *Op Cit.*
115. *Op Cit.*
116. Colledge, J. *Ships of the Royal Navy: Vol 1* (London 1969) .
117. Pope, *At Twelve …* ', p.114.
118. *Op Cit.*
119. Lavery, B. *Ship of the Line: Vol One* (London 1982).
120. Lyon, D. *The Sailing Navy List* (London 1993) p.18.
121. *Op Cit*, p.40.
122. *Op Cit.*
123. *Op Cit*, p.72.
124. *Op Cit.*
125. *Op Cit*, p.66.
126. *Op Cit.*
127. *Op Cit*, p.42.
128. *Op Cit*, p.45.
129. *Op Cit.*
130. *Op Cit*, p.198.

Chapter Four

1. Tunstall, B. *Byng and the loss of Minorca* (London 1928) p.68.
2. Harding, R. *Amphibious Warfare in the Eighteenth Century* (Royal Historical Society 1991) .
3. Harding, *Amphibious Warfare … passim.*
4. See Preceding Chapter.
5. Bl Add 35895 folio 366.
6. Tunstall, *… loss of Minorca* pp.64–65.
7. *Op Cit.*
8. Bl Add35895 Op Cit.
9. Tunstall, *Op Cit*, p.67.
10. *Op Cit.*
11. Bl Add 35895 *Op Cit.*
12. Tunstall, *Op Cit*, p.69.
13. *Op Cit.*
14. *Op Cit.*
15. Tunstall, *Op Cit*, p.70.
16. *Op Cit.*
17. See Pope, D. *At Twelve Mr Byng was Shot*' (London 1987) and Tunstall, *… loss of Minorca Op Cit*, as examples of the debate.
18. Tunstall, *Op Cit.*
19. *Op Cit.*
20. Tunstall, *Op Cit.*
21. *Op Cit.*
22. Richmond, H (ed) 'Papers Relating to the Loss of Minorca' *Navy Records Society* 1911 p.22.
23. *Op Cit.*
24. Richmond, *… Minorca, passim.*
25. See Chapter 3.
26. Richmond, . *The Navy in the War Vol. 2* 1738–1749 (Cambridge 1920) *passim.*
27. Baugh, D. *New Dictionary of National Biography*, *Op Cit*, Admiral Byng.
28. Corbett, J. *England in the Seven Years War: Vol I* (London 1907) p.104.
29. *Op Cit.*

30. Ware, C. 'George Byng Viscount Torrington', in *Precursors of Nelson*, ed. Harding and La Fevere (London 2000).
31. See Chapter Two.
32. Rodger N, *Command of the Ocean* (London 2004) *Op Cit*, pp.265–66.
33. *Op Cit*.
34. Tunstall, *Op Cit*, p.75–77.
35. See Preceding Chapter.
36. *Op Cit*.
37. Quoted in Tunstall, *Op Cit*, p.76.
38. Quoted in Black, *George II*, *Op Cit*, p.112.
39. *Op Cit*.
40. TNA ADM1/: Tunstall, *Op Cit*, p.84.
41. *Op Cit*.
42. *Op Cit*.
43. *Op Cit*.
44. Bl Add 35895 folio 10.
45. Tunstall, *Op Cit*, p.88.
46. Entick, J. *The General History of the Late War Containing its Rise, Progress, and Events, in Europe, Asia, Africa, and America* (London 1763–1764) pp.293–321.
47. *Op Cit*.
48. *Op Cit*.
49. *Op Cit*.
50. *Op Cit*.
51. *Op Cit*, p.302.
52. Pope, *At Twelve …*', pp.126–8.
53. *Op Cit*.
54. *Op Cit*.
55. Tunstall, *Op Cit*.
56. Pope, *At Twelve …*', *Op Cit*.
57. *Op Cit*.
58. Tunstall, *Op Cit*.
59. Pope, *Op Cit*.
60. TNA ADM52/996.
61. Pope, *Op Cit*, p.129.
62. *Op Cit*.
63. *Op Cit*.
64. *Op Cit*.
65. *Op Cit*.
66. *Op Cit*.
67. *Op Cit*.
68. *Op Cit*.
69. *Op Cit*.
70. *Op Cit*, pp.131–32.
71. Richmond, *Op Cit*, *passim*.
72. Pritchard, J. *Louis XV's Navy 1748–1762* (McGill-Queen's University Press 1987) *Op Cit*.
73. Pritchard, *Op Cit*.
74. Lavery, B. *Ship of the Line: Vol One* (London 1982) *passim*.
75. *Op Cit*.
76. Pope, *Op Cit*.

77. *Op Cit.*
78. *Op Cit.*
79. *Op Cit.*
80. For opinions on what Byng might have done , see Pope, *At Twelve...*', pp.132–34, and Tunstall, *...loss of Minorca*, pp.113–18.
81. Pope, *At Twelve...*', p.135.
82. *Op Cit.*
83. Tunstall, *Op Cit.*
84. *Op Cit.*
85. Pope, *Op Cit.*
86. *Op Cit.*
87. TNA ADM 51/165 log *Captain.*
88. Pope, *Op Cit.*
89. TNA ADM 51/4301, log *Princess Louisa.*
90. TNA ADM 51/4301, *Op Cit.*
91. TNA ADM 51/4301 *Princess Louisa.*
92. TNA ADM 51/165 log *Captain.*
93. Lavery, B. *The Arming and Fitting of English Ships of War, 1600–1815* (London 1986).
94. Pope, *Op Cit.*
95. Pope, *Op Cit*, p.139.
96. Falconer, W. *Universal Dictionary of the Marine* (London 1780).
97. See Last Chapter: Mathews and Lestock court martial.
98. Pope, *At Twelve...*', p.140.
9 9. National Maritime Museum, (hereafter NNM) ADM/L/C48 lieutenant's log *Captain.*
100. NNM ADM/L/C48 *Captain.*
101. Pope, *At Twelve...*', pp. 140–41 gives a dramatic review of proceedings..
102. *Op Cit.*
103. Quote in Pope, *At Twelve...*', p.141.
104. Corbett, *England and the Seven Years War...*, *Op Cit.*
105. Corbett, *Op Cit*; Pope, *At Twelve...*', *passim*; and also Tunstall, *Op Cit*, all have variations on this theme..
106. Pope, *passim.*
107. *Op Cit.*
108. *Op Cit.*
109. See Tunstall and Pope, *Op Cit.*
110. Pope, *At Twelve...*', pp.141–43.
111. Tunstall, *Op Cit.*
112. *Op Cit.*
113. NNM ADM/L/C48 *Captain.*
114. NMM ADM/L./R 33 *Ramillies.*
115. Pope, *At Twelve...*', *Op Cit.*
116. Quoted in Pope, *Op Cit*, pp.143–44.
117. Tunstall, *Op Cit.*
118. NMM ADM/L/R *Ramillies.*
119. Pope, *Op Cit.*
120. Tunstall, *Op Cit.*
121. See Pope, *At Twelve...*', p.146 as an example.
122. Fearne, C. *The Trial of the Honourable Admiral John Byng* (London 1757) p.309.
123. Fearne, *Trial...*, p.307.

124. Pope, *Op Cit*, p.146; Tunstall, *Op Cit*, pp.120–21.
125. Tunstall, *Op Cit*, p.121.
126. Tunstall, *Op Cit*.
127. Pope, *Op Cit*.
128. *Op Cit*.
129. Tunstall, *Op Cit*.
130. Pope, *Op Cit*, p.149.
131. Pope, *Op Cit*, p.150.
132. Tunstall, *Op Cit*, p.123.
133. Dull, *Op Cit*, p.52.
134. NMM ADM/L/C48.
135. NMM ADM/L/C48.
136. Tunstall, *Op Cit*.
137. Pope, *Op Cit*, p.151.
138. Tunstall, *Op Cit*, p.124.
139. Fearne, *Trial…*, Appendix XXIII.
140. Pope, *Op Cit*, p.152.
141. Tunstall, *Op Cit*, p.124.
142. Fearne, *Op Cit*, p.347: Durrell's evidence.
143. Tunstall, *Op Cit*.
144. NNM ADM/L/R33.
145. NMM ADM/L/R33.
146. Pope, *Op Cit*.
147. Fearne, *passim*.
148. Pope, *Op Cit*.
149. Fearne, *Op Cit*.
150. *Op Cit*.
151. Tunstall, *Op Cit*.
152. Quoted in Pope, *At Twelve…*', p.156.
153. *Op Cit*.
154. Dull, *Op Cit*, p.52.
155. Dull, *Op Cit*, pp.52–53.

Chapter Five

1. NMM, ADM/L/C48 *Captain*; Tunstall, *Op Cit*, pp.129–30.
2. NMM ADM/L/C48 *Captain*.
3. Fearne, *Op Cit*.
4. Pope, *Op Cit*, p.158; Tunstall, *Op Cit*, p.131.
5. Chesterfield, P.D.S. *Letters to his Son: on the Fine Art of Becoming a Man of the World and a Gentleman*, (London 1901).
6. Walpole, H. *History of George II* (London 1789).
7. Tunstall, *Op Cit*, p.130.
8. Pope, *Op Cit*.
9. Tunstall, *Op Cit*, p.132.
10. Quoted in Pope, *At Twelve…*', p159.
11. *Op Cit*.
12. *Op Cit*.
13. Fearne, *Op Cit*, pp.36–7.
14. *Op Cit*.

15. *Op Cit.*
16. Pope, *Op Cit.*
17. Pope, *Op Cit*, p.161.
18. Tunstall, *Op Cit*, p.133.
19. *Op Cit.*
20. Falconer, W. *Universal Dictionary of the Marine* (London 1780).
21. *Op Cit.*
22. Hervey, A *Journal* (London 1953) p.208 and *passim*.
23. Corbett, *Op Cit.*
24. Hervey, *Op Cit*, pp.208–213.
25. Pope, *Op Cit*, p.161.
26. TNA ADM/1/383 Byng's despatch and enclosure 25 May 1756.
27. Pope, *Op Cit.*
28. Black, *Op Cit.*
29. See for example Baugh's article on Byng in the *New Dictionary of National Biography*.
30. Richmond, H (ed) 'Papers Relating to the Loss of Minorca' *Navy Records Society* 1911 Introduction.
31. Pope, *Op Cit*, p.163.
32. Dull, *Op Cit*, p.53.
33. TNA ADM/1/383 Byng's despatch 25 May 1756.
34. Dull, *Op Cit*, p.53.
35. *Op Cit.*
36. Tunstall, *Op Cit.*
37. Pope, *Op Cit.*
38. *Op Cit.*
39. Pope, *Op Cit*, p.165.
40. Hervey, *Journal, Op Cit.*
41. Tunstall, *Op Cit.*
42. TNA ADM/2/1331 letters and orders dated 8 June 1756.
43. TNA ADM/2/1331 secret orders dated 8 June 1756.

Chapter Six
1. Pope, *Op Cit.*
2. Cardwell, J. *Art and Arms, Literature, Politics and Patriotism during the Seven Years War* (Manchester University Press 2004) p.4.
3. Cardwell, *Art and Arms…* p.48.
4. *Op Cit.*
5. *Op Cit.*
6. *Op Cit.*
7. *Op Cit.*
8. *Op Cit.*
9. *Op Cit.*
10. *Op Cit.*
11. Bl Add51,387, letter dated 26 June 1756.
12. Hervey quoted in Cardwell, *Art and Arms…*, p.48.
13. Newcastle to Hardwicke, 19th July 1756 quote in Cardwell, *Art and Arms…*, p.49.
14. *Op Cit.*
15. Cardwell, *Op Cit*, p.51.
16. *Op Cit.*

17. Pope, *Op Cit*, p.166 *passim*.
18. Cardwell, *Op Cit*, p. 50: Pope, *Op Cit*.
19. Quoted in Cardwell, *Art and Arms...*, p.50.
20. *Op Cit*.
21. Tunstall, *Op Cit*, p.45, Pope, *Op Cit*, Chapter 3.
22. Cardwell, *Op Cit*.
23. *Op Cit*.
24. Quoted in Cardwell, *Art and Arms...*, p.51.
25. Cardwell, *Op Cit*, p.52.
26. TNA ADM/1/383 despatch dated 25 May 1756.
27. Cardwell, *Op Cit*.
28. Cardwell, *Art and Arms...*, p.67.
29. Pope, *Op Cit*.
30. Cardwell, *Op Cit*.
31. *Op Cit*.
32. Quoted in Pope, *Op Cit*, p.168.
33. Pope, *Op Cit*.
34. TNA ADM/ 3/64 dated 7 -8 June 1756.
35. TNA ADM/3/64, *Op Cit*.
36. Pope, *Op Cit*.
37. *Op Cit*.
38. Pope, *Op Cit*.
39. *Op Cit*.
40. *Op Cit*.
41. Quoted in Pope, *Op Cit*, p.175.
42. *Op Cit*.
43. TNA ADM 1/383 letter dated 11 June 1756.
44. Quoted in Pope, *Op Cit*, p.176.
45. *Op Cit*.
46. Quoted in Rodger, N. *The Wooden World*, (London 1986) p.248.
47. Rodger, *Op Cit*, p.248.
48. *Op Cit*.
49. Rodger, *Op Cit*, p.248–49.
50. Pope, *Op Cit*, p.177.
51. *Op Cit*.
52. TNA ADM2/ despatch dated 2 July 1756.
53. Tunstall, *Op Cit*, p.141.
54. TNA ADM/1/383 despatch dated 2 July 1756.
55. TAN ADM/1/383, *Op Cit*.
56. *Op Cit*.
57. See Chapter One.
58. Pope, *Op Cit*.
59. Hervey, *Journal*, *Op Cit*, pp.217–18.
60. Quoted in Cardwell, *Op Cit*, p.56.
61. *Op Cit*.
62. Cardwell, *Op Cit*, p.58.
63. TNA ADM1/923 letter dated 29 June 1756.
64. TNA ADM 2/76 despatches dated 27 July 1756.
65. Pope, *Op Cit*.

66. TNA ADM1/923 letter dated 26 July
67. TNA ADM 2/.76 despatch dated 28 July 1756
68. TNA ADM/1/923, *Op Cit*.
69. Black, *Op Cit*, p.112.
70. Pope, *Op Cit*.
71. *Op Cit*.
72. *Op Cit*.
73. *Op Cit*.
74. Quoted in Pope, *Op Cit*, p.198.
75. *Op Cit*.
76. Quoted in Pope, *Op Cit*.
77. *Op Cit*.
78. Bl Add15955.
79. *Op Cit*.
80. Bl Add 32866 letter date 31 July.
81. Quoted in Pope, *Op Cit*, p.200.
82. TNA ADM 1/4322, Secretary of War letter dated 31 July 1756.
83. Pope, *Op Cit*.
84. *Op Cit*.
85. Pope, *Op Cit*, p.203.
86. Cardwell, *Op Cit*, p.61.
87. Cardwell, *passim*.
88. Bl Add.ch 76400.
89. Tunstall, *Op Cit*, p.164.
90. See Previous Chapter.
91. Listed in Cardwell, *Art and Arms ...*, p.65.
92. Pope, *Op Cit*, p.204.
93. Cardwell, *Op Cit*, p.66.
94. Cardwell, *Op Cit*.
95. Entick, *History of the Late War*, Op Cit.
96. Cardwell, *Op Cit*.
97. *Op Cit*.
98. Pope, *Op Cit*.
99. *Op Cit*.
100. *Op Cit*.
101. Cardwell, *Op Cit*.
102. *Op Cit*.
103. *Op Cit*.
104. Cardwell, *Op Cit*, p.79.
105. *Op Cit*.
106. *Op Cit*.
107. *Op Cit*.
108. Cardwell, *Op Cit*.
109. Walpole, *Op Cit*.
110. TNA ADM/2/518 letter dated 14 August 1756.
111. Pope, *Op Cit*, p.216.
112. Inspection by author December 2006.
113. Fearne, *Op Cit*, p.37–41.
114. Pope, *Op Cit*, p.217.

115. Fearne, *Op Cit*, pp.41–45.
116. *Op Cit*.
117. Black, *Op Cit*, p.238.
118. Black, *Op Cit*.
119. Quoted in Pope, *Op Cit*, p.225.
120. Quote in Black, J. *Pitt the Elder* (Cambridge University Press 1992) p.122.
121. Black, *Pitt the Elder*, p.122.
122. *Op Cit*.
123. *Op Cit*.
124. *Op Cit*.
125. *Op Cit*.
126. *Op Cit*, p.127.
127. TNA PRO/30/29/1/14.
128. Quote in Black, *Op Cit*, p.128.

Chapter Seven

1. Pope, *Op Cit*, p.318.
2. *Op Cit*.
3. *Op Cit*.
4. Quoted in Pope, *Op Cit*, p.229.
5. Quoted in Tunstall, *Op Cit*, p.207.
6. TNA ADM3/64 meeting 19 November 1756.
7. Tunstall, *Op Cit*, p.204.
8. TNA ADM3/64, *Op Cit*.
9. TNA ADM3.64 Board meeting dated 24 November 1756.
10. Pope, *Op Cit*, p.231.
11. Hervey, *Journal*, *Op Cit*, pp.229–31.
12. Cardwell, *Op Cit*.
13. Pope, *Op Cit*.
14. Bl Add 32869 letter to Hardwicke.
15. *Op Cit*.
16. Bl Add 32869.
17. TNA ADM1/4322 letter from Secretary of War.
18. Pope, *Op Cit*, p.235.
19. Black, *Op Cit*, Chapter Six.
20. Quoted in Pope, *Op Cit*, p.236.
21. TNA ADM2/516 despatch dated 14 December 1756, Admiral Smith at the Downs.
22. TNA ADM2/516, *Op Cit*.
23. *Op Cit*.
24. TNA ADM2/519.
25. Coad, *Royal Dockyards*, *Op Cit*.
26. Pope, *Op Cit*, p.238.
27. Tunstall's phrase, *Op Cit*, p.210.
28. Ware, *Precursors...*, *Op Cit*, p.129–49.
29. Keppel, T. *Life of Admiral Keppel, passim*.
30. Eder, M. *Crime and Punishment in the Royal Navy in the Seven Years War* (Ashgate 2004) p.53.
31. *Op Cit*, p.53.
32. *Op Cit*, p.54.

33. *Op Cit*, p.58.
34. *Op Cit*.
35. *Op Cit*.
36. Tunstall, *Op Cit*; and Fearne, Court Martial.
37. Quoted in Pope, Op Cit, p.240.
38. Pope, *Op Cit*, p.241.
39. Eder, *Op Cit*.
40. Tunstall, *Op Cit*.
41. Pope, *Op Cit*, p.243; and Winfield, *Op Cit*, p.15.
42. Winfield, *Op Cit*.
43. Bl Add 3359.
44. Bl Add 3359.
45. Pope, *Op Cit*, p.243.
46. *Op Cit*.
47. Fearne, *Op Cit*.
48. Pope, *Op Cit*.
49. *Op Cit*.
50. Fearne, *Op Cit*.
51. *Op Cit*.
52. *Op Cit*.
53. *Op Cit*.
54. *Op Cit*.
55. *Op Cit*.
56. *Op Cit*.
57. Quoted in Pope, *Op Cit*, p.247.
58. Pope, *Op Cit*.
59. Fearne, *Op Cit*.
60. *Op Cit*.
61. *Op Cit*.
62. *Op Cit*.
63. Quoted in Pope, *Op Cit*, p.249.
64. *Op Cit*.
65. Pope, *Op Cit*, p.249; Tunstall, *Op Cit*, p.217.
66. Fearne, *Op Cit*.
67. *Op Cit*.
68. Pope, *Op Cit*, p.251.
69. Fearne, *Op Cit*.
70. *Op Cit*.
71. Pope, *At Twelve ...*, p.250.
72. Fearne, *Op Cit*.
73. Tunstall, *Op Cit*.
74. Harding, *Amphibious Warfare ...*, *Op Cit*.
75. Fearne, *Op Cit*.
76. Fearne, *Op Cit*.
77. Quoted in Tunstall, *Op Cit*, p.219.
78. *Op Cit*.
79. Fearne, *Op Cit*.
80. Quoted in Pope, *Op Cit*, p.253.
81. *Op Cit*.

82. Fearne, *Op Cit*.
83. *Op Cit*.
84. Fearne, *Op Cit*.
85. Quoted in Tunstall, *Op Cit*, p.221.
86. Fearne, *Op Cit*.
87. Quoted in Pope, *Op Cit*, p.255.
88. *Op Cit*, p.255.
89. *Op Cit*.
90. *Op Cit*.
91. *Op Cit*.
92. Hervey, *Journal*, *Op Cit*, pp.233–36.
93. *Op Cit*, pp.233–36.
94. *Op Cit*.
95. Tunstall, *Op Cit*, p.223.
96. Fearne, *Op Cit*.
97. *Op Cit*.
98. *Op Cit*.
99. *Op Cit*.
100. *Op Cit*.
101. *Op Cit*.
102. *Op Cit*.
103. *Op Cit*.
104. *Op Cit*.
105. *Op Cit*.
106. *Op Cit*.
107. Pope, *Op Cit*, footnote p.264.
108. Fearne, *Op Cit*.
109. *Op Cit*.
110. *Op Cit*.
111. Tunstall, *Op Cit*, p.227.
112. Fearne, *Op Cit*.
113. Quoted in Pope, *Op Cit*, p.263.
114. *Op Cit*.
115. Pope, *Op Cit*.
116. Fearne, *Op Cit*.
117. *Op Cit*.
118. *Op Cit*.
119. *Op Cit*.
120. *Op Cit*.
121. *Op Cit*.
122. *Op Cit*.
123. *Op Cit*.
124. *Op Cit*.
125. *Op Cit*.
126. *Op Cit*.
127. Pope, *Op Cit*, pp.268–269.
128. Fearne, *Op Cit*.
129. *Op Cit*.
130. TNA ADM52/1074, log *Culloden*; TNA ADM 51/1010 log *Trident*; Pope, *Op Cit*, p.269.

131. Pope, *Op Cit*.
132. Fearne, *Op Cit*.
133. *Op Cit*.
134. *Op Cit*.
135. *Op Cit*.
136. Quoted in Tunstall, *Op Cit*, p.239.
137. Tunstall, *Op Cit*.

Chapter Eight
1. Fearne, C. *The Trial of the Honourable Admiral John Byng* Verdict.
2. Quoted in Pope, *Op Cit*, p.206.
3. Bl Add 35985 Folio 34.
4. Bl Add 35985 Folio 34.
5. Quoted in Pope, *Op Cit*, p.278.
6. TNA ADM2/519.
7. Pope, *Op Cit*, p.279.
8. *Op Cit*.
9. Quoted in Cardwell, *Arm and Art ... Op Cit*, p.174.
10. Pope, *Op Cit*, pp.279–82.
11. *Op Cit*.
12. *Op Cit*.
13. Fearne, *Op Cit*.
14. Quoted in Pope, *Op Cit*, p.286.
15. Fearne, Verdict.
16. *Op Cit*.
17. *Op Cit*.
18. *Op Cit*.
19. *Op Cit*.
20. Pope, *Op Cit*, pp.290–93.
21. Fearne, *Op Cit*.
22. Pope, *Op Cit*, p.291; Tunstall, *Op Cit*, p.246-47.
23. *Op Cit*.
24. Quoted in Tunstall, *Op Cit*, p.247.
25. Tunstall, *Op Cit*, p.247.
26. Pope, *Op Cit*, pp.294–95.
27. TNA ADM2/519 letter dated 28 January 1757.
28. TNA ADM3/64 Board minutes dated 29 January 1757.
29. TNA ADM52.660 master's log 31 January 1757.
30. See Prelude.
31. Quoted in Tunstall, *Op Cit*, p.248.
32. Pope, *Op Cit*, pp.296–7.
33. Quote in Pope, *Op Cit*, p.297.
34. *Op Cit*.
35. TNA ADM3/64 Admiralty minutes dated 9 February 1757.
36. TNA ADM3/64, *Op Cit*.
37. Pope, *Op Cit*, p.298.
38. *Op Cit*.
39. *Op Cit*.
40. TNA ADM3/64 Board of Admiralty minutes 16 February 1757.

41. TNA ADM3/64 *Op Cit.*
42. *Op Cit.*
43. *Op Cit.*
44. Pope, *Op Cit*, p.299.
45. Tunstall, *Op Cit.*
46. TNA ADM3/64 Board of Admiralty minutes 17 February 1757.
47. Quoted in Pope, *Op Cit*, p.300.
48. *Op Cit.*
49. Pope, *Op Cit*, p.301.
50. TNA ADM1/5116/2.
51. TNA ADM3/64 Admiralty Minutes February 1757.
52. Pope, *Op Cit*, p.301.
53. Quoted in Pope, *Op Cit*, p.302.
54. Black, *George II Op Cit*, pp.112–13.
55. Hervey, *Journal*, *Op Cit*, pp.236–7.
56. Black, *George II*, *Op Cit.*
57. Black, *Pitt*, *Op Cit*, *passim.*
58. *Op Cit.*
59. Keppel, *Admiral Keppel*, *Op Cit*, pp.238–40.
60. Hervey, *Journal Op Cit*, p.307.
61. Keppel, *Op Cit.*
62. *Op Cit.*
63. *Op Cit.*
64. TNA ADM3/64 Admiralty minutes 26 February 1757.
65. Bl Add35895 Folio 53.
66. Quoted in Pope, *Op Cit*, p.311.
67. *Op Cit.*
68. Keppel, *Op Cit*, Vol II, *passim.*
69. Pope, *Op Cit.*
70. Walpole, *Op Cit*, *passim.*
71. *Op Cit.*
72. Quoted in Pope, *Op Cit*, p.314.
73. Walpole, *Op Cit.*
74. Pope, *Op Cit*, p.315; Walpole, *Op Cit.*
75. Pope, *Op Cit.*
76. Eder, *Crime and Punishment*, *Op Cit*, Chapter 7.
77. Quoted in Pope, *Op Cit*, p.315.
78. Pope, *Op Cit*, p.316.
79. TNA ADM3/64.
80. TNA ADM3/64.

Chapter Nine

1. BlAdd 24059.
2. Bl Add 24058.
3. Bl Add 24058.
4. *Op Cit.*
5. TNA ADM51/3914 Captain's log *Monarch* 6 March 1757.
6. TNA ADM 51/3914, *Op Cit.*
7. TNA ADM52/660 Master's log *Monarch* 6 March 1757.

8. Hervey, *Journal*, *Op Cit*, pp.242–43.
9. Hervey, *Op Cit*.
10. Hervey, *Op Cit*.
11. *Op Cit*.
12. Pope, *Op Cit*, p.319.
13. Pope, *Op Cit*.
14. Hervey, *Op Cit*, p.243.
15. TNA Prob 11/831 Folio 210 will of the Hon John Byng Vice Admiral of the Blue, proved 27 July 1757.
16. Baugh, D. *British Naval Administration in the Age of Walpole*, (Princeton 1965) p.110.
17. Austen, J. *Pride and Prejudice*.
18. TNA Prob 11/831 Folio 211.
19. TNA Prob 11/831 Folio 211.
20. *Op Cit*.
21. TNA Prob 11/831 Folio 210.
22. TNA Prob 11/831, *Op Cit*.
23. Pope, *Op Cit*, p.321.
24. TNA Prob 11/831, *Op Cit*.
25. Quoted in Pope, *Op Cit*, p.322.
26. TNA ADM3/64 board minute dated 4 March 1757.
27. TNA ADM52/660 Master's log *Monarch* 14 March 1757.
28. *A letter to a Gentleman in the Country from his friend in London* (London 1757).
29. Pope, *Op Cit*, p.328.
30. Pope, *Op Cit*.
31. Quoted in Pope, *Op Cit*, p.329.
32. *A Letter to a Gentleman...*, *Op Cit*.
33. *Op Cit*.
34. *Op Cit*.
35. *Op Cit*.
36. TNA ADM52.660, *Op Cit*.
37. *A Letter to a Gentleman...*, *Op Cit*.
38. Quoted in Pope, *Op Cit*, p.333.
39. Quoted in Cardwell, *Art and Arms*, *Op Cit*, p.175.
40. Middleton, *Bells of Victory*, *Op Cit*.
41. Pope, *Op Cit*, p.334.
42. Richmond, *Op Cit*, Vol II, *passim*.
43. Baugh, *British Naval Administration...*, *Op Cit*, p.110.
44. Corbett, *Op Cit*, *passim*.
45. *A Letter to a Gentleman...*, *Op Cit*.

Bibliography

Manuscript sources

The British Library

Byng (John). Admiral. Biographical note of 19th century. Add. 41378 ff. 71–71 b.

Byng (John). Vice Admiral. Correspondence with Sir B. Keene 1756. Copy Add. 43437 ff. 69, 125, 185. Add. 43438 f. 8.

Byng (John). Admiral. Despatch to J. Cleveland 1756. Copy. Add. 41355 ff. 164–167b.

Byng (John). Letters to G. Goad 1658–1659. Add. 33572 ff. 370–374.

Byng (John). Admiral. Memoranda by S. Martin, junior, rel. to 1756. Add. 41356 ff. 2–3b.

Byng (John). Admiral. Verdict at the court-martial of 1757. Copy. Add. 41355 ff. 168–169.

Byng (John). Hon. Admiral. Letter to the Duke of Newcastle 1748. Add. 32714 f. 383.

Byng (John). Hon. Admiral. Memorandum relating to [1745–57]. Add. 33056 f. 318.

Byng (John). Hon. Admiral. Papers relating to his action against the Toulon fleet 1757. Add. 31959.

Byng (John). Hon. Admiral. 4th son of 1st Viscount Torrington. Letter to Lord Sandwich 1748. Copy. Add. 37682 f. 214.

Byng (John). Admiral. Vice Admiral. J. Forbes's reason for refusing to sign his death warrant. 1757. Copy, circ. 1796. Add. 45364 f. 40.

Byng (John). Admiral. Letter describing Lords' debates relating to Admiral Byng 1757. Add. 71170 f. 22.

Byng (John). Admiral. Letter to the Admiralty from his sister. 1757.

Byng (John). Hon. Admiral. 4th son of 1st Viscount Torrington. Letter to Lord Sandwich 1748. Copy.

Byng (John). Hon. Admiral. 4th son of 1st Viscount Torrington. Papers relating to 1756, 1757. Add. 35895.

Byng (John). Hon. Capt., afterwards Admiral. Letters to Adm. Haddock 1740, 1741. Eg. 2529 ff. 32, 35, 96, 172.

The National Archives Kew

Admiralty

ADM 1 in letters.

ADM 2 out letters.

ADM 3 Minute books.

ADM 36 Ships' Muster Books.

ADM 52 Masters' Logs.

ADM 53 Captains' Logs.

State
SP 36/72 1745 Oct 25–31.
SP 36/72 1745 Oct 25–31.
SP 36/72 1745 Oct 25–31.
SP 54/27/1D 1746 Jan 2.
SP 54/27/53 1746 Jan 28.
SP 54/28/8 1746 Feb 5.
SP 54/28/15C 1746 Feb 6.
SP 54/28/20D 1746 Feb 9.
SP 54/28/24C 1746 Feb 10.
SP 54/28/24F 1745 Feb 12.
SP 54/28/37A 1746 Feb 22.

Secondary Sources
Anderson, F. *Crucible of War* (Norton 2000).
Baugh, D. *British Naval British Administration in the Age of Walpole* (Princeton 1965).
Black, J. *George II* (Exeter University Press 2007).
Black, J. 'Hanover and British Foreign Policy, 1714–1760', in *English Historical Review* 120: 486 (2005).
Black, J. *Natural and Necessary Enemies, England and France in the Eighteenth Century* (London 1986).
Black, J. *Pitt the Elder* (Cambridge University Press 1992).
Cardwell, J. *Art and Arms, Literature, Politics and Patriotism during the Seven Years War* (Manchester University Press 2004).
Chesterfield, P.D.S. *Letters to his Son: on the Fine Art of Becoming a Man of the World and a Gentleman,* (London 1901).
Coad, J. *The Royal Dockyards 1690–1850* (Scolar Press 1989).
Colledge, J. *Ships of the Royal Navy: Vol 1* (London 1969).
Corbett, J. *England and the Mediterranean: Vol. I* (London 1930).
Corbett, J. *England in the Seven Years War: Vol I* (London 1907).
Corbett, T. *Account of the Expedition of the British Fleet to Sicily under Sir George Byng* (London 1739).
Davies, J D. *Gentlemen and Tarpaulins* (Oxford 1991).
Dull, J. *The French Navy* (University of Nebraska 2005).
Eder, M. *Crime and Punishment in the Royal Navy in the Seven Years War* (Ashgate 2004).
Eherman, J. *The Navy in the War of William III* (Cambridge 1953).
Entick, J. *The General History of the Late War Containing its Rise, Progress, and Events, in Europe, Asia, Africa, and America* (London 1763–1764).
Entick, J. *History of the Late War* (London 1765).
Falconer, W. *Universal Dictionary of the Marine* (London 1780).
Fearne, C. *The Trial of the Honourable Admiral John Byng* (London 1757).
Graham, J. *Annals of the Viscount and 1st and 2nd Earls of Stair: Vol 2* (1875).
Harding, R. *Amphibious Warfare in the Eighteenth Century* (Royal Historical Society 1991).
Hatton, R, *George I* (Thames and Hudson 1978).
Hervey, A *Journal* (London 1953).
Horstein, S. *Trade in the Mediterranean* (Scolar Press 1989).
Kamen, H. *Charles V* (Yale 2006).
Lavery, B. *The Arming and Fitting of English Ships of War, 1600–1815* (London 1986).
Lavery, B. *Ship of the Line: Vol One* (London 1982).
Lloyd,C. *The Navy and the Nation* (London 1947.

Luff, W. 'Mathews v Lestock: Parliament , Politics and the Navy in the Mid-Eighteenth-Century England', in *Parliamentary History* Vol 10; pt 1 (1991).

Lyon, D. *The Sailing Navy List* (London 1993).

McLynn, F.J. *Charles Edward Stuart* (London 1988).

New Dictionary of National Biography 'George Anson' (Oxford 2004) http://www.oxforddnb.com/

New Dictionary of National Biography 'George Byng' (Oxford 2003–2008).

New Dictionary of National Biography: Vol 8 'Streynsham Masters' (Oxford 2003).

Owen, J. *War at Sea under Queen Anne: 1702–1708* (Cambridge 1938).

Pope, D. *At Twelve Mr Byng was Shot* (London 1987).

Pritchard, J, *Louis XV's Navy 1748–1762* (McGill-Queen's University Press 1987).

Richmond, H. *The Navy in the War: Vol. I; 1738–1749* (Cambridge 1920).

Richmond, H. *The Navy in the War Vol. 2 1738–1749* (Cambridge 1920).

Richmond, H. *Byng and the Loss of Minorca* (London 1911).

Rodger, N. *Command of the Ocean* (London 2004).

Rodger, N. *The Insatiable Earl: A Life of John Montagu, 4th Earl of Sandwich* (Harper Collins 1993).

Rodger, N. *The Wooden World: the Anatomy of the Georgian Navy* (London 1986).

Simms, B. *Three Victories and a Defeat, the Rise and Fall of the First British Empire* (Allen Lane 2007).

Spinney, D. *Rodney* (London 1968).

Tunstall, B. *Byng* (London 1928).

Walpole, H. *History of George II* (London 1789).

Ware, C. 'George Byng Viscount Torrington', in *Precursors of Nelson*, ed. Harding and La Fevere (London 2000).

Wilkinson, C. *The Royal Navy and the State in the Eighteenth Century* (London 2006).

Williams, B. *Stanhope, a Study in Eighteenth Century War and Diplomacy* (Oxford 1932).

Williams, G. *The Prize of all the Oceans* (Yale 1999).

Winfield, R. *British Warships in the Age of Sail, 1714–1792* (London 2007).

Woodfine, P. *Britannia's Glories: the Walpole Ministry and the War With Spain* (the Royal Historical Society 1998).

Index